"Andy is a gifted, insightful communicator who has written a critically important book. The great challenge in life is crafting a meaningful and motivating personal vision for our time on earth. To that end, *Visioneering* is a MUST read."

JOEL MANBY
PRESIDENT & CEO, SAAB CARS USA

"It has been my observation that there is much confusion about what vision is and is not. Andy Stanley, with keen insight, has written a book that is extremely biblical and, consequently, practical to anyone who is interested and concerned about vision. Without vision, churches, families, businesses, and ministries have no hope. This is a 'must read.'"

RON BLUE
RONALD BLUE & COMPANY

"It didn't take me long to appreciate Andy Stanley. His disarming communication, his passionate style, and his biblical insights are memorable—as you will discover in this book. Vision is a nonnegotiable for success and no one explains it any better than Andy."

DR. JOHN C. MAXWELL
FOUNDER, THE INJOY GROUP

"Helen Keller said the only thing worse than having no sight is to have sight but no vision. Andy Stanley challenges us to look beyond just physically seeing things as they are and, instead, seeing things as God wants us to see—from His perspective."

BOB RECCORD
NORTH AMERICAN MISSION BOARD

"When Andy writes about visioneering, it is not theoretical exercise. It is biblical. It is practical. It is real. North Point Community Church is a thriving, vibrant community of faith because Andy practices what he preaches as a God-called man of vision."

BRYANT WRIGHT
SENIOR PASTOR, JOHNSON FERRY BAPTIST CHURCH

"Anyone who knows my good friend Andy well, knows that he lives daily what he so masterfully writes about regarding 'visioneering.' Reading this book will be like getting a new prescription for your outdated glasses, allowing you to see with greater clarity the God-given vision for your future."

RANDY POPE
PERIMETER CHURCH, DULUTH, GEORGIA

ACKNOWLEDGMENTS

Authors are somewhat like NASCAR drivers. They drive alone. But they don't race alone. Racing is a team sport. Although I wrote alone, I certainly did not produce this manuscript alone.

Visioneering was inspired by the courage and passion of those who partnered with me to begin North Point Community Church. I am especially grateful to the Leadership Team and our original Steering Committee. Together, we experienced firsthand the thrill of embracing a divinely-authored vision.

I am grateful as well to the folks at Multnomah for giving me this opportunity to share these remarkable principles outside the walls of our church. A special thanks to John Van Diest for inviting me to join the Multnomah family. And to my new friend, Jeff Gerke, thanks for coaching and encouraging me to the finish line. I couldn't ask for a finer editor.

visioneering

ANDY STANLEY

Multnomah®Publishers *Sisters, Oregon*

VISIONEERING
published by Multnomah Publishers, Inc.

© 1999 by Andy Stanley
International Standard Book Number: 1-57673-538-9 (hardback)
International Standard Book Number: 1-57673-787-X (paperback)

Cover images by Tony Stone Images
Cover design by Uttley DouPonce DesignWorks

Scripture quotations are from:
New American Standard Bible® (NASB) © 1960, 1977, 1995
by the Lockman Foundation. Used by permission.

Also quoted:
The Holy Bible, New International Version (NIV) © 1973, 1984 by International Bible
Society, used by permission of Zondervan Publishing House

Multnomah is a trademark of Multnomah Publishers, Inc., and
is registered in the U.S. Patent and Trademark Office.
The colophon is a trademark of Multnomah Publishers, Inc.

Printed in the United States of America

For information:
MULTNOMAH PUBLISHERS, INC.
POST OFFICE BOX 1720
SISTERS, OREGON 97759

Library of Congress Cataloging-in-Publication Data:

Stanley, Andy.
    Visioneering: fulfilling God's purpose through intentional living / by Andy Stanley.
        p. cm. Includes bibliographical references.
    ISBN 1-57673-538-9 (alk. paper)
    1. Success—Religious aspects—Christianity. 2. Nehemiah (Governor of Judah)
    I. Title.
    BV4598.3.S73   1999   99-15763
    248.4—dc21   CIP

02 03 04 05 — 10 9 8 7

TABLE OF CONTENTS

This book is lovingly dedicated to my dad, Charles Stanley,
on whose shoulders I have been privileged to stand.
It was from that vantage point that I caught a glimpse
of what could be and should be for my life.

INTRODUCTION

Visioneering. A new word. An old concept. A familiar process. Where definitions fall short, a story often achieves clarity. So let's begin with a story.

On December 17, 1903, at 10:35 A.M., Orville Wright secured his place in history by executing the first powered and sustained flight from level ground. For twelve gravity-defying seconds he flew 120 feet along the dunes of the Outer Banks of North Carolina.

In the field of aviation, this historic event represents a beginning. But for Orville and Wilbur Wright, it was the end of a long and tedious journey. A journey initiated by a dream common to every little boy. The desire to fly. But what most children abandon to the domain of fantasy, Orville and Wilbur Wright seized upon as potential reality. They believed they could fly. More than that, they believed they should fly.

Wilbur described the birth of their vision this way.

> Our personal interest in it [aviation] dates from our childhood days. Late in the autumn of 1878, our father came into the house one evening with some object partly concealed in his hands, and before we could see what it was, he tossed it into the air.
>
> Instead of falling to the floor, as we expected, it flew across the room till it struck the ceiling, where it fluttered awhile, and finally sank to the floor. It was a little toy, known to scientists as a "hélicoptère," but which we, with sublime disregard for science, at once dubbed a "bat."
>
> It was a light frame of cork and bamboo, covered with paper, which formed two screws, driven in opposite directions by rubber bands under torsion. A toy so delicate lasted only a short time in the hands of small boys, but its memory was abiding.[1]

This childhood experience sparked in the boys an insatiable desire to fly. The only thing they lacked was a means. So they immediately went to work removing the obstacles that stood between them and their dream.

They began building their own hélicoptères. In doing so they stumbled upon the principles of physics that would pave the way to their first successful manned flight. In short, they began to engineer their vision. They took the necessary steps to ensure that what they believed could be, would be. This process captures the essence of visioneering.

Visioneering is the course one follows to make dreams a reality. It is the process whereby ideas and convictions take on substance. As the story of the Wright brothers illustrates, visioneering is the engineering of a vision. If I were to boil it down to a formula, it would look something like this:

VISIONEERING = INSPIRATION + CONVICTION +
ACTION + DETERMINATION + COMPLETION

DESTINATIONS

Life is a journey. And as you know, every journey has a destination. In the pages that follow we are going to spend some time discussing your destination. Not heaven and hell. Your destination in this life. Where you will end up in the various roles you play; what you will accomplish personally, professionally, domestically, and spiritually.

Everybody ends up somewhere in life. A few people end up somewhere on purpose. Those are the ones with vision. They may have other things going for them as well. But they certainly have vision. Not necessarily *a* vision (singular). Vision for each of the key roles they are assigned along the way.

Life is a multifaceted journey. It calls for a multifaceted vision.

Whether you are aware of it or not, you have multiple visions for your life. That is, you have a mental picture of what you want the various arenas of your life to look like down the road.

If I were to ask you to describe how you picture your life in ten years, chances are you could paint a fairly clear picture. No doubt you could outline a financial profile. You could describe what you hope to achieve relationally. You have some idea of where you want to be professionally. In other words, you would be able to look beyond what is and paint a picture of what could be—and in some cases what should be—true of your life. That's vision.

A *clear* vision, along with the courage to follow through, dramatically increases your chances of coming to the end of your life, looking back with a deep abiding satisfaction, and thinking, *I did it. I succeeded. I finished well. My life counted.*

Without a clear vision, odds are you will come to the end of your life and wonder. Wonder what you could have done—what you should have done. And like so many, you may wonder if your life really mattered at all.

Vision gives significance to the otherwise meaningless details of our lives. And let's face it, much of what we do doesn't appear to matter much when evaluated apart from some larger context or purpose.

But take the minutia of this very day, drop it into the cauldron of a God-ordained vision, stir them around, and suddenly there is purpose! Meaning! Adrenaline!

It is the difference between filling bags with dirt and building a dike in order to save a town. There's nothing glamorous or fulfilling about filling bags with dirt. But saving a city is another thing altogether. Building a dike gives meaning to the chore of filling bags with dirt. And so it is with vision.

Too many times the routines of life begin to feel like shoveling dirt. But take those same routines, those same responsibilities, and view them through the lens of vision and everything looks different. Vision brings your world into focus. Vision brings order to chaos. A clear vision enables you to see everything differently.

Specifically, vision weaves four things into the fabric of our daily experience.

1. PASSION

Vision evokes emotion. There is no such thing as an emotionless vision. Think about your daydreams. The thing that makes daydreaming so enjoyable is the emotion that piggybacks on those mind's eye images. When we allow our thoughts to wander outside the walls of reality, our feelings are quick to follow.

A clear, focused vision actually allows us to experience ahead of time the emotions associated with our anticipated future. These emotions serve to reinforce our commitment to the vision. They provide a sneak preview of things to come. Even the most lifeless, meaningless task or routine can begin to "feel" good when it is attached to a vision. Through the avenue of vision, the feelings reserved for tomorrow are channeled back into our present reality.

When I was in high school I never dated anybody who lived on my side of town. Our church was located in the middle of Atlanta. Consequently, we drew families from all around the city. Being the preacher's son, my primary realm of influence (and acceptance) was church. So I dated church girls.

Unfortunately, none of the girls I was interested in lived near Tucker. They lived thirty or forty miles away. So I would put up with the traffic, the gas bills, and even leaving their houses early enough to be home by curfew. Why? It was worth it!

On Friday afternoon, the thought of being across town elicited in my teenage heart emotions that were strong enough to make the headache and expense of driving across town worth it. That's vision. I was committed to what could be (being on the other side of Atlanta) as opposed to what was (sitting at home in Tucker).

Let's face it, you did similar things as a teenager. Thoughts of what could and should be—and the emotions associated with those thoughts—drove you to all kinds of extremes. Some of which you probably regret. But think about how powerful, how compelling, those thoughts and feelings were. The emotions associated with being there (wherever *there* was) were enough to motivate you through the drudgery of getting there.

Vision is always accompanied by strong emotion. And the clearer the vision, the stronger the emotion.

2. MOTIVATION

Vision provides motivation. The mundane begins to matter. The details, chores, and routines of life become a worthwhile means to a planned-for end. Dike builders are a motivated bunch. Saving a town is enough to keep you working through the night. But just filling bags with dirt for the sake of bag-filling will leave you looking at your watch.

Vision-driven people are motivated people. Find me a man or woman who lacks motivation and I'll show you someone with little or no vision. Ideas, yes. Dreams, maybe. Vision, not a chance.

Vision is a big part of the reason you completed college or graduate school. A lack of vision is the reason many never finish. Think of all the seemingly wasted hours of study and class time. Even then you knew that much of what you were memorizing for tests was a waste of time and effort. But you did it. Why? Because of what could be. A degree. And beyond a degree, a career. For four (or in my case, five!) long years you endured science labs, European history, research papers, and lectures. And you hung in there through it all—motivated by the thought of graduation and the rewards it would bring.

That is the power of vision.

3. DIRECTION

Maybe the most practical advantage of vision is it sets a direction for our lives. It serves as a road map. In this way, vision simplifies decision making. Anything that moves us toward the realization of our vision gets a green light. Everything else is approached with caution.

I have loved music all my life. God has blessed me with a measure of musical talent. I played in bands through high school and college. I have written a couple dozen songs. Like most serious musicians, I accumulated quite a collection of gear: recording equipment, guitars, keyboards, drum machines, and several miles of cable. Through the years it became an expensive and time-consuming hobby.

When Sandra and I were married, she allowed me the luxury of setting up a small studio in the basement of our condominium. In that environment time stood still. It was not unusual for me to retreat to my studio after dinner and emerge just in time for breakfast.

Four years after we were married, Andrew came along. Twenty months later, Garrett was born. As Andrew began to look less like a baby and more like a little boy, I started to give serious thought to my relationship with my children. I began focusing on what could be and what should be. Having spent ten years working with teenagers, I had a frighteningly clear picture of what could be and what should not be!

So, a few months before Garrett was born I made a decision. It was one of the easiest decisions I have ever made. But it came as a shock to those who knew my love for music. I decided to sell my studio gear. Why? I could see a storm brewing on the horizon. I knew I would be torn between my family and the studio. Something had to go.

My vision for my family dictated that I put musical pursuits on hold. There was no way I would be able to develop the relationship I envisioned with my children while pursuing my musical aspirations.

Vision will prioritize your values. A clear vision has the power to bring what's most important to the surface of your schedule and lifestyle. A clear vision makes it easy to weed out of your life those things that stand in the way of achieving what matters most. Vision empowers you to move purposefully in a predetermined direction. Once you have clarified your vision, or visions, many decisions are already made. Without vision, good things will hinder you from achieving the best things.

My observation is that people without clear vision are easily distracted. They have a tendency to drift from one activity, pleasure, or relationship to another. Without vision, there is no relational, financial, or moral compass. Consequently, they often make foolish decisions. Decisions that rob them of their dreams.

4. PURPOSE

Vision translates into purpose. A vision gives you a reason to get up in the morning. If you don't show up, something important won't be accomplished. Suddenly, you matter. You matter a lot! Without you, what could be—what should be—won't be. A vision makes you an important link between current reality and the future. That dynamic gives your life purpose. And purpose carries with it the momentum to move you through the barriers that would otherwise slow you down and trip you up.

Your set of visions are unique to you. No one else will share your particular passions for what could be. Others may applaud them. They may buy into the aspects of your vision that interface with their life. And they may work with you in the areas where you share a common vision. But your vision-set is unique to you. This uniqueness gives your life purpose. You have a reason for getting up and showing up.

THE DIVINE ELEMENT

Granted, you have probably heard or read this type of stuff before. Self-help books are full of this kind of hype. We have all read something about goal setting. If you believe—you can achieve! You know the drill.

But here is where we part ways with the secular motivational gurus of our culture. The average person has the right to dream his own dreams and develop his own picture of what his future could and should be. But at the cross, those of us who have sworn allegiance to the Savior lost that right. After all, we are not our own. We have been bought with a price. Remember the rest? We are to glorify—or honor—God with our bodies (1 Corinthians 6:19–20).

Honoring God involves discovering his picture or vision of what our lives could and should be. Glorifying God involves discovering what we could and should accomplish. We were created and re-created with his purposes in mind. And until we discover his purpose—and follow through—there will always be a hole in our soul.

With that in mind, rethink the implications of this familiar verse:

For we are His workmanship, created in Christ Jesus for good works, which God prepared beforehand so that we would walk in them. (Ephesians 2:10)

Don't let this slip by. You are his workmanship. Say it out loud, "I am God's workmanship." Do you know what that means? It means you are the product of God's vision. God has decided what you could be and should be. You are the outcome of something God envisioned. And through Christ he has brought about, and continues to bring about, changes in you in accordance with his picture of what you could and should be.

But his vision for you is not complete. You have a part. Look at the next phrase. We have been envisioned and then crafted for a particular purpose. And that purpose is to do good works which God has envisioned us doing.

God has a vision for your life. That is, he has a mental image of what you could and should be as well as what you could and should do. In my first book, *Like a Rock,* I focused on his vision of what you could and should become. In this book, we are going to focus on what he wants you to accomplish.

Honestly, I can't get over the fact that the God of the universe has something in mind for us to do. After all, doesn't he have other things to think about? But the apostle Paul assures us that God has prepared something specific for us to do.

MORE TO THIS LIFE

All that to say, as Christians, we do not have a right to take our talents, abilities, experiences, opportunities, and education and run off in any direction we please. We lost that right at Calvary. But then, why would we dream of such a thing? God has a vision for your life. What could possibly be more fulfilling than that?

At the same time, we have no right to live visionless lives either. If God—think about it—if God has a vision for what you are to do with your allotment of years, you had better get in on it. What a tragedy to miss it. Missing out on God's plan for our lives must be the greatest tragedy this side of eternity.

Granted, this world offers a truckload of options when it comes to possible visions to pursue. But you were tailor-made, carefully crafted, minutely detailed for a selected divine agenda. It is what you were created and re-created for. God's visions for your life are *the* things that will give your life impact beyond this life. For, as we will see, God's visions always have an eternal element. His individual vision for your life is a small part of a plan he envisioned and put in motion long before you or I came on the scene—but now I'm jumping ahead.

Without God's vision, you may find yourself in the all too common position of looking back on a life that was given to accumulating green pieces of paper with pictures of dead presidents on them. Granted, that is a vision. Maybe that has been your vision up until now. And you may have been vastly successful at the accumulation game.

But let's face it, at each milestone in your pursuit of more stuff, you feel like you did as a kid after all the presents were opened on Christmas morning. *Is that all there is?* Chances are, the memories of your successes elicit little or no passion. They are just memories. After all, a closing is a closing. A sale is a sale. A deal is a deal.

Accumulating money or stuff is a vision of sorts. But it is the kind of vision that leaves men and women wondering. Wondering if there was more. Wondering what they could have done—should have done—with their brief stay on this little ball of dirt.

You cannot wring enough life or meaning out of secular accomplishment to satisfy your soul. The hole you are trying to fill has an eternal and spiritual dimension that only matters of eternity and spirituality can satisfy. This is why it is imperative that you discover and participate in God's multifaceted vision for your life. It is what you were made for. Your homespun visions—as challenging and demanding as they may be—fall short. They will always leave you wondering.

We serve an intensely creative God. We talk about the fact that no two snowflakes are alike—but God has never made two of anything alike. God's vision for you does not include pressing you into someone else's mold. He is not in the business of conforming us to the image of other Christians. Your uniqueness and individuality will reach its pinnacle in the context of your pursuit of God's plan for your life. Manmade visions all begin to look alike after a while. Unless you discover God's unique vision for your future, your life may very well be a rerun.

Having said all that, let's begin. Our study will center around the life and vision of Nehemiah. Several things make his story particularly relevant to our modern day situation. The one I find most encouraging is that there are no overt miracles associated with his story. This is a tale of hard work, prayer, and (behind the scenes) divine intervention. Nothing out of the ordinary here.

Let's face it, if we could heal at will, part the Red Sea with the flick of a wrist, or walk on water, it would make the process of accomplishing our goals much simpler. We are tempted to look with suspicion at the Old and New Testament heroes who had a supernatural ace up their sleeves.

But not Nehemiah. He was just a regular guy who caught a divine glimpse of what could and should be. And then went after it with all his heart.

gins as a concern.

ts not necessarily require immediate action.

3. Pray for opportunities and plan as if you expect God to answer your prayers.

4. God is using your circumstances to position and prepare you to accomplish his vision for your life.

5. What God originates, he orchestrates.

6. Walk before you talk; investigate before you initiate.

7. Communicate your vision as a solution to a problem that must be addressed immediately.

8. Cast your vision to the appropriate people at the appropriate time.

9. Don't expect others to take greater risks or make greater sacrifices than you have.

10. Don't confuse your plans with God's vision.

11. Visions are refined—they don't change; plans are revised—they rarely stay the same.

12. Respond to criticism with prayer, remembrance, and if necessary, a revision of the plan.

13. Visions thrive in an environment of unity; they die in an environment of division.

14. Abandon the vision before you abandon your moral authority.

15. Don't get distracted.

16. There is divine potential in all you envision to do.

17. The end of a God-ordained vision is God.

18. Maintaining a vision requires adherence to a set of core beliefs and behaviors.

19. Visions require constant attention.

20. Maintaining a vision requires bold leadership.

CHAPTER ONE

A VISION
IS BORN

The soul never thinks without a picture.
ARISTOTLE

What is a vision?
Where do they come from?

Visions are born in the soul of a man or woman who is consumed with the tension between what is and what could be. Anyone who is emotionally involved—frustrated, brokenhearted, maybe even angry—about the way things are in light of the way they believe things could be, is a candidate for a vision. Visions form in the hearts of those who are dissatisfied with the status quo.

Vision often begins with the inability to accept things the way they are. Over time that dissatisfaction matures into a clear picture of what *could be*. But a vision is more than that. After all, what *could be* is an idea, a dream, but not necessarily a vision.

There is a always a moral element to vision. Vision carries with it a sense of conviction. Anyone with a vision will tell you this is not merely something that *could* be done. This is something that *should* be done. This is something that must happen. It is this element that catapults men and women out of the realm of passive concern and into action. It is the moral element that gives a vision a sense of urgency.

Vision is a clear mental picture of what could be, fueled by the conviction that it should be.

Vision is a preferred future. A destination. Vision always stands in contrast to the world as it is. Vision demands change. It implies movement. But a vision requires someone to champion the cause.

For a vision to become a reality, someone must put his or her neck on the line. Vision requires visionaries, people who have allowed their minds and hearts to wander outside the artificial boundaries imposed by the world as it is. A vision requires an individual who has the courage to act on an idea.

And that brings us to our story.

ONCE UPON A TIME...

Around 587 B.C., the Babylonians invaded Judah and destroyed the city of Jerusalem, along with Solomon's temple. This was the third of three campaigns into that region. On all three occasions the Babylonians took a number of Israelites as captives and resettled them in Babylon. Daniel, Shadrach, Meshach, and Abednego were taken during the first invasion.

About seventy years after the first Babylonian invasion, Cyrus, king of Persia (who had since conquered the Babylonians), gave the Jews permission to return to Jerusalem to rebuild the temple.

Under the leadership of a man named Zerubbabel, these exiled Jews returned to Jerusalem and rebuilt the temple. Things were looking up for a while. It seemed as if Israel was on the verge of becoming a blessed nation once again. But the people refused to turn away from the very sins God had judged their ancestors for in the days of Daniel and Nebuchadnezzar.

The temple was not being maintained. Sacrifices had ceased. The Jews continued to adopt the religious practices and culture of the surrounding nations. By the time our story begins, the political, social, and spiritual conditions in Jerusalem were deplorable.

Meanwhile, back in Persia, a Jewish fellow named Nehemiah heard about the plight of his homeland—and he felt something. In fact, what he felt, he felt so deeply that he wept. And as we will see later, Nehemiah was not the sort of man who wept at the drop of a hat. He wasn't weak. And he certainly wasn't emotionally unstable. But he was burdened. And his burden drove him to a prolonged period of prayer and fasting (Nehemiah 1:4).

Little did he know these deep feelings were the initial birth pains of a vision that people would be reading about thousands of years later. The point is, Nehemiah's vision didn't begin as a vision. It began as a concern, a burden. A burden for his nation and its people.

BUILDING BLOCK #1

A VISION BEGINS AS A CONCERN.

A God-ordained vision will begin as a concern. You will hear or see something that gets your attention. A thought related to the future will generate an emotion. Something will bother you about the way things are or the way things are headed. Unlike many passing concerns, these will stick with you. You will find yourself thinking about them in your free time. You may lose sleep over them. You won't be able to let them go because they won't let you go.

Nehemiah's concern over the condition of Jerusalem consumed him. It broke his heart. Thoughts of what *was* as opposed to what *could be* brought tears to his eyes. It changed his countenance. Everyone who knew him was aware that something was botherng Nehemiah. This was not a casual concern. This was a vision in the making.

So what did he do? Nothing. He *did* absolutely nothing. He didn't steal away across the desert in the night. He didn't fabricate a reason to leave Persia. He didn't even share his burden with other concerned Jews.

But neither did he allow his daily responsibilities to distract him from the burden that had gripped his heart. No, Nehemiah chose the third and most difficult option. He chose to wait. Nehemiah knew what so many of us have a hard time remembering: What could be and should be can't be until God is ready for it to be. So he waited.

BUILDING BLOCK #2

A VISION DOES NOT NECESSARILY REQUIRE IMMEDIATE ACTION.

I talk to a lot of people with a lot of good ideas. In many instances I sense God is in the process of birthing a vision in their hearts. In almost every case, they are ready to start NOW! Once they feel their idea is from God, they assume all systems are go and they need to quit their jobs, step out on faith, and begin. But the story of Nehemiah, along with numerous other biblical accounts, illustrates the truth that a clear vision does not necessarily indicate a green light to begin. In fact, I have witnessed a good many people with what seemed to be God-ordained visions charge out of the starting gates too early. And the result is always the same. Failure. Discouragement. Disillusionment.

A vision rarely requires immediate action. It always requires patience.

WHY WAIT?

Why is this the case? Why can't we just plunge ahead?

Developing or discovering a vision for a particular area of our lives takes time. Visioneering is a process. Sometimes it is a painful process. Because of the time required, it can be agonizing. But it is a process that yields a product worth every bit of the agony along the way.

Revving our vision engines at the starting line feels like a waste of time. After all, there are things to be done. People to rescue. Organizations to begin. What is the use of waiting?

This sense of "time is awasting" is the very thing that compels people to move out too soon. The assumption is, since we aren't moving on, nothing's going on. But that is not the case at all. Three important things are taking place while we wait.

1. THE VISION MATURES IN US.

Not every good idea is vision material. But every vision begins as an idea. Not all burdens are vision material. But every vision begins as a burden. Time allows us to distinguish between good ideas and visions worth throwing the weight of our life behind. Waiting gives us a chance to examine our emotions and sort our minor concerns from major ones. After all, if what concerned you yesterday is of little concern today, odds are that was not vision material. I will give you several tips on distinguishing good ideas from God ideas at the end of this chapter.

Just as you cannot rush the development of a child in the womb, so we cannot rush the development of a vision. God determines the schedule for both. Acting too quickly on a vision is like delivering a baby prematurely. They are always weak. And in some cases a preemie cannot survive the rigors of life outside the womb. So it is with a vision. Immature visions are weak. They rarely make it in the real world.

The world is hard on a vision. After all, a vision is about change. And change is not welcomed in most arenas of life. For a vision to survive, it must be mature and healthy before being exposed to the cynical, critical, stubborn environment in which it is expected to survive. And maturity requires time.

As a college student, I had two friends who felt called to career missions. Chip felt the call during a missions conference in our church. For David, it was a sequence of events that tipped him off as to God's call on his life.

Knowing these guys as well as I did, I'm sure that if they had had the opportunity to sign up and ship out on the day they sensed God's call on their lives, they would have both headed for the airport. Fortunately, the system didn't work that way.

During the process of finishing college, Chip slowly began to lose interest. After college he got married and took a job in another city. His explanation? "I thought that was what God was calling me to do at the time. I realize now I am to be a missionary in the corporate world." Of course, that just sounded like a good excuse at the time. But Chip has followed through with that vision. He is very active in his local church and is effective in the ministry of lifestyle evangelism.

David, on the other hand, went to the Philippines and planted a church. As I write, he and his wife Kathy have just begun their second church plant in that area of the world.

Let's face it, a good motivational speaker can cast such a compelling vision that before you know it you feel like it is your own. And in some cases, it may become your own. Time will tell. With time, you will be able to distinguish between God's ideas for you and other people's ideas. As we wait, God will shape and mature ideas into visions that can survive in the real world.

2. WE MATURE IN PREPARATION FOR THE VISION.

Not only does our vision mature, we mature as well. Often, we are not ready to move out in pursuit of a vision. The tendency is to assume that since I know what I am to do, I'm ready to do it. But the two don't always coincide. God has to grow us into our vision. Like a child trying on her mommy's wedding dress, it doesn't fit—yet. But in time, after some growing up, it will look like it was made for her.

If you saw *The Empire Strikes Back,* you remember the scene in which Luke wants to go rescue his friends before he has finished his Jedi Knight training. Yoda begs him to wait. "Luke, you must complete the training."

But Luke has seen the future, and he knows his friends' lives are in danger. "I can't keep the vision out of my head. They are my friends; I must help them."

Yoda finally issues a dire warning, "If you leave now, help them you could, but you will destroy all for which they have fought and suffered."

But Luke is determined to go. He is so locked in on what could and should be that he feels compelled to leave immediately. So he does. And do you remember what happened? Everything worked out great!

But back in this galaxy, action before preparation usually spells disaster.

In the case of a divinely ordered vision God goes to work in you to prepare you for what he knows lies ahead. Like Luke, the need often seems so urgent it seems foolish to wait. But God is sovereign. Keep that in mind. Your vision is simply an extension of his vision. And his timing is perfect. The apostle Paul said it this way:

> For it is God who is at work in you, both to will and to work for
> His good pleasure. (Philippians 2:13)

He is working in you to prepare you to act on his purposes. And I think we can assume his purposes are in accordance with his timetable. Maybe that's why he inspired the apostle to write the next phrase: "Do all things without grumbling or disputing" (v. 14).

I assume *all things* includes waiting on him. Don't you hate that? The complaint most associated with the process of visioneering is God's timing. Once the vision is clear we assume we are ready. Otherwise, why would he have given us the vision in the first place?

My guess is that without a vision, our willingness to allow God to prepare us would be greatly diminished. Who would suffer the headache of college or graduate school without the vision of job opportunities? Your vision will enable you to endure the preparation. Vision always precedes preparation. Initially, your vision will exceed your competency. Within the context of that tension, God will go to work on you.

Good Idea/Bad Timing

Remember Moses? Poor guy. He had the right idea, but his timing and methods were terrible. His vision was to free his people from Egyptian slavery. And that was a God-thing if there ever was one. So what did Moses do? He went to work. He killed an Egyptian.

Now I don't know if he actually sat down and calculated how long it would take to deliver Israel by killing one Egyptian at a time. But at best, it would have taken several lifetimes.

So what did God do? He sent him to the University of Sinai. This was not a four-year study program. He was a freshman for ten years. His sophomore, junior, and senior experiences were equally as long. And there were no spring breaks.

It took Moses forty years to grow into the vision God had designed for him. Forty years! Meanwhile, back in Egypt, another generation or two dies at the hands of Egyptian taskmasters. What was God thinking? Didn't he know the urgency of the matter? Israel didn't have forty years to wait. Why give a man a vision and then send him to the desert?

We could spend pages speculating as to why God does the things he does. Suffice it to say, that is the way he works. He did the same thing with the apostle Paul. He told him specifically that he would be used to reach the Gentiles (Acts 9:15–16). And then he sent Paul to the desert as well (Galatians 1:17–18).

So what's the deal with the desert? I don't know. But I do know the time between catching a glimpse of what God wants to do through us and the time when we are led to move out often feels like a desert experience. The desert always feels like a complete waste of time. It is only when we are able to look back that our desert experiences make sense.

Our Hero

Nehemiah, on the other hand, got off pretty easy by comparison. By his account, he only had to wait four months before the wheels started turning. But he had to wait nonetheless. As the story unfolds, it becomes evident his service to the king of Persia was in fact his desert experience. For this was a man with immense leadership ability who awoke every day to do a job that tapped little or none of those skills.

Can you relate? Do you wake up every day to circumstances that have absolutely nothing remotely to do with the vision you sense God is developing in you? Then you are in good company. Joseph reviewed his vision from an Egyptian dungeon. Moses spent years following sheep. David, the teenage king, spent years hiding in caves. And Nehemiah was the cupbearer to the very king whose ancestors had destroyed the city he longed to rebuild! Be encouraged. God has you there for a reason.

I don't know your situation. But from what I read in the Scriptures, I would guess the time required for God to grow you into his vision for your life will be somewhere between four months and forty years. And if you feel you are on the forty-year track, here's one other bit of information you might want to chew on. There seems to be a correlation between the preparation time and the magnitude of the task to which we are called. Leading God's people out of four hundred years of slavery required more than a four-year degree. It required forty years of preparation. But then again, we are still talking about it today.

3. GOD IS AT WORK BEHIND THE SCENES PREPARING THE WAY.

There is a third important process taking place between the birth of a vision and our pursuit of it. In the case of a divinely ordered vision, God is working behind the scenes to prepare the way. This is why it is so important that we wait on his timing. Remember, your personal vision is only one small piece of the puzzle.

Ultimately, we are taking part in a massive assault that began one dark afternoon on a hill just outside of Jerusalem. God's vision for your life is much bigger than you. Apart from his intervention and preparation, you and I are incapable of pulling off even our small part of the operation. We dare not move ahead too early.

Nehemiah certainly knew how this worked. And he knew that apart from divine intervention there was no way in the world he would be able to take part in the reconstruction of Jerusalem. So he bided his time and prayed. Oh yeah, and he did one other thing. He thought about it a lot. He dreamed about it. In fact, as we will see in the next chapter, he went so far as to think through exactly what it would take to pull off a project of that magnitude. And unbeknownst to him, God was working behind the scenes the whole time.

AUTHENTICATING YOUR VISION

One of the most difficult aspects of visioneering is distinguishing between good ideas and God ideas. We all have good ideas. Everybody is concerned or burdened about something. But how do you know which ideas to act on? Certainly Nehemiah was not the only Jew whose heart was broken over the condition of Jerusalem. How did he know *he* was the one to do something about it?

As a pastor I have counseled with dozens of men and women who were in the process of determining the source of a concern or burden they carried. I have watched many of these successfully launch and maintain what appear to be visions forged in heaven. While developing the material for this book I interviewed several Christian men and women who have visioneered ideas into successful enterprises. You will be introduced to several of these in the course of our time together.

These encounters have led me to conclude two things concerning the distinction between good ideas and God ideas:

1. A GOD-ORDAINED VISION WILL EVENTUALLY FEEL LIKE A MORAL IMPERATIVE.

If it is God who has begun painting a picture of what could and should be on the canvas of your heart, over time you will begin to sense that not to follow through would be tantamount to an act of disobedience. Your vision will begin to feel like a moral imperative. As the burden in you grows, you will feel compelled to take action.

This is why waiting is so important. Time allows your heavenly Father to transition what begins as an idea into a moral compulsion. The vision simply will not go away. Your only alternative to following through will be to say, "No. No, I'm not going to move in that direction. I'm not going to pick up this burden and act on it."

2. A GOD-ORDAINED VISION WILL BE IN LINE WITH WHAT GOD IS UP TO IN THE WORLD.

A second indicator is that there will always be alignment between a divinely originated vision and God's master plan for this age. There will always be a correlation between what God has put in an individual's heart to do and what he is up to in the world at large.

As we said at the outset, at Calvary we lost our right to devise our own plans and pursue our own agendas. Like a good father, our heavenly Father has a vision for each of his children, a vision that lends support to his work in this world.

All divinely inspired visions are in some way tied into God's master plan. Whether it is loving your wife, investing in your kids, witnessing to your neighbor, launching a ministry, or starting a company, every divinely placed burden has a link to a bigger picture. As a believer, there is a larger, more encompassing context for everything you do.

It was Israel's strategic role in God's plan that made Nehemiah's vision so compelling. As we will see, it wasn't the condition of the walls that broke his heart. It was the spiritual condition of his people.

If the idea or burden you are mulling over is from God, there will be an overt connection between it and God's providential will. It will become apparent how the thing you feel compelled to do connects with what God is up to in this generation.

Initially, you may not see a connection. If not, wait.

YOUR PART

There are several productive things you can do while you wait. To begin with, investigate. In chapter 6 we will explore the importance of investigation in detail. In the meantime, ask some questions. Talk to people who have pursued similar visions. Read. Observe. Learn everything you can.

Investigation will accomplish one of three things. It will: confirm the divine origin of your vision, give further definition and focus to the vision, or tip you off that you were mistaken about the vision altogether.

In chapter 2 we will discover what Nehemiah did while he waited. Remember, with a vision, timing is critical. Waiting does not reflect a lack of faith. Usually it is evidence of wisdom.

VISIONEERING

PROJECT #1

1. You have multiple visions for your life. Some are clearer than others. To begin clarifying what you believe your future should hold, write a one-sentence summary of how you believe life ought to be in the following areas. In other words, describe your preferred future.

   • Career

   • Finances

   • Spouse

   • Children

   • Ministry

   • _____

2. Visions are often born in the soul of a man or woman who is gripped by a tension between what is and what should be. Are you gripped by a particular tension? If so, take a minute to describe your dilemma.

   • What's bothering you?

   • What is the solution?

   • What should be?

3. Have any of your burdens begun to feel like a moral imperative?

4. Do you see a connection between your various visions and what God is up to in this world? Describe the connection. How does your picture of a preferred future support God's providential will?

....

CHAPTER TWO

PRAYING AND PLANNING

Vision is the art of seeing things invisible.
JONATHAN SWIFT

L et's talk further about that dreaded period of time when it appears impossible to move ahead with your vision. You know: those weeks and months and possibly years when circumstances don't permit you to be proactive. That season when you are not free to take action.

You don't have the finances to finish school. Your present job doesn't allow you the flexibility to pursue your business idea. Everybody says you need more experience. Your family responsibilities leave you with no free time. You are in the wrong part of the country. You've got debts to pay.

Visions often die during this stretch of inactivity. It is discouraging to continue dreaming about something that appears to have no potential of ever happening. Besides, there is so much in life that must be done, why waste time dreaming about the impossible? Too many hours on the starting blocks can cause us to lose sight of what could be and should be. After a prolonged period of waiting, a vision can slip into the realm of what won't ever be.

IN THE MEANTIME...

So what should you do in the meantime? What can you do to keep your dream alive? Nehemiah did two things. He prayed and he planned.

When Nehemiah heard about the condition of Jerusalem, there was not one thing he could do to remedy the situation. Nothing. He was in the wrong place with the wrong job working for the wrong guy. And he had no way of changing any of that. He wasn't free to act on his vision.

But Nehemiah was not inactive. The four months between hearing about the condition of the walls and finally being able to do something about it was productive time for Nehemiah. He used this time to prepare for the day when God would release him to pursue his vision. He didn't allow the downtime to discourage or distract him. Nehemiah didn't allow his dream to die. He used the time for praying and planning.

1. HE PRAYED.

Prayer is critical to vision development. Here's why: We see what we are looking for; we often miss what we don't expect to see.

Each spring Sandra's family rents a big house on the beach for a come one, come all, family vacation. Aunts, uncles, grandparents, cousins—everybody shows up at some point during the week. One afternoon, my brother-in-law announced he was going to go down to the beach to look for shark teeth. My boys immediately lit up. "Can we go wif' (with) you Uncle Wob (Rob)?"

"Sure," he said. And down to the beach they ran.

As they galloped off, I thought to myself, *There aren't any shark teeth on the beach. I've been walking up and down that beach all week, and I haven't seen any shark teeth. He shouldn't get my boys' hopes up like that.*

An hour later, to my utter amazement, they returned with a handful of shark teeth. I couldn't believe it. "Where did you get those?" I asked skeptically.

Garrett proudly announced, "Day wur on da sand, Daddy."

You know why I hadn't seen any shark teeth? I hadn't been looking for them. They were there all along. But it took someone who was look-ing for them to find them.

We see what we are looking for. We often miss what we don't expect to see. Prayer keeps us looking. Prayer keeps the burden fresh. It keeps our eyes and hearts in an expectant mode. Prayer doesn't force God's hand. But it keeps us on the lookout for his intervention. Prayer sensitizes us to subtle changes in the landscape of our circumstances. When he begins to move, we are apt to recognize it. Praying almost ensures we won't miss opportunities God brings our way. Looking for something doesn't necessarily mean you will find it. But it sure increases the odds of seeing it if it is there to be seen.

Nehemiah prayed for two things in reference to his vision. First, he prayed for an opportunity. Take a look:

> "O Lord, I beseech You, may Your ear be attentive to the prayer of Your servant and the prayer of Your servants who delight to revere Your name, and *make Your servant successful today and grant him compassion before this man.*" Now I was the cupbearer to the king. (Nehemiah 1:11, emphasis mine)

Nehemiah wanted an opportunity to share his vision with the king. He knew it would take divine intervention for such an opportunity to present itself. So he prayed that God would grant him "success." Success in what? Success in casting his vision to the one man who stood between him and his dream.

I doubt this was the first time he had prayed that prayer. He probably prayed it every time he was about to go in to see the king. Yet time and time again he had gone before Artaxerxes to fulfill his duty and was never given an opportunity to discuss his homeland. But Nehemiah continued to pray.

Our tendency is to pray for miracles. But in most situations, it is more appropriate to pray for opportunities. More than likely you need an opportunity rather than something supernatural.

If you are a parent, you probably have a vision for your children. Instead of simply praying that they would become men and women of character, pray for opportunities to build character into their lives. Your vision involves you. You have a role. You have a part to play.

If you have a vision for unbelieving friends, don't simply pray that they will be saved. Pray for an opportunity to speak to them about Christ.

If you pray for an opportunity, more than likely you will recognize it when God brings it along.

Dreamers and Visionaries

It is interesting that Nehemiah never prayed for God to rebuild the wall. What he prays for is an *opportunity* to go rebuild it himself. That is the difference between a dreamer and a visionary. Dreamers dream about things being different. Visionaries envision themselves making a difference. Dreamers think about how nice it would be for something to be done. Visionaries look for an opportunity to do something.

Nehemiah was a man with a vision, not a dream. He wasn't expecting God to do something independently of him. He was looking for an opportunity to work alongside God. So he prayed for an opportunity. And as we will see in the next chapter, God gave it to him.

The Prayer of Favor

In addition to an opportunity, Nehemiah prayed for favor. Nehemiah prayed for God to cause King Artaxerxes to take an interest in and support his vision.

> Make Your servant successful today and grant him compassion before this man. (v. 11b)

The term *compassion* means *favor* or *mercy*. Nehemiah wanted the king to feel something when he heard about the plight of the Jews in Jerusalem. This was a long shot. The king was not known to be a compassionate man. It was not in his nature. In fact, when Nehemiah finally got his big chance to speak to the king, he was, in his own words, "very much afraid" (2:2).

Unless God intervened in the king's heart, there was no way in the world he was going to feel sympathetic toward Israel. After all, his predecessors were the ones who tore the city apart to begin with. So Nehemiah prayed for compassion and mercy. He asked God to sway the king's heart in his direction. And he did. King Artaxerxes became a primary player in the reconstruction of the wall. But there I go getting ahead of myself again.

Think about this. If God could sway King Artaxerxes to finance the rebuilding of the wall around Jerusalem, he can certainly change the heart of those who stand between you and the vision God has given you. Humanly speaking, there was no way in the world King Artaxerxes was going to support Nehemiah's vision. But prayer takes us well beyond human possibilities.

Real Estate Opportunities

In 1995 I was part of a group who began a new church just north of Atlanta in the city of Alpharetta. Before we officially began looking for property, Sandra and I rode through the area to get a feel for what was available. As we drove along, we found ourselves in a new office development called Royal 400. I turned to her and said, "This would be ideal. This is where we need to locate our church."

One month later one of our church trustees and I were sitting in the office of the gentleman who owned Royal 400. As it turned out, he was a Christian. In fact, he had been very generous to churches and Christian organizations through the years. I was optimistic about the meeting. I was sure this was more than a coincidence.

After a long and informative meeting, he said he wished he could help us, but he was unable to at that time. We had initiated the meeting with the hopes that we could buy a piece of his property. It became obvious during the meeting he wasn't interested in selling us anything in the Royal 400 development. I assumed he just didn't want a church in his office park. That was certainly his prerogative. So we thanked him and went on our way.

Several weeks later we found out he was in the process of selling the entire development to what was to become the largest investment firm in the country. At that point it made perfect sense why he didn't offer to sell us any land. He was in the middle of putting this deal together.

The fellow who told us about the sale suggested we contact the group in New York that was about to purchase the development. This seemed a little premature, seeing as they had not even closed on the land. But we went ahead and contacted them. We even went so far as to make an offer on an eighty-three acre tract.

The broker representing the group in New York was skeptical. The

New York group was buying the land as an investment. The real estate market in that area was heating up. They were going to want top dollar and a fast closing. He was confident they would not be willing to sell us an option. Nor would they be willing to allow us to take an unreasonable amount of time to close.

Looking at it from their perspective, we were a big risk. We had been in existence for all of four months. We had no members. No assets. We had no credit. We had no history. And we had very little money in the bank. And here we were trying to purchase a five-million-dollar piece of property. There was no reason in the world they should have taken a chance on us.

To complicate matters even further, several parties involved with the decision-making arm of this firm weren't wild about a church in the park to begin with. Churches generally drive property values down.

And if that wasn't enough, we had no direct dealings with the people in New York. Everything was being communicated through a broker.

This was a long shot to say the least. But we also knew this was the ideal location for our church. So we prayed. And we prayed and we prayed. Specifically, we prayed that God would give us favor with the group that was buying the property.

After about a month of communication through their broker, they decided to give us a chance. We were amazed. The brokers on both sides were surprised as well. We negotiated the price of the land before it was really theirs to negotiate. Nine months later we closed on what would soon become the home of North Point Community Church.

Focus your prayers on what you know needs to happen in order to get your vision off the launching pad. Pray for those people who have the power, resources, or influence to make your vision possible. Pray that God would give you favor in their presence. Then start preparing your speech.

2. HE PLANNED.

In addition to praying for opportunities and potential players, spend some time planning a strategy. This will feel like the biggest waste of time imaginable. Don't allow the seeming improbability of your vision to keep you from developing a strategy. Besides, at this point, what else can you do?

Go ahead and develop a plan. Assuming you had the resources, what would you do? Assuming you had the time, what would you do first? Second? Third? Plan as if you knew someone were going to come along and give you an opportunity to pursue your vision.

"Absurd" you say? "A foolish exercise"? Nehemiah didn't think so. He developed a plan. Think about how ludicrous it was for him to even think about having the opportunity and the resources to pursue his vision. Yet, he devised a plan anyway. Nehemiah's Strategy for Rebuilding the Wall in Jerusalem looked something like this:

- Step 1—Convince the king to allow me to leave his service in order to rebuild the wall around a city that in years past posed a military threat to this area.
- Step 2—Convince the king to lend financial support to the building project.
- Step 3—Procure letters from the king to the governors in the surrounding areas asking them to provide me safe conduct along the way.
- Step 4—Work out a deal with Asaph, keeper of the king's forest, to procure enough lumber to build the city gates as well as a home for me.
- Step 5—Ask the king for the title of Governor of Judah.
- Step 6—Organize and equip the inhabitants of Jerusalem.
- Step 7—Begin construction.

Compared to his plans, yours probably won't look so extraordinary after all. In fact, it may be a good idea to review Nehemiah's plans from time to time just to stay encouraged. And as we will see in the next chapter, he had all of this worked out before there was any movement on the part of the king.

Nehemiah spent his time in the starting blocks praying and planning. If God granted him an opportunity to cast his vision before the king, he would be ready. There would be no doubt in Artaxerxes' mind that this fellow was serious. This was not some fanciful wish or dream. This was a vision. And given an opportunity, Nehemiah was prepared to follow through.

Get Ready

At a minimum, you have a vague idea of what should and could be in the key areas of your life. Do you have a plan?

If the right opportunity came along, do you know what you would do? If that guy you have been praying for were to ask you about your faith, do you know what you would say? If suddenly you had an opportunity to switch careers, do you know what steps you would need to make the transition successfully? You probably have a vision for how you want your children to turn out. Do you have a plan? You have a vision for your marriage. Do you have a plan?

In many instances, opportunity apart from preparation results in missed opportunity. There are opportunities you will not be able to take advantage of if you haven't done your homework. Nehemiah certainly would have missed his. Without a plan, without some preparation, you may miss yours.

Michael's Story

When I met Michael, the two things I noticed first were his car and his clothing. His car was a bomb. But he dressed like he just stepped out of GQ magazine. He was a study in contrasts. He drove a big 1973 green Impala. It was huge by modern standards. And beat-up by any standards. Yet there he was, dressed to kill. Shined shoes. Straps. Starched shirt. Great tie. Very professional. So what's with the car?

Michael had a vision. His vision was to be in business for himself. Which business? He didn't know. When? He didn't know. How would he make the transition from supporting himself with his current job to investing the time needed to get a start-up company off the ground? He didn't know that either.

But Michael wasn't discouraged. He developed a plan. At this stage in the life of his vision, there were several big unknowns. Several pieces of the puzzle involved people he hadn't even met. But that was okay. In the meantime he decided to do what he could do with what he knew. And what he knew was that owning his own business would require start-up capital.

With that in mind, Michael and his wife Susie chose a standard of living well below what they could afford. His job demanded a professional appearance. So he couldn't cut corners there. But his boss had no say so over the car he drove. So he drove the Impala. After driving the Impala for a few more years, he gave it away and bought a Ford Escort.

Why? What was he saving for? Well, he didn't know exactly. What he knew was that if the right opportunity came along, he wanted to be ready. Lowering his standard of living was pretty much the only part of his plan he had any control over. Like Nehemiah, he did what he knew to do. And he prayed God would honor his vision and grant him an opportunity.

Seven years later his opportunity came along. Sure enough, it required a hefty chunk of capital. But Michael was ready. The uninformed outsider may be tempted to comment on how "lucky" he was. Michael wasn't *lucky*. He was *ready*. He had a vision. And in the beginning that was all he had. But in the interim, he did what he could. He prayed, he dreamed, and he planned. Now Michael can drive whatever he wants. And he doesn't need to dress up anymore!

One of the exciting things about being a believer is watching God unveil his plan for our lives. On one hand we have no idea what he desires to do through us. At the same time we are called to make ourselves available. Envisioning the future and planning for it are parts of the availability process.

Why should God bring an opportunity your way if you are not in a position to take advantage of it? If you were God, to whom would you give opportunities? Wishful thinkers? Dreamers? Or planners?

I know it seems futile. Remember, most visions appear futile in the early stages. President Kennedy was talking about putting a man on the moon before the technology to do so even existed. Vision usually precedes just about everything necessary to bring it into the sphere of reality. I say "just about everything" because there is usually at least one thing the visionary can do. Plan.

Ready Ahead of Time

While working as minister to students in my father's church, I began writing a church constitution. Not necessarily for the First Baptist Church of Atlanta. I really didn't know what church it was for. All I knew was that one day I hoped to have an opportunity to pastor a church. I was content where I was. But I had a feeling I wouldn't be a minister to students forever. I didn't have a timetable in mind. In fact, I assumed I would stay at FBA in some capacity indefinitely.

What I did know was that if I was ever to assume the responsibility of senior pastor I wanted to work within a church structure that reflected a specific vision and mission. So I began developing a detailed outline of how I thought a church ought to be set up. I went so far as to have a fellow develop several charts to illustrate my ideas. I worked on this off and on for two years. And honestly, I had no idea where or if it would ever be implemented.

Four years later I had the privilege of working with a team of like-minded people to form North Point Community Church. One of the first issues that came up was the form of church government we would adopt. I can't imagine what it would have been like to begin that process from scratch. Especially with everything else that was going on at the time.

My years of pondering and planning paid off. My ideas made sense to the rest of the team. After a few minor changes, we adopted the basic structure I had outlined as the framework for our new church constitution.

STAYING ALIVE

New visions die easily. And understandably so. There is little to go on. Praying and planning will help you keep your vision alive. And that is critical. When your vision dies, part of you dies as well. So pray. Pray for opportunities. Pray for the people who could help you launch your vision. And while you wait, plan! Develop a strategy. Dream on paper. Find the one or two things you *can* do and get busy.

You don't know what God is up to. It is better to be ready even if nothing happens than to run the risk of missing out if he brings an opportunity your way.

BUILDING BLOCK #3

PRAY FOR OPPORTUNITIES AND PLAN AS IF YOU EXPECT GOD TO ANSWER YOUR PRAYERS.

VISIONEERING

PROJECT #2

Work through this exercise for each of your visions.

1. What opportunities do you need to begin praying for?

   _____

   _____

   _____

   _____

2. Who are the people who could help you accomplish your vision?

   _____

   _____

   _____

   _____

3. What changes would need to take place in their thinking in order for them to support your effort?

   _____

   _____

   _____

   _____

4. Write a simple plan.

   Step 1._____

   Step 2._____

   Step 3._____

   Step 4._____

5. What can you do now?

_____

_____

_____

_____

CHAPTER THREE

....

POSITIONS
PLEASE!

Goals can be energizing—when you win.
But a vision is more powerful than a goal. A vision is enlivening,
it's spirit-giving, it's the guiding force behind all great human endeavors.
Vision is about shared energy, a sense of awe, a sense of possibility.
BENJAMIN ZANDER, CONDUCTOR,
BOSTON PHILHARMONIC ORCHESTRA

Let's begin with some good news. From the outset, just about every God-ordained vision appears to be impossible. The reason that's good news is because you were beginning to suspect you were crazy to even consider pursuing some of the ideas swirling around in your head. And if you have dared to share your vision with others, they may have confirmed your suspicion. They just looked at you skeptically and said something along the lines of, "Now that's an interesting idea." Which you rightly interpreted to mean, "That'll never happen."

Maybe that's why Nehemiah kept his mouth shut for such a long time. For four months he kept it all inside. After all, who would have taken him seriously? Think about it.

He was a slave. He worked for the king. He couldn't exactly slip out unnoticed. And besides, the Babylonians had torn down the walls around Jerusalem for a reason. A defenseless city posed no threat. The Persians

41

certainly weren't going to stand by while somebody reestablished Israel as a military presence in that region. Nehemiah was crazy to even consider such a thing.

Add the fact that the walls had been torn down for almost 150 years. If the people who lived in Jerusalem hadn't made any effort to rebuild before now, what made Nehemiah think that if he showed up it would make any difference? After all, he had no authority. He was just the cup-bearer to the king. The king whose predecessors had torn the wall down to begin with.

No doubt you can relate to some of Nehemiah's feelings as he considered the magnitude of his vision. Perhaps you are a pastor with a vision for bringing needed change to your church. Maybe you are married to an unbeliever and you are envisioning a Christian marriage. You may be considering a major career change. It could be that you are contemplating beginning your own business. Whatever the case, when you look at the landscape of your circumstances, it is overwhelming. It just doesn't look like there's any way in the world to pull it off.

That is always the case when God puts something in our hearts for us to do. The task always appears to be out of reach. And the reason it appears that way is because it is. God-ordained visions are always too big for us to handle. We shouldn't be surprised. Consider the source.

There are always more questions than answers when God births a vision in our hearts. There are always obstacles. There is always a lack of resources. A man or woman with a vision usually feels alone. Even isolated. Often there is little to go on other than gut-level, unquenchable, insatiable desire. And hopefully a sense of destiny: a feeling that this is what you were made for, an assurance that God has called you out into uncharted waters with a divine purpose in mind. If any of that rings true for you, you may be on the brink of something divine.

POSITIONING THE PLAYERS

"So," you ask, "if I am on the brink of something divine, why am I stuck here, doing something not remotely related to what I feel God has put in my heart to do?" No doubt Nehemiah asked that question every time images of Jerusalem passed through his mind. "Lord, what am I doing in Persia? You have called me to be a builder, not a bartender!"

Ah, but God knew exactly what he was doing. He had Nehemiah in the right place, doing the right thing, at the right time. Unbeknownst to Nehemiah and Artaxerxes, God had spent years preparing and positioning these men for what was about to unfold.

Consider this: from the time Nehemiah was a little boy, God had been engineering his circumstances to ensure him a place among the palace servants. From there God maneuvered him through the ranks of influential Persian officials so he was noticed for his integrity and trustworthiness. Eventually, he was recommended to the king by some unknown palace staffer. And then one day he was appointed to the position of cupbearer.

On the surface, it would appear God was moving Nehemiah in a direction that would make it impossible for him to ever realize his dream. But just the opposite was true. God landed Nehemiah a job that gave him an inside track to the king. But he had more than a job. As cupbearer, Nehemiah had a special relationship with the king as well. Every day the king entrusted his life to the man who served his wine. It was the cupbearer's responsibility to protect the king from being poisoned by his enemies. Artaxerxes' own father had been murdered by a trusted servant. He knew all too well the possibility of betrayal from within the inner circle.

Like a master strategist, God had been working behind the scenes, putting all the players into position. And now the curtain was about to go up, signaling the beginning of a divinely scripted, perfectly cast play.

Of course that's easy for me to say. I've read the end of the story. I know how everything turns out. But Nehemiah didn't. He had no idea his years of servitude to the king had any divine significance. For all he knew, God had forgotten him and his people. For years his prayers had seemingly gone unanswered. He saw no improvement nor hope of improvement. Every day was basically the same. His leadership gifts and organizational skills lay dormant as he served Artaxerxes month after month after month. After all, he was merely the cupbearer to the king. But God had Nehemiah right where he wanted him. He was perfectly positioned.

BUILDING BLOCK #4

GOD IS USING YOUR CIRCUMSTANCES TO POSITION AND PREPARE YOU TO ACCOMPLISH HIS VISION FOR YOUR LIFE.

POSITIONS PLEASE!

Believe it or not, God wants to do the same thing in your life. His desire is to work through your circumstances to maneuver you into proper position. This is easy to see when we are looking back. It is something we have to take by faith when looking ahead. Often there is no tangible connection between our circumstances and the vision God has given us.

In 1969, while pastoring the First Baptist Church of Bartow, Florida, my dad received a call from a friend asking him if he would be interested in coming to First Baptist Church of Atlanta as an associate pastor.

Humanly speaking, it was not a good career move. My dad had always been a senior pastor in previous churches. As a senior pastor, he had an opportunity to preach two or three times per week. Preaching was a major part of what he perceived to be God's vision for his life. By going to Atlanta he would lose that opportunity.

FBA was a large multiple-staff church. He would have far fewer preaching opportunities. And he ran the risk of being pegged as an associate pastor for life. Nothing about going to Atlanta indicated this was a vision-oriented move. But as he prayed, he felt we should relocate to Atlanta.

After a few weeks in his new position, he discovered things were not as they had been presented to him. He would not have the authority he had been promised. He would have far less responsibility than he had expected. And upon moving into his new office he discovered the desk drawers were locked, and nobody knew where the keys were!

Looking back, it is evident our move to Atlanta was God's way of positioning my dad for what lay ahead. But at the time it seemed like a colossal mistake. Life in Bartow had been great. After a month in Atlanta, Bartow seemed like paradise.

Three years after our moving to Atlanta the senior pastor resigned, and the church put together a pulpit committee to find a new senior pastor. Meanwhile my dad filled the pulpit on Sunday mornings. As you can imagine, most of the people loved him. Unfortunately, the power brokers of FBA didn't.

My dad posed a threat to their control of the church, and consequently he was asked to resign. Not formally. They never came out and asked him in a legitimate business meeting. But behind the scenes—one on one, over dinner—promises were made. It was church politics at its worst.

Once again, circumstantially, this was all moving in the wrong direction. From a ministry standpoint, things couldn't have been better. Every week people were responding to his preaching. The services were being broadcast all over the city. And now he was facing pressure to resign. What was God up to?

Things finally came to a head. A business meeting was called for the express purpose of forcing his resignation. He had said all along that if the people voted him out, he would have no problem leaving. He would accept that as God's will. But he had no peace about resigning.

When the big night rolled around, things took an unexpected twist. After several hours of bantering back and forth, a vote was called for. The congregation stood by him. They did not vote him out. In fact they elected him as senior pastor that very night! The opposition was furious. They left the church and saw to it that the local CBS affiliate dropped FBA from its programming schedule.

As it turned out, their departure, and the decision by the local station to cancel the broadcast, laid the groundwork for the birth of In Touch Ministries. Looking back, it is as if God had scripted the whole thing. He brought my father in through the back door. He got him into position. Then he birthed an international ministry.

You don't know what God is up to behind the scenes of your life. You don't know how close you are to a breakthrough. It is no accident you are where you are. And it is not necessarily a problem that you are not where you assume you ought to be. God is very much in control. He works all things to the good of those who are "called according to his purpose" (Romans 8:28). His vision for your life is his purpose.

God is using your circumstances to prepare you to accomplish his vision for your life. Your present circumstances are part of the vision. You are not wasting your time. You are not spinning your wheels. You are not wandering in the wilderness. If you are "seeking first" his kingdom where you are, then where you are is where he has positioned you. And he has positioned you there with a purpose in mind. Like Nehemiah, it may be difficult for you to make the connection at this point. But in time, it will come together. It always does.

CONGRATULATIONS!

One of the things that makes this stage in the development of a vision so difficult is our confusion regarding success. There is a tendency to confuse *success* with the *rewards* of success. If you are where God wants you, fulfilling the responsibilities he has given you, you are successful. In fact, when that is the case, you are as successful as you will ever be. Granted, you may not be seeing or experiencing the rewards of your success. But you are successful nonetheless.

Success is remaining faithful to the process God has laid out for you. Certainly there are significant and enjoyable mile markers along the way. But success is not the mile marker. Success is not the raise, promotion, recognition, Christian home, or wonderful children. Those are simply enjoyable mile markers along the way. Success is staying faithful to the process that contributed to those things becoming a reality. Unfortunately, we often don't consider ourselves successful until we experience the rewards.

In 1995 the Atlanta Braves finally won a World Series. But no one would say they became a successful team in the ninth inning of game six in the 1995 World Series. When did they become successful? Certainly winning their division title was a mile marker, a reward. But when did they become successful? They were successful the entire season. In fact, their success began in previous seasons as they began making the decisions necessary to build a championship team. Winning the World Series was the fulfillment of a vision. But success came long before the exhilaration of winning that final game.

Think about it. When was Nehemiah successful? I know when he *felt* like a success. The day they laid the last brick on the wall. That was one of the most exhilarating days of his life. But Nehemiah was successful long before then.

He was successful the day he embraced the vision God laid on his heart. Why? Because he was faithful to what God had called him to do that particular day. He was successful the night he laid in bed and developed a mental inventory of what it would take to rebuild the gates. Why? Because he did everything he could do to advance the vision God had given him. He was successful the morning he asked God to grant him favor before the king. He was successful before the king granted his request. Why? Because he was doing all he knew to do.

When did my dad become successful? I know when he became famous. But when was he successful? The day he embraced the vision God gave him for his life. He was successful long before he was known. His success/faithfulness in those early years is what enabled him to enjoy the rewards of his success during these latter years. But he is no more successful now, in God's eyes, than he was then.

When are parents successful? When their child emerges from adolescence without a police record? When their daughter or son graduates from college? When their grown son lands his first job? When their daughter brings home the first grandchild? No. Those are the rewards of successful parenting. Those are significant mile markers. But a parent who has a good relationship with a responsible, mature adult child has been successful for years. Every day of responsible parenting was a day of success.

Don't miss this important distinction. As a parent, my ultimate vision is responsible children with whom I can enjoy an adult relationship for life. But I can be a successful parent long before I reach that rewarding mile marker.

You are a success every day you get up and show up for duty. Every day of faithfulness where you are with what you have is a successful day. Rewarding? Maybe. Successful? Absolutely. You are as successful now as you will be the day you see your vision materialize. Others may not recognize your success until then. But that does nothing to diminish the significance of what was taking place along the way.

If you measure your success by whether or not your vision has materialized, you are a candidate for discouragement. After all, there are days when it seems we are moving at light speed in the wrong direction. It is possible to go for weeks, months, even years, with no sign of progress. Confusing success with the rewards of success is one of the primary reasons people abandon their dreams.

CELEBRATING LITTLE SUCCESSES

If I don't consider myself successful until I *see* something happen, then I am only inches away from considering myself a failure. And we won't allow ourselves to fail any longer than we have to. Once feelings of failure begin to take root, we have a compelling reason to abandon the vision. After all, if I don't really want to do something anyway, I don't feel so much like a failure when I retreat. Retreating from the vision becomes a form of self-defense.

In the meantime we must see success for what it is: faithfulness to the process. And we must celebrate little successes along the way. Instead of cursing your surroundings, celebrate your faithfulness in spite of them. The problem with cursing your current surroundings is that, like anything else you curse, it becomes a focus. And *to focus on what's around you diminishes your ability to focus on what's before you.*

Unfortunately, it is easy to lose sight and give up. It is easy to get so fixated on our surroundings that we give in to the little voice that whispers, "Who are you kidding?"

"You're not going anywhere to rebuild anything."

"She's never coming home."

"He's not going to become a Christian."

"You're never going to have the resources to do that."

"Nobody's going to go for that."

"Your kids are too far gone."

"You'll never have a marriage like that."

"Nobody's going to listen to you."

It is hard to ignore that little voice when everything around you seconds the motion. It is next to impossible to regain perspective in an environment hostile to your dreams.

But it is even more difficult to live life wondering. Wondering what God would have done. Wondering how close you were to experiencing a breakthrough. Wondering what would have happened had you not given up.

WAITING TIME

In *I Was Wrong*, Jim Bakker describes the terrible depression he went through while in prison. During one of his lowest moments, he received an encouraging letter from a pastor friend, Bob Gass. Bob believed God was not through with Jim. It was his conviction that prison was part of God's vision for Jim's life. Later, Jim came to share that conviction. In the book he documents the remarkable changes that took place in his life as a result of those dark days in prison.

Part of Jim's depression stemmed from the fact that he had a forty-five-year sentence, and he was unable to minister inside the prison. From his vantage point he was facing forty-five pointless, fruitless, wasted years of life. You can certainly understand why he was depressed.

In his letter, Bob Gass made a statement that must have sounded like "preacher talk" to Jim at the time. But which later proved to be true. He wrote, "Waiting time will not be wasted time."[1] As hard as that was for Jim to believe, I imagine it was just as hard for Nehemiah to believe. Waiting time is not wasted time for anyone in whose heart God has placed a vision. Difficult time. Painful time. Frustrating time. But not wasted time.

God has you where he wants you. He is the master strategist. You are an important component in his strategy. He is the head. You are a member of the body. He is in control. You are to surrender to that control.

In the meantime, God is using your circumstances to position and prepare you to accomplish his vision for your life.

VISIONEERING
PROJECT #3

1. What does remaining faithful in your current situation entail?

_____

_____

_____

2. What is the main thing about your current situation that makes it difficult for you to believe God is preparing you for his vision?

_____

_____

_____

No doubt Nehemiah would have answered this question, "I am cupbearer to the king of Persia." And yet that was the very thing God used to launch the vision. Would you be willing to pause and express your faith in God's ability to use your present circumstances to position you for the fulfillment of his vision for your life?

....

CHAPTER FOUR

THE GOD OF HOW

The vision of an organization acts as its magnetic north.
THE LEADERSHIP CHALLENGE

hris had a vision. His vision was to share the gospel with every student at Dunwoody High School. Chris first let me know about his vision at the beginning of his senior year. He and I met together on Tuesday afternoons for discipleship. As his youth pastor I was both thrilled and humbled. Thrilled at his zeal. Humbled by memories of my senior year. I don't know about you, but my senior year "visions" were not what you would consider positive illustration material. Anyway, Chris told me about his vision, and we went to work trying to figure out a way to make it happen.

One of our obstacles was that Chris was not what you would consider a mainstream kind of guy. He wasn't the president of anything. He wasn't on any teams. He didn't date a cheerleader. He wasn't an honor student. He didn't even dress like everybody else. Chris was a skater.

Now in certain communities around Atlanta, being a skater would put you in one of the top echelons in your local junior high or high school. But not at Dunwoody. At Dunwoody High, skaters got no respect. There weren't that many to begin with. And the handful that were there were alternative before alternative was cool. Bottom line, Chris wasn't going to be asked to speak to the student body in this lifetime. He had no leverage. All he had was a vision.

But Chris wasn't discouraged. He felt this was something God would have him pursue. He felt it was his responsibility to make sure everybody in his school had at least one opportunity to hear a clear gospel presentation once before he or she graduated. So we explored every option imaginable. We thought about writing everybody a letter. We discussed doing a phone blitz. I suggested dropping notes in everybody's locker. But none of these ideas seemed right. The year came and went and Chris's vision never came to fruition—or so it seemed.

Like Nehemiah, however, Chris was faithful to do what he could while trusting God to do what he couldn't. During his senior year, Chris took advantage of every opportunity to share his faith with other students. One of the fellows he had an opportunity to share with was Mark.

Mark grew up with his mom in Miami. His folks had split up when he was younger, and his dad eventually moved to Atlanta. When Mark hit adolescence, he did so with a vengeance. He fell prey to the allurement of alcohol and drugs. He was flunking out of school. By the end of his tenth grade year, his mom had had enough. She packed him up and sent him to Atlanta to live with his dad.

Mark didn't want to leave his friends in Miami. He didn't really want to live with his dad. As far as he was concerned, life... Well you get the picture. With that in mind, imagine his first day at Dunwoody High School. He had an attitude that preceded him by about ten minutes everywhere he went. This was not a kid you walked up to and greeted in the halls. Consequently, nobody reached out to Mark. Nobody except, you guessed it, Chris.

One of the most remarkable things about Chris was that nobody intimidated him. He wasn't put off by Mark. He saw him for what he was: an angry, hurt young man in need of a friend and a Savior. So Chris went right up, introduced himself, and showed him around. As it turned out, they both liked some of the same music. In fact, Mark was a drummer and Chris played bass. That weekend, Chris invited Mark to spend the night with him at his parents' house.

At this juncture in Chris's life, he assumed all bets were off with his vision. There was no way he was going to be able to share the gospel with the student body. God hadn't provided a vehicle. The best he could do was get in as many one-on-one exchanges as possible before the year ended.

Little did he know God had not given up on the vision. He was still quietly at work behind the scenes. And Mark was going to play a key role in seeing to it that Chris's vision became a reality.

Late that evening, after several hours of listening to music, Mark opened up with Chris. He told him about his life in Miami. He shared his reluctance about coming to Atlanta. He admitted he was pretty much mad at the world.

When he finished, Chris, a seventeen-year-old high school student, told Mark that he had a heavenly Father who loved him in spite of all he had done. He told him about Christ dying for his sin so he could be forgiven. That night, Mark put his trust in Christ and became a Christian. Then Chris told him about his cool youth pastor (me!) and about his church. The next Sunday Mark showed up. He joined our student ministry.

The school year came and went. Chris graduated and went to college. Meanwhile Mark had one more year at DHS. I asked Mark to be in my discipleship class. Through that year we became good friends.

Then one Wednesday night, right before our student Bible study, Mark ran up to me with a look of panic on his face. "Andy, you won't believe it." Mark started every sentence that way. "You won't believe it, I have been asked to speak to the whole student body during our Arrive Alive assembly."

Every year, on the Friday afternoon just before spring break, DHS conducted a campuswide assembly program dedicated to warning students about the dangers of drinking and driving. Typically, they would invite someone who had a gory tale to tell. The stories usually involved a head-on collision, multiple broken bones, and a long hospital stay. Occasionally, the speaker would show a scar or two.

The idea was to motivate students to be careful while they were away on spring break. Often, they would put a car that had been totaled by a drunk driver on the campus lawn as a visual aid.

Well, Mrs. Dolworth, the principle of DHS, knew Mark had been heavily involved with alcohol and drugs before coming to her school.

Furthermore, she was aware that a remarkable change had taken place in his life. She thought it would be a good idea if Mark, being a student, would follow the featured speaker at the assembly. So she called Mark and asked him to share his story.

"Do you think I should tell them my *whole* story?" he asked.

I smiled. "Mark, when I speak at a public school, they won't even announce where I work. They introduce me as an adolescent counselor. God has given you a unique opportunity. You are a student. You can say anything you want. Yes, I think you ought to tell them your whole story."

I will never forget walking into the DHS gym that Friday afternoon. My heart was pounding so hard I could hear it. I rarely get nervous when I speak. But I was so nervous for Mark I wasn't sure I was going to be able to stay.

The gym was packed. It was literally standing room only. Students, faculty, teachers—they were all there. Mrs. Dolworth introduced their keynote speaker. He had graduated from DHS several years prior. He did a good job telling his story. Lots of blood and guts. The students loved it. But his conclusion was flat. After thirty minutes of car wrecks and life-threatening injuries he said, "So students, hang together. You have each other. Thank you." And he sat down.

Everyone clapped politely. Then Mrs. Dolworth walked to the center of the gymnasium and announced, "This afternoon we have one of our own DHS students who is going to share for just a few minutes about some changes that have taken place in his life. Please welcome Mark Hannah."

I thought I was going to die. Mark walked slowly out to center court, took the microphone off the stand and began. "When I first came to Dunwoody High School, I hated everything and everybody." He talked about his life in Miami. He shared about his intense anger. He delved into his experience with alcohol and drugs.

You could have heard a pin drop—except for the fact that my heart was beating so hard I'm sure it must have distracted the people around me.

Then Mark turned the corner. "One day a guy named Chris Folley introduced himself to me and invited me to his house. That night I told him all about my life. I told him how much I hated everybody. He listened. And then he told me Jesus loved me. He explained how he died on the cross for my sins. He said I could be forgiven. That night I prayed with Chris and my life changed.

"Everything hasn't been easy since then. I still have my struggles. But now I don't have to face them alone. If you have any questions about anything I've said, I would be happy to talk with you afterwards. Thank you."

With that, he placed the microphone back in the stand and sauntered back to his assigned place on the bleachers. Meanwhile, the entire student body stood to their feet in applause. They clapped and cheered for what must have been several minutes. It was too much for me. I left the gym and headed for my car.

Strangely enough, it wasn't until I walked outside that the significance of what had just happened hit me. "Lord, this was about Chris, wasn't it?"

Even as I type these words, tears fill my eyes as I think back to one senior in high school who was faithful to do what he could while trusting God to do what he couldn't. Chris's concerns were in alignment with the Father's. So he went to work behind the scenes to ensure that the vision became a reality.

WHAT BEFORE HOW

The story of Chris and Mark illustrates an agonizingly important principle: *what* always precedes *how.* You will know what God has put in your heart to do before you know how he intends to bring it about. Often, you will know *what* long before you understand *how.* Chris had to wait almost two years. His *how* came so late in the game he assumed what he thought should be, wouldn't be. After all, he had already graduated. It is not that his plan failed. We were never able to come up with a plan to begin with. His *how* came about independently from his planning. But not independently from his faithfulness.

This was certainly Nehemiah's experience. He knew what God had called him to do. He didn't have a clue as to how or when God would pull it off. For four months, nothing happened. And he apparently had no indication anything was even about to happen. He was at a standstill. And he knew that humanly speaking, there was absolutely no way this vision was ever going to get off the ground.

But God had a plan. God knew how to secure Nehemiah's release from service to the king. He had a plan for financing and overseeing the rebuilding of the walls. God had the *how* all worked out. What he needed was a *who*. By embracing and internalizing the burden God placed on his heart, Nehemiah became God's answer to *who*.

Many visions die in the time between what and how. And understandably so. When *how* seems out of sight, it is tempting to put *what* out of mind. Why put ourselves through the agony? Why live in a constant state of frustration? In Nehemiah's case, why walk around looking like you just lost your best friend (2:1)? At some point it is just easier to lower your sights, jettison your vision, and shoot for a target you have some hopes of hitting.

For this reason, it is dangerous to become too preoccupied with trying to figure out how to bring about your vision. Plan the best you can. But remember, a divine vision necessitates divine intervention. And that brings us to building block #5:

BUILDING BLOCK #5

WHAT GOD ORIGINATES, HE ORCHESTRATES.

You probably need to put this one on your bathroom mirror for a month or two. *How* is never a problem for God. It is usually a big problem for us. But *how* is God's specialty. If the Old and New Testament teach us anything, they teach us that nothing is too difficult for God. What he originates, he orchestrates.

Case in point: Mary. Talk about a vision. Gabriel appears and paints an all too clear picture of what is about to transpire in her life. And she asks the question any of us would have asked in that situation: *How?*

Mary said to the angel, "How can this be, since I am a virgin?" (Luke 1:34)

Remember the angel's answer? "Nothing will be impossible with God" (v. 37).

How is never a problem with God. When he puts something in your heart to do, he goes to work behind the scenes to ensure that it happens. In the meantime, we are to remain faithful to him and focused on the vision. You are not responsible for figuring out how to pull off God's vision for your life. You are responsible to do what you know to do, what you can do. And then you must wait.

Think back for a minute. Can you remember one Old or New Testament story in which the responsibility of figuring out how a divine vision would be fulfilled fell to the men or women to whom God gave the vision? Did Moses have to come up with a way to get the Israelites out of Egypt? Across the Red Sea? Through the desert? Was it David's responsibility to figure out how to get Saul out of the way so he could ascend the throne of Israel? When Jesus told the apostles to feed the five thousand, were they responsible for figuring out how to make five loaves and two fish go that far? Were the disciples responsible for figuring out how to get the gospel to the uttermost parts of the earth?

No. In every situation, God orchestrated events in such a way that those involved recognized the thumbprint of God. These were ordinary men and women who just did what they knew to do while never losing sight of the vision God had birthed in their hearts.

GOOD IDEAS VERSUS GOD IDEAS

If we were talking about good ideas, that would be different. Good ideas are limited to our potential, connections, and resources. If you are simply pursuing a good idea, then you need to devote a great deal of time and energy trying to figure out how to pull it off.

A divine vision, on the other hand, is limited only by God's potential and resources. That means anything is possible. If it is just a good idea, you have to *make* it happen. When God gives you a vision, there's a sense in which you stand back and *watch* it happen.

The challenge is that sometimes you have to stand back for a long time. Since we never know exactly when or how God is going to intervene, it is imperative that we remain vision focused. We must focus on what he has called us to do, not on how he is going to pull it off.

Staying vision focused keeps us God focused. The vision is a reminder of our dependency. We remain aware that if God doesn't do something, there is no going forward. For that reason, people with vision live with a sense of expectancy. They look for God to do something. They live by faith in the truest sense of the word. That is, they are living as if God is going to do what they believe he has promised to do.

In light of a divine vision, our daily faithfulness takes on new significance. It is no longer faithfulness for faithfulness' sake. There is something important at stake. If the visionary doesn't act, something significant won't get done. Believers with vision live with the knowledge that how may come about independently from their planning. But it will not come about apart from their faithfulness. Faithfulness is critical to success.

Find me a believer who is no longer faithful to the cause of Christ, and I will show you a man or woman who has no vision from God, no sense of divine destiny. Such people have either lost it or never had it. Visionary believers are marked by their intense faithfulness to their vision and to their Savior. For them, the question of *how* is not an obstacle. It is simply an opportunity for God to do what he does so well—the impossible.

The apostle Peter is a good example of someone who was prone to lose focus. Remember the water-walking incident? He was fine as long as he didn't worry about *how* he was going to walk on water. He did okay as long as he focused on the One who called him out of the boat. He was a water walker as long as he did what he knew to do while trusting Christ to do what he couldn't.

But the minute he lost focus, the moment his focus shifted off of *what* and *who* and onto *how*, he was treading water. He didn't know *how* to walk on water. But that wasn't a concern as long as his focus was right. As long as he kept his eyes on Jesus, *how* wasn't an issue.

So it is with us. Once God puts something in our hearts for us to do, we are to lock in on *what* it is he has called us to do. Our responsibility is to do what we know to do, and wait for him to fill in the blanks. Nehemiah did what he could do. Chris did what he could do. God did what he could do. And in the end, everything got done.

How is God's specialty.

- He knows how to reach your husband/wife/boss/neighbor.
- He knows how to protect your children even though their daddy is gone.
- He knows how to get a prayer group started where you work.
- He knows how to get your business venture off the ground.
- He knows how you can pay for school.
- He knows how to get you over your hurt.

- He knows how to put your marriage back together.
- He knows how to get that ministry started.
- He knows how to get your church turned around.

CHARGE!

Whereas some are tempted to give up when confronted with the question of *how* something will come to be, others are prone to go to the opposite extreme. These are the Navy SEAL Christians. The ones for whom no task is too challenging, no mountain too high, no problem too complex. Their life verse is Philippians 4:13a, "I can do all things." They operate under the assumption that once God gives them a vision, that's their green light to go. And since all things are possible with God, and God lives in them, nothing is impossible for them, either.

They are not afraid to grab a tiger by the tail, tug on Superman's cape, or spit into the wind. They are fearless. And to be honest, I'm somewhat envious of people who demonstrate that kind of courage. Their sense of abandonment to the cause is admirable. But often their timing is terrible.

Peter started out that way. He wasn't going to let anybody arrest Jesus. If it meant cutting off every ear in the Roman Empire, he was determined to stand by his man. After all, they were on a mission. But what a mess that turned out to be.

Maybe you can relate. You may be wired to charge in immediately once the direction is set. Had you been Nehemiah, you would have packed your bags the day you heard about the mess in Jerusalem. At nightfall, you would have been over the wall and on your way. After all, God commissioned you to rebuild a wall. And, no, you don't know how you are going to get it built. But hey, where there's a will there's a way. And where there's a God's will, there's a God's way. Besides that, you certainly can't get it built as long as you are living in Persia, bowing and scraping to a king who has no concern for you or your people.

But as convincing as your speech may have sounded, as impressive as your bravado may have come across, you would have been dead wrong.

NOT UNTIL IT'S TIME

Several years ago, Sandra and several of her friends felt a burden for the young women in our church. They were particularly concerned for those who were either geographically separated from their mothers or whose relationship with their mothers made communication difficult.

Sandra asked if they could pursue beginning a women's ministry built around the idea of older women mentoring younger women. I thought it was a great idea. So I began asking her dozens of *how* questions.

"How are you going to find the women who need to be mentored?"

"How are you going to find women to mentor these women?"

"Will you train the mentors?"

"How long will the program last?"

"Who's going to be in charge?"

"How will you pair the women up?"

"Do you have a curriculum for the women to follow?"

Nothing is worse than being asked these kind of questions when your vision is in its embryonic stage. If we aren't careful, we can *how* a person's vision to death. I wasn't trying to be obnoxious. I was expressing interest—and maybe a little concern.

Of course she didn't have answers to any of these questions. But she did have a great response. She said, "We would like to take a year to pray and plan."

A year? They wanted to wait an entire year before launching the women's ministry. In church work, this is unheard of. Customarily, you start before you are ready. You publicize it before you have staffed it. Then you spend years complaining about how nobody is committed anymore.

For twelve months Sandra and her team met and prayed and planned. At the end of the year they went public with their plans. From day one, it was evident God had given them a strategy. I sat back in amazement as this team of relatively young ladies mobilized and trained the older women in our congregation. Then with what had to be divine guidance they paired younger with older. We heard story after story of how the women they put together were a perfect match. That was five years ago. Many of those women continue to meet together to this very day. God knew *how* to launch a women's ministry in our church. He just needed somebody to step up to the plate and wait for the right pitch.

It is amazing what can be accomplished when we wait on God to lead us out. It is equally amazing the mess we can make of things when we charge out on our own. A divine vision is not dependent upon us making something happen. It is dependent upon God making something happen. Jesus explained it to his disciples this way:

> I am the vine, you are the branches; he who abides in Me and I in him, he bears much fruit, for apart from Me you can do nothing. (John 15:5)

To which we are tempted to respond, "Now wait, certainly I can do *something.*" True. But nothing of any eternal consequence. God's vision for your life is chock-full of eternal consequence.

When left to our own ingenuity, we can foul up a vision in short order. But God's work, done in God's way, in God's time, is always successful. And it comes off in such a way as to point back towards the source: God.

ONE MORE TIME

Just in case you missed it the previous twelve times, *how* is not a problem for God. If God has a problem, it's us. We are prone to allow the question of *how* either to overwhelm us or to catapult us into a self-propelled frenzy of activity.

If you feel overwhelmed, remember, you are invited to tap into the inexhaustible resources of God. He is not expecting you to come up with everything that is needed to accomplish the vision he has birthed in you.

If, on the other hand, your healthy self-esteem deceives you into thinking that you have what it takes to get the job done, remember: this is a God thing. God has called you. He is not depending upon you. You are a player. You are not the whole team.

In either case, God is looking for dependence. A dependence that actively waits upon him to answer the question *how?*

VISIONEERING
PROJECT #4

1. How do you normally respond to a challenge?
   ___ I am easily overwhelmed.
   ___ I have a tendency to charge ahead.
   ___ I don't like to move ahead until most of my questions are answered.
   ___ Other. Explain:

2. Imagine yourself in Nehemiah's situation. Based on your track record, how do you think you would have responded if God had given you the vision of rebuilding the walls around Jerusalem?

3. I love to spend time with people who are pursuing a vision. I always come away from those conversations challenged and encouraged. Who do you know and respect who is pursuing a vision?

Set up a time to talk with that person about how he or she approached the question of *how* when they initially stepped out to pursue the vision.

CHAPTER FIVE

FAITH, THE ESSENTIAL INGREDIENT

The testing of your faith produces endurance.
JAMES 1:3

F ew things provide our faith with a more thorough workout than a divinely-ordered vision.

Spiritually speaking, faith is confidence that God is who he says he is and that he will do what he has promised to do. Faith is not a power or a force. It is not a vehicle by which we can coerce God into something against his will. It is simply an expression of confidence in the person and character of God. It is the proper response to the promise or revelation of God.

Embracing and owning a vision is in itself an act of faith. To do so is to live by faith in the truest sense. When we embrace a vision in its infancy, before anything has really "happened," we are making a statement about our confidence in the person and character of God. Pursuing a divine vision is really an act of worship. It is a declaration of our confidence in God. It is a proclamation of how important we believe his agenda to be. And God is honored.

Acting on your faith is the ultimate expression of devotion, admiration, and adoration. Acting on your faith demonstrates that you believe God is who he says he is, and he will do what he has promised to do.

Nothing is more honoring to your heavenly Father than making life decisions based upon what he has claimed about himself. This is especially true when circumstances seem to dictate a different response.

The difficult thing for us is that the more contrary the circumstances, the more honor God receives. That is, the more unlikely the fulfillment of our vision, the more faith that is required. And consequently, the greater the potential for God's glory.

That being the case, Nehemiah was set up for maximum impact in the glory department. His vision was against the wind in every way imaginable. No one, including Nehemiah, was going to rob God of his fair share of credit if this deal came down. This, of course, was good news for God. But it was a faith-stretching, trust-wrenching ordeal for Nehemiah.

THE LEGACY OF FAITH

Nehemiah was only one of many Bible characters who lived with the tension of faith and vision. The Scriptures are full of stories of men and women who wrestled with this relationship. The Bible heroes we so often celebrate were not simply men and women of faith, they were visionaries, as well. They were committed to what could be and what should be in spite of what they saw around them.

Think of the honor Noah and his family brought God by obeying God and building the ark. Noah's faith fueled his vision. He was taking God at his word. It was going to rain. There would be a flood. Noah was not only a man of faith, he was a man of vision.

> By *faith* Noah, being warned by God about things not yet *seen*, in reverence prepared an ark for the salvation of his household, by which he condemned the world, and became an heir of the righteousness which is according to *faith*. (Hebrews 11:7, emphasis mine)

The same was true of Abraham. He envisioned a homeland where God would multiply his children to the point of international significance. But it was vision supported by faith. After all, he didn't know where God was taking him. And Sarah was unable to have children. Yet notice what is said of Abraham.

> By faith Abraham, when he was called, obeyed by going out to a place which he was to receive for an inheritance; and he went out, not knowing where he was going. (v. 8)

His faith fueled his vision. Without great faith, there would have been no forward progress for Abraham. The vision would have died in Haran. But Abraham believed God. He believed his promise of a new homeland and a family that would bless the earth. He believed not because he could see. His faith was grounded in the character of God. If God said there would be a nation, there would be a nation. And God was honored by Abraham's faith.

The same pattern can be found in the story of Joshua at Jericho, Gideon and the Midianites, and David in his pursuit of the throne. All these men were given visions of what could and should be. And each stepped out in faith, putting all his hopes in God's faithfulness to his word.

Pursuing a vision requires faith. Pursuing a great vision requires great faith. Pursuing a vision will test, stretch, and at times exhaust your faith. And while you are pulling your hair out down here, God revels in the glory he receives.

While we wait and wait and wait, and trust and trust and trust, he basks in the glory reflected back to him by his faithful servants. He glories in our willingness to take him at his word. He delights in our perseverance in the face of debilitating odds. Our faith and ensuing faithfulness bring him immense honor—honor he rightly deserves.

All of this points ahead to a truth we will explore in greater detail later. But I can't resist stating it now. God-inspired visions ultimately lead back to God. Regardless of our role, we are never the focal point of a genuine God-ordained vision. He is.

MEANWHILE, BACK IN PERSIA

Back in Persia, Nehemiah's faith was being stretched beyond recognition. He was all too aware of his dependence upon God. And no doubt God was basking in the glory it brought him.

And then something entirely unexpected happened. While Nehemiah was serving the king, Artaxerxes noticed that his cupbearer was sad. This was the first time Nehemiah had revealed his emotions to the king (Nehemiah 2:1). Instead of throwing him out of the throne

VISIONEERING

room, which was common when a servant expressed anything other than delight in the king's presence, the king actually asked Nehemiah why he was so distraught.

In an unprecedented act of courage, one that could have cost him his position as well as his life, Nehemiah launched into an abbreviated yet detailed description of the dilapidated condition of his homeland.

I imagine there was a long pause as the king pondered Nehemiah's response. Then King Artaxerxes popped the magic question. The question that provided Nehemiah with the opportunity he had been waiting and praying for. This was the big moment. And Nehemiah knew he probably wouldn't get a second chance.

> Then the king said to me, "What would you request?" (Nehemiah 2:4a)

Nehemiah's heart must have been beating out of his chest. He was going to have an opportunity to lay out his whole plan before the one man in the world who could do anything about it. His response? "So I prayed to the God of heaven" (v. 4b).

Throughout the process, Nehemiah never lost sight of his dependence. Even with the opportunity of a lifetime staring him in the face, he dared not step out on his own. He was sufficiently broken of his self-will. There was no independent, macho, let-me-at-'em-God spirit in Nehemiah. He was so locked into the source of his strength that not even the emotionally charged events that day in the throne room knocked him off-center. He didn't utter a word before asking God for help.

Think about it. He had rehearsed this speech a thousand times. He was prepared. But he was not depending upon his preparation. He wasn't depending upon the king. He was as dependent as ever upon his God.

This is the kind of faith God is developing in you as you wait in the starting blocks of your vision.

This attitude is reflected again in Nehemiah's account of how the throne room scene ended.

> And I said to the king, "If it please the king, let letters be given me for the governors of the provinces beyond the River, that they

66

may allow me to pass through until I come to Judah, and a letter to Asaph the keeper of the king's forest, that he may give me timber to make beams for the gates of the fortress which is by the temple, for the wall of the city, and for the house to which I will go." And the king granted them to me because the good hand of my God was on me. (Nehemiah 2:7–8)

Notice who got the credit. Nehemiah knew it wasn't his patience, his preparation, his communication skills, or his persuasive personality that had made this moment possible. "The king granted them to me because the good hand of my God was on me." Only God could have engineered these circumstances. And Nehemiah was quick to give credit where credit was due. He recognized the source of his success.

THANKS, GOD; I BELIEVE I CAN HANDLE IT FROM HERE

Few things distort our perspective like public success. The rewards that accompany success can turn a humble man or woman into a tyrant. Success often leads to self-sufficiency. Rare is the successful individual who has not lost sight of what he would be without God.

Success in secular pursuits is not the only kind of success that ruins a person. Launching a successful vision of any kind can lead to the same place. My profession stands as a case in point. How ironic that men and women who credit God with their *call* to ministry are often slow to give him credit for their *success* in ministry.

The depth and authenticity of our faith determines in part our ability to handle success. Faith focuses us on our inadequacy and his adequacy. Mature faith is able to maintain that perspective even when faith becomes sight.

Strange as it may sound, it is more difficult to maintain a faith walk when we begin to see our dreams come true. When hopes become realities it is easy to shift our faith onto the thing we have dreamed of and off of the One who was the source of our provision.

Rare is the visionary who is able to maintain a spirit of dependency and humility in the face of public success. So God works overtime to ground, strengthen, stretch, and mature our faith in the initial stages of the visioneering process. Our ability to go the distance depends on it.

Let's face it, it's much easier to trust God when we have little to trust him for. What do we have to lose? But when faith becomes sight, when at last the vision takes tangible shape, there is something in each of us that says, "God may have gotten me this far, but it is up to me to maintain things." And with no conscious decision on our part, we shift strategies. We take control.

A fellow came to see me one afternoon to discuss a personnel problem he was having in his company. A disgruntled former employee was suing him. Jack was countersuing, and the whole thing had turned into a big mess.

Not knowing exactly how to help him, I said, "Jack, how did you get into this line of work to begin with?" He smiled, sat back, and told me an incredible story of how God had given him a vision for this company. Step by step, God had paved the way for Jack to pursue his vision and build his company into a multi-million-dollar enterprise.

Then, without any prompting from me, he shook his head and said, "I don't have any business suing this guy. I don't have any business suing anybody." Then he confessed that lawsuits had become a way of life. It was a standard business procedure. He continued, "I didn't start out this way. I didn't sue my way into business." Again, he shook his head and just sat back in his chair.

As we continued talking, it became clear to both of us that somewhere along the way, Jack had taken the reins. Somewhere he had bought into the notion that God could get him where he wanted to be but that Jack would have to work hard to keep himself there. Like many of us, Jack succumbed to the pressure to take responsibility for maintaining the vision, as if that were too great a task for God.

Success has a way of weaning us off our dependency on God. In the throes of success it is easy to take responsibility for maintaining our success. Without ever meaning to, we shift from a God orientation to a self orientation.

For that reason, God uses the time before our vision is launched to fasten our faith to him. He allows us to rev our engines in the starting blocks long enough for us to overheat and shut down. He allows us to wait until our faith is in him and him alone. For that is our only hope for seeing our vision through to a truly successful ending.

The bigger the vision, the more important it is that your faith be grounded in his ability, not yours. The bigger the vision, the more pressure you will feel to take credit for your success. Before God can entrust you with the rewards that accompany success, you must be dependent. He brings you to that place by stretching and even straining your faith. But as the capacity of your faith increases, so too your potential to pass along to him the glory he deserves.

So be encouraged. The agony you are experiencing is normal. The loneliness you feel is to be expected. The sleepless nights when you stare up at the ceiling and think, "What have I gotten myself into?" are part of the process. All of those experiences will ultimately lead you to the conclusion, "God, if you don't come through, I'm sunk!" And that is exactly where he wants you to be—and stay. For this reason, men and women of vision are men and women of faith. And through their faith, God is honored.

A LEAP OF FAITH

We have a brick retaining wall that runs for about sixty feet behind our house. Andrew, my five-year-old, has been dying to walk along the top of the wall since he was old enough to walk. This afternoon he took his maiden voyage.

At each end, the wall is about three feet high. From there it bumps up to five feet. In the center it is eight feet tall. The highest section runs for about thirty feet before dropping back down to five feet.

After a long and repetitive lecture about how he is never to climb up on the wall unless Daddy is watching, and after answering a series of questions regarding other adults that might be acceptable supervisors, I nervously set him up on the three-foot section of wall. Without hesitation he traversed the lower section. He managed to pull himself up to the five-foot section and had no problem there, either.

When he reached the highest section of wall, I could tell his confidence and bravado were waning. He walked almost the entire length of the wall before he finally looked down at me and said, "Daddy, I don't want to do this anymore."

Immediately, I stretched out my arms and said, "Jump."

He looked at the wall. Then he looked down at me. Then he looked back at the wall. And again down at me. He bent his knees slightly and said, "Are you going to catch me?"

To which I responded, "No, I am going to move at the last minute and let you fall to the ground." Just kidding.

"Yes, Andrew," I said. "I will catch you."

Without another moment of hesitation, he jumped into my arms. When I started to put him down, he clung to my neck. So I stood there holding him for a few precious, insightful seconds.

When he jumped he was still very much afraid. But his confidence in me was stronger than his fear of jumping. He honored me with his act of courage. There was never any question as to whether I could or would catch him. The issue was whether his confidence in me would supersede his fear. It did. And in that moment, I experienced in a small way what our Father experiences when we act on our faith in spite of our feelings and surroundings.

The higher the wall, the greater the honor.

Great visions are like high walls.

VISIONEERING
PROJECT #5

1. *Evaluate the success of others.*

I have two mentors. One of the things that attracted me to these men initially was the magnitude of their visions. In fact, one of them frequently opens our conversations by asking me, "Andy, what are you working on big?" Considering his definition of "big," I usually have a hard time coming up with a good answer.

Both men have achieved a great deal of success in their chosen fields. Both have received some national acclaim. Yet neither of these men has lost sight of who is ultimately behind their success. This is probably *the* thing I appreciate most about them. Success has not caused them to shift from dependence to independence. They are genuinely humble men.

Do you know anyone like that? Is there anyone in your network of relationships who has been a Christian for at least fifteen years, has been successful in his or her chosen field, and who appears to have an active faith in God? If so, initiate a conversation with him or her related to the subject of this chapter. Ask the following questions.

How did you get started (with respect to the area of vision and success)?

When you started out, did you feel God was leading you?

Did you ever feel God had abandoned you as you pursued your vision?

If so, what did you do?

What was the most faith-stretching experience you had along the way?

As you began to experience the rewards of success, did it ever go to your head?

Is there anything in particular that helps you keep your success in perspective?

What would you do differently if you had it to do over?

2. *Evaluate your prayers.*

I think it is safe to assume that most Christians are not attempting anything that requires God's intervention. They are not looking for God to do anything special. They are not aware that they need him to do anything special. They are trusting that he will step in once they breathe their last breath. But other than that, they live as if they have everything under control.

If you want to know how you score on this issue, listen to your prayers and prayer requests. What do you pray for? What are the things you find yourself praying for night after night? Those are your passions. Those are the things that matter most to you. Pretty scary, huh? A little embarrassing? Somewhat self-centered?

What was your response the last time someone asked you for a prayer request? Did you have to think for a moment? Was your response kind of...well...less than inspiring? Or did your eyes light up as you thought about that thing, that person, that ministry you were trusting God for? Other than heaven, and possibly your health, what are you consciously depending on God to do?

CHAPTER SIX

....

TAKING
INVENTORY

If your vision is for a year, plant wheat.
If your vision is for ten years, plant trees.
If your vision is for a lifetime, plant people.
CHINESE PROVERB

When last we saw our hero, he was doing cartwheels down the hallways of the palace. King Artaxerxes had released Nehemiah to pursue his vision of rebuilding the walls around Jerusalem. The pace was picking up. Things were starting to happen. The vision had been launched.

Just as the king had promised, Nehemiah was given a letter granting him permission to take trees from the royal forest. In addition, he was given letters addressed to the governors in the regions through which he would be traveling. These would guarantee him safe passage to Jerusalem. In addition, the king commissioned several of his own military officers and their horsemen to accompany Nehemiah on his trip.

For the next five months Nehemiah was absorbed with his vision. What a thrilling time that must have been. After years of routine and menial service to the king, he must have felt like a caged bird that had been set free. For the first time in a long time, maybe in his life, Nehemiah's organizational skills were being put to good use.

Within a few weeks he and his entourage were on their way to cut timber for the city gates. Once that task was completed they slowly made their way toward Jerusalem. Altogether, they traveled about one thousand miles.

There was no way for Nehemiah to know what he would find when he arrived in Jerusalem. He knew what God had put in his heart to do. But he also knew that without the support of the residents of Jerusalem, success would be impossible. Once again, he was facing circumstances over which he had no control. After an amazing start, Nehemiah was face-to-face with the prospect that this whole project might still be shut down. In spite of his momentum, if God didn't intervene again, there would be no wall.

This was familiar territory for Nehemiah.

WALK BEFORE YOU TALK

Finally, there on the horizon was the city of Jerusalem. It must have been an emotional moment for Nehemiah as the silhouette of this revered city grew in the distance. In all likelihood, this was the first time Nehemiah had set foot on his native soil. He had wept over descriptions of Jerusalem. No doubt he wept as he approached the city.

Nehemiah's arrival did not go unnoticed. It wasn't every day that a Persian official rode into town with an armed escort. Besides that, what was with all that lumber?

Chances are, news of their presence was all over town before the last horseman passed through what was left of the front gate. Who were these people? Why had they come? Who was in charge? Nobody knew. And Nehemiah didn't tell a soul (2:12). In fact, Nehemiah didn't share his vision with anyone in Jerusalem for at least three days! Imagine that. When I get a good idea, I have a hard time keeping my mouth shut for three minutes. But Nehemiah knew it was too early to announce his intentions. Instead, Nehemiah spent some time taking inventory of the situation.

> And I arose in the night, I and a few men with me. I did not tell anyone what my God was putting into my mind to do for Jerusalem and there was no animal with me except the animal on

which I was riding. So I went out at night by the Valley Gate in the direction of the Dragon's Well and on to the Refuse Gate, inspecting the walls of Jerusalem which were broken down and its gates which were consumed by fire. (Nehemiah 2:12–13)

Nehemiah did some walking before he did any talking. He did not ride into town and announce his intentions. Instead, he did some fact-finding. He wasn't driven by the emotion of the moment. As excited as he must have been, he kept a level head.

BUILDING BLOCK #6

WALK BEFORE YOU TALK; INVESTIGATE BEFORE YOU INITIATE.

When God first lays something on your heart for you to do, don't tell anybody. To begin with, nobody is going to be nearly as excited as you are. Their lack of zeal has the potential to shut you down before you get started. To share a vision prematurely usually guarantees a less than warm reception.

Beyond that, there is usually some background work that needs to be done before you go public with your idea. Like Nehemiah, you will probably need to do some fact-finding, some exploration, some homework before you start telling people what you are up to. Remember, a vision does not necessarily require immediate action. But it will probably require some in-depth investigation.

It is neither heroic nor smart to take bold, uninformed action to further a vision—regardless of the source. And, on the flip side, it is not evidence of a lack of faith to ask the hard questions wisdom dictates you ask.

It is wise to know what you are up against. Initially, you may be overwhelmed by the magnitude of a God-given vision. But even at the risk of being frightened or intimidated, it is important to know everything that can be known before moving ahead. Jesus alluded to this when he inquired of his disciples, "Which one of you, when he wants to build a tower, does not first sit down and calculate the cost, to see if he has enough to complete it?" (Luke 14:28). In other words, get the facts. Walk before you talk.

Nehemiah's midnight ride was not fueled by a lack of faith. He wasn't having second thoughts. He didn't investigate the walls in order to make up his mind about doing the project. He investigated because he was committed to the project. When he finally announced his intentions to those who would do the work, he knew exactly what they were up against. Nobody could accuse him of not understanding the magnitude of the project.

Once you announce your vision, you open it up to discussion—and criticism. Everyone you share with will respond with the question, HOW? And if you have not taken the time to investigate properly, you run the risk of having someone squash your enthusiasm. All because you are not able to answer their questions.

In most environments, if your vision cannot be presented in great rational detail, it will be passed off as a crazy idea. So it is important to know all you can know before announcing your intentions. Granted, there is a sense in which every vision is impractical. In the early stages of the visioneering process, many of the questions you will be asked will have no answer. But you ought to know all there is to know before you open your vision up for questioning.

As simple and obvious as this principle may seem, it is easy to overlook when the excitement of a new idea takes over. I am amazed at the number of people I have encountered through the years who have gotten fixed on an idea, announced it to the world, and then collided head on with the realities surrounding their "vision." Many of these fatal collisions could have been avoided if they had done their homework.

AVOIDING A COLLISION

Investigation will accomplish at least one of three things. It will confirm the divine origin of your vision, give it further definition and focus, or tip you off that you were mistaken about the vision altogether.

VISION CONFIRMED

One of the most dramatic illustrations of how God can use investigation to confirm a vision is found in the book of Joshua. The people of Israel had just finished a forty-year tour of the desert. This little excursion was initiated by God after the people allowed themselves to be intimidated by the magnitude of the vision he had set for them. Moses had sent a group of spies into Canaan to get some idea as to what they were up against once they crossed the Jordan River. His purpose for sending them was not to decide *if* they should move into Canaan, but to discover what to expect *when* they made their move.

After the spies reported what they had seen, the Israelites decided to abort the mission. They concluded that it would be best to return to Egypt. This was not exactly what God had in mind. So, he led them around in the desert until the entire generation of doubters died! Then he turned to Joshua and said, and I paraphrase, "All right, let's try this one more time. Take my people into Canaan."

Once God decides something needs to be done, it is never a matter of *if*. The issue is usually *who?* Who will step forward, embrace the vision, and move ahead by faith?

Now it is Joshua's turn to lead (or coax) the people into Canaan. Like Moses, he sent spies into the promised land to get a feel for what they would encounter. To their amazement and encouragement, they discovered the people of Canaan were scared to death of the Israelites. In fact, they were still talking about how the Israelite God had parted the Red Sea.

When the spies returned this was their report.

> And they said to Joshua, "Surely the LORD has given all the land into our hands, and all the inhabitants of the land, moreover, have melted away before us." (Joshua 2:24)

That's all Joshua needed to hear. Vision confirmed. All systems go. The next morning the nation began a campaign God had ordained hundreds of years before Joshua drew his first breath. This was a God thing. The information gathered by the spies confirmed it.

The primary difference between the first group and the second group of spies was not what they saw. It was how they interpreted what they saw. Both groups saw the same high walls and fortified cities. They both saw the oversized people and productive land. The spies Moses sent interpreted the data from the standpoint of Israel's military potential and strength. Their conclusion? "We would be better off in Egypt."

Joshua's spies, on the other hand, interpreted the data differently. They didn't go in to evaluate the possibility of the task. They were not there to determine whether or not their army was capable of defeating the

Canaanite forces. They were looking for confirmation, evidence that this was the right time and the right place to advance the vision. They didn't merely look, they listened. And their investigation led to confirmation.

Remember, God-ordained visions will often appear to be impossible from a purely pragmatic perspective. But upon further investigation, if it is, in fact, a vision from God, there will be an element of confirmation mixed somewhere within the data you accumulate. And if in the face of overwhelming odds you still have a burning desire to move ahead, chances are you have latched onto something divine.

VISION DEFINED

In addition to confirming a vision, investigation serves to further define and focus a vision. Nehemiah's original plan probably involved restoring the walls around Jerusalem to their original specifications and coverage. But after examining the debris, he revised his plan. He narrowed his focus. As a result, the wall constructed under his leadership had a significantly smaller footprint than the previous one.

Imagine how foolish Nehemiah would have sounded had he ridden into town and announced they were going to rebuild the wall to its original size and glory. To begin with, that was not what God had commissioned him to do. That would have been Nehemiah's vision, not God's. And second, he would have failed. Early on, it would have become apparent to the workers that the task was impossible. They would have given up.

Nashville or Bust

Matt had an insatiable desire to be involved in Christian music. He first began sensing this while in high school. So like most of us at that age, he started looking for an instrument he could master. He tried guitar. That didn't suit him. He bought a bass. He lost interest in that as well. Finally, he settled on drums.

As he neared the end of his senior year, it became apparent he wasn't going to be able to make a living playing the drums. In fact, as much as he hated to admit it, he didn't have the talent needed to make it as a musician. Yet he still had a burning desire to be connected with the world of Christian music.

As you would imagine, people encouraged him to give up on his childhood fantasy and go to college so he could get a real job. He packed his bags and went to Auburn University to study marketing. During his freshman year, however, it occurred to him there was a business side to the Christian music industry he had never looked into.

The more Matt discovered about this previously unexplored "scene" behind the scene, the more interested he became. After a year at Auburn, he transferred to Belmont University in Nashville and applied for an internship position with a Christian recording company. One thing led to another, and within three years he was working as a publicist for one of the top Christian recording artists in the country.

In the process of looking into the business side of the Christian music industry, Matt's vision was redirected. God used his investigation to shift and sharpen his focus. Had Matt not taken the time to look behind the scenes, he would have abandoned his vision. He would have concluded he just wasn't cut out for the music business. What a tragedy that would have been.

This world is filled with people who stopped one question short of finding an avenue that would allow them to pursue their vision. Don't let the discouragement of a few slammed doors cause you to walk away from the vision God has birthed in your heart. Investigate. Look around. Think outside the lines.

Few destinations have only one point of access. The same is true of your vision. If your initial approach is blocked, look for alternatives. Don't give up too quickly. You may be one question away from discovering the key that will unlock the door that stands between you and God's vision for your life. God will use this period of investigation to confirm, sharpen, and, sometimes, redirect your vision.

VISION ABORTED

Clayton had a vision for his son. Little Clay would grow up to be an all-star quarterback, just like his dad. There was just one problem. Little Clay didn't have the talent or stamina to be an all-star. Worse than that, he wasn't really all that interested in football. In fact, Clay wasn't interested in sports at all.

For years I watched the tension build between father and son. It began with Clay doing everything he could to live up to his dad's expectations. He managed to stick it out through the sixth and seventh grade. But once he entered junior high, he was starting to resent the constant pressure. To make things worse, it was evident to Clay's coaches that Clay was not cut out to play football.

But his dad wouldn't hear of it. He pushed and pushed until Clay finally refused to play. That was the beginning of several years of outright rebellion. A little investigation on Clayton Sr.'s part would have revealed what everybody else seemed to know: Clay Jr. was not destined to be an all-star. Had Clayton aborted his vision early on, and encouraged Clay in the areas where he was gifted, years of heartache and conflict could have been avoided.

Investigation may lead you to conclude your vision wasn't really a vision to begin with. It may have just been a good idea. Or, as in Clayton's case, it may have been a bad idea! What strikes you as a vision may, in fact, be somebody else's vision. A motivating speaker can make us feel "called" to take part in his or her particular vision. Mix a few statistics with some heartrending stories, flash a few pictures up on the screen, and I'm ready to sign up.

It is important to distinguish between a worthwhile cause and a personal vision. Like many people, I contribute to and volunteer for some worthwhile causes. But they are not necessarily part of the vision God has given me for my life.

I have a friend who pioneered a unique ministry to underprivileged children who live in inner-city Atlanta. Every time I listen to Karen talk about how God is using her organization to rescue children from their drug-infested environments, my heart swells up inside me.

I have told her on many occasions I am willing to do whatever I can to assist her. I have directed several potential donors in her direction. But Karen and I don't share the same vision. She is consumed with what could be and should be in the lives of those kids. And I believe with all my heart her vision is from God. But it is not God's vision for *my* life.

Investigation will help you distinguish between a good cause and a God-ordained vision. Investigation will either confirm your vision, focus your vision, or cause you to wonder. If after a thorough survey of the landscape, you come away with a clearer picture of what could be, and a hotter passion for what should be, chances are you have struck gold.

If your investigation leaves you with a fistful of facts and a general concern for a group or situation, that's probably not where God is leading you to focus your life. Recognizing a need does not necessarily translate into vision. A general sense of sadness about the condition of a group of people is not a vision. That is compassion. Vision will always involve compassion. But compassion is only one component of vision.

Before you sign on for anything, ask some questions. Ask lots of questions. Experiment. Volunteer. Explore. Get your feet wet. Try things out.

Don't commit in response to the passion of the moment. That's not the way to go about finding a mate, and it's not the way to find a vision, either. What's true of relationships is true of a vision. Emotional commitments are only as strong as the emotion. As the emotions subside—well, you know the rest.

VISIONCASTING

Investigation is not only important for our sake. It is important for the sake of those who work alongside us. Divinely ordained visions often involve representatives from the entire body of Christ. Whether you are envisioning a new organization or a new level of relationship with a family member, you will need support. And team members need to know the facts.

In the next chapter we are going to look at the subject of visioncasting. Before you can successfully cast your vision to another person or group of people, you must have a firm grip on current reality. You need to know what you are up against. More importantly, you need to know what you are leading other people up against. You need to know everything there is to know about the environment you are expecting other people to follow you into.

Nehemiah knew. He had firsthand knowledge of the magnitude of the project he wanted the people of Jerusalem to tackle. This knowledge gave him the edge he needed to cast a compelling vision.

One of the reasons we lean toward sharing our vision too soon is we feel the burden of the vision resting on our shoulders. A vision is always accompanied by a sense of responsibility. That nagging sense of responsibility sets us up for the "If I don't do something, nothing will get done" mentality. Our natural tendency is to take the vision and run with it, as if it is exclusively our vision. It is easy to forget that a God-ordained vision is not our responsibility. We have a role to play. And our role is our responsibility. But the vision itself is God's responsibility.

Once again my mind goes back to Mary, the mother of Jesus. She was so confident in the divine nature of her vision for her Son, that she was content to fulfill her responsibility as a mother while waiting for God to bring about the fulfillment of the vision.

The classic example of this takes place only hours after Jesus is born. Without warning, shepherds suddenly appear with news that angels had announced the birth of her Son. Her vision was confirmed. It was going to be just as the angels had promised. Soon after the shepherds departed, other strangers arrived to see the baby.

> And they [the shepherds] came in haste and found their way to Mary and Joseph, and the baby as He lay in the manger. And when they had seen this, they made known the statement which had been told them about this Child. And all who heard it wondered at the things which were told them by the shepherds. (Luke 2:16–18)

Don't you know there was something in Mary that wanted to stand up and announce to the world everything the angel told her when she first discovered the divine identity of her Son? Can you imagine the excitement she must have felt as people showered her and Joseph with questions regarding the claims of the shepherds? As she looked around at the pitiful environment in which her Son was born, surely she wanted to send word to somebody who could do something about their housing. This was not just any baby. Angels had announced his birth. His life and health must be protected at all costs.

But she didn't do any of that. Luke tells us, "Mary treasured up all these things, pondering them in her heart" (Luke 2:19). There was no sense of urgency. Mary was not controlled by her natural, maternal instinct. She didn't give in to the desire to tell everyone what she knew about her Son. Apparently she didn't feel the need to make something happen. Instead, she rested in the knowledge that this was God's vision. And therefore, God would bring it about in his timing. She had a responsibility. But the vision was God's responsibility.

What could be and should be won't be until God allows it to be. Timing is a critical part of the visioneering process. There's no rush. Investigate!

VISIONEERING
PROJECT #6

1. Develop a plan for investigating the environments surrounding your various visions.
   - Is there someone you should talk to?
   - Are there books you should read?
   - Is there a location you should visit?

2. There are three things that keep people from fully investigating their visions. Which line of reasoning are you most tempted to use?
   - *Impatience*—"I don't have time to walk around a bunch of broken-down walls. Besides, I already know what the problem is. It is time to start rebuilding."
   - *Pride*—"What's the point of walking around looking at broken-down walls? What could I possibly learn that I don't already know?"
   - *Fear*—"I'm afraid that if I found out how bad things really are, I might get discouraged."

....

CHAPTER SEVEN

GOING PUBLIC,
PART I

Then the LORD answered me and said,
"Record the vision and inscribe it on tablets,
that the one who reads it may run.
For the vision is yet for the appointed time;
it hastens toward the goal, and it will not fail.
Though it tarries, wait for it; for it will certainly come, it will not delay."

HABAKKUK 2:2–3

All God-ordained visions are shared visions. Nobody goes it alone. But God generally raises up a point person to paint a compelling verbal picture. A picture that captures the hearts and imaginations of those whom God is calling to embrace the task at hand.

Eventually, you will need to share your vision with somebody. It may be from a platform or across the dinner table. Regardless of the context, the day will come for you to go public with what God has put in your heart to do. If God is developing in you a picture of what could and should be, you will be called upon to verbalize that picture. Painting a verbal picture is the essence of visioncasting.

After examining the walls, Nehemiah knew the time had finally come to let the people of Jerusalem know the purpose of his trip. It was time to cast his vision. I imagine this was a speech he had rehearsed in his mind a thousand times. This was truly the moment he had been waiting for.

As is the case with anyone who is casting a vision, Nehemiah had no idea how the people would respond. After all, he was a newcomer. They had been content to live without the benefit of protective walls for generations. For all he knew, they might run him out of town, or laugh, or, worse yet, just ignore him.

But a man with a vision from God is a man on a mission. And he cannot be silent forever. Nehemiah managed to gather the people together. And then he cast his vision for the city.

> Then I said to them, "You see the bad situation we are in, that Jerusalem is desolate and its gates burned by fire. Come, let us rebuild the wall of Jerusalem that we may no longer be a reproach." And I told them how the hand of my God had been favorable to me, and also about the king's words which he had spoken to me. (Nehemiah 2:17–18a)

THE FOUR COMPONENTS OF AN EFFECTIVE VISION

This short quote from Nehemiah's speech includes four vital components. Every compelling vision includes these four components:

1. The problem
2. The solution
3. The reason something must be done
4. The reason something must be done *now*

BUILDING BLOCK #7

COMMUNICATE YOUR VISION AS A SOLUTION TO A PROBLEM THAT MUST BE ADDRESSED IMMEDIATELY.

In order to share your vision convincingly, you must be able to state the problem your vision addresses along with a solution to the problem. Furthermore, you must be able to give a compelling reason why something must be done and why it must be done now. Until you can address these four issues clearly and succinctly, you are probably not ready to begin talking about your vision.

Let's look at each of these components in detail.

1. THE PROBLEM

The problem facing the people in Jerusalem was apparent. The walls were broken down. And yet Nehemiah began his speech by verbalizing the obvious.

> You see the bad situation we are in, that Jerusalem is desolate and its gates burned by fire. (v. 17a)

Why would Nehemiah feel it was necessary to make such a statement? They knew the condition of the walls. Some of the people listening to Nehemiah had lived in Jerusalem all their lives. They passed in and out of the burned gates every day. They didn't need him telling them their gates were burned.

How would you feel if a houseguest went around pointing out everything in your home that was broken, cracked, stained, outdated, or in need of painting? Chances are, you would take offense. After all, it is your house. And besides, you know better than anyone what needs attention.

But once your guest left, chances are you would get to work fixing some of those things. Not because you weren't aware they needed fixing. But because suddenly you saw those old problems through somebody else's eyes.

The people living in Jerusalem had grown so accustomed to the fact that the walls were torn down that they hardly noticed anymore. They had ceased to be concerned. They had learned to live with it. The inconveniences and the dangers it imposed had become part of their lifestyle. Over the years they had lost sight of what could be and what should be. And nobody seemed to remember what used to be.

Nehemiah's words were a wake-up call. In essence he was saying, "Open your eyes! Things are bad! We're in trouble." His fresh set of eyes brought a new perspective. And without much prodding the people of Jerusalem took a fresh look at their situation. In that moment they were able to see their city through Nehemiah's eyes. And once that happened, they caught his vision.

Visioncasting will always include an element of waking people out of their apathy. Visioncasters rarely bring new information to the table. What they bring is an impassioned concern about an existing problem. They bring fresh eyes. Often it boils down to a contemporary interpretation of an age-old problem. Like the innocent child in the fairy tale, the vision-caster declares, "The king isn't wearing any clothes." And if he or she is effective, the audience will declare, "You are right! Let's do something about it."

What is the problem your vision addresses? The problem is not the vision. The solution is the vision. But the problem provides a clear context for presenting the vision. Identifying and clearly stating the problem pricks the interest of your audience. It engages their minds.

In some cases, your explanation of the problem will reorient people to something they have known about but have learned to live with. To the degree you enable people to see the world around them the way you see it, to that degree they will be willing to listen to your solution to the problem. As long as your audience is blind to the needs at hand, they will have little interest in hearing you out.

Think about it this way. Every successful organization addresses a problem or fills a void in a market. New businesses begin in response to perceived needs. Parachurch organizations are launched in response to unmet needs or untapped ministry opportunities. What problem will your vision potentially solve? What need will be met? What point of tension or conflict do you propose to ease?

When you have a clear, concise answer to those questions, you have taken the first step in preparing to cast your vision. As long as you are unsure or your answer lacks focus, don't say a word. Ponder, investigate, pray. But resist the urge to cast.

2. THE SOLUTION

Everybody in Nehemiah's audience was in agreement concerning the problem. The walls were torn down. Nobody would dispute that. Having established the problem, Nehemiah went on to propose a solution. "Come, let us rebuild the wall of Jerusalem."

Once again, the solution is obvious. But it took somebody saying it to motivate the people to do anything about it. And in verbalizing the solution, Nehemiah cast his vision. Simply put, Nehemiah envisioned Jerusalem as a walled city.

A vision is always a solution to a problem. It addresses a felt or perceived need.

Can you state your vision or visions succinctly? If given the opportunity, could you communicate convincingly, in one sentence, exactly what you feel God is calling you to do? Are you able to paint a clear verbal picture of what could be and should be?

This is critical to visioncasting. Whereas a clear explanation of the problem engages the mind, the solution engages the imagination. A vision invites us to imagine the future in a way that demands change in the present. A vision necessitates a willingness on the part of the audience to overlook present reality for the time being and imagine what could be.

With very little prompting, Nehemiah's audience was able to envision Jerusalem as a walled city. This vision ignited a desire in them to alter the present for the sake of a potential future. Nehemiah tapped into their imagination. And consequently, they signed on to the vision.

In order for others to share your passion, they must be given a clear picture of how your vision will alter the future. They must know in no uncertain terms where you are taking them. So, you must paint a verbal picture that serves as an imagined target, something everyone can shoot for and work toward together. You must engage their imaginations.

WHAT ABOUT YOU?

Has your vision gripped your imagination? Do you daydream about what could and should be? Do you have a clear mental picture of how the future could be? If not, do yourself and everybody else a favor and don't talk too much about your vision. It is too early. You are not ready.

I'm reminded of something Howard Hendricks said on many occasions during my seminary years. The context was preaching, but it certainly pertains to our discussion. "Men," he'd say, "if it's a mist in the pulpit, it will be a fog in the pew."

His point, of course, was that what may start out as a slightly confusing message from the lips of the preacher will ultimately result in mass confusion among the congregation. If the speaker is unable to communicate clearly, there is little hope the audience will comprehend clearly.

The same is true of visioncasting. If the visioncaster has a difficult time conveying the meat of his or her vision, there is little chance anyone will walk away with a clear picture of what the future could look like.

The horsepower behind a well-cast vision is a thoroughly developed verbal picture of what could be, a picture that can be accurately reproduced in the minds of the listeners. For it is only when the listeners' imaginations have been engaged that true visioncasting has taken place. When the pictures and images that fill the mind and heart of the visioncaster are accurately transferred to the minds and hearts of the audience, the vision has been cast. Like an artist who transfers mental images and colors to canvas, so the visioncaster paints a picture in the imagination of his audience.

But it is not enough to engage the imagination. There is still the question of incentive. That leads us to the third and fourth facet of visioncasting. We will pick up with these in chapter 8.

No one accomplishes a God-given vision alone. Whether your vision involves the salvation of a friend or the launching of an organization, it is going to take a team. A team whose imaginations are in alignment. A group whose hearts have been knitted together by what could and should be.

If God has birthed a vision in you, he is in the process of developing a similar vision in the hearts of others around you. When the time comes to share your vision, it will ring true in the souls of those he has been preparing.

In the meantime, your responsibility is to continue to develop a clear verbal picture of the problem your vision is intended to solve and how your vision will solve it. After all, a vision is a solution. And when the time comes for you to cast your vision, perhaps your audience will respond like Nehemiah's:

"Let us arise and build." So they put their hands to the good work. (v. 18b)

VISIONEERING
PROJECT #7

1. What problem does your vision propose to solve? (Use the lines on the next page for your answer.)

- Another way of asking this question is "What might or might not happen if your vision does not materialize?
- It could be your vision is intended to keep something from becoming a problem. This is usually the case when someone develops a vision for his or her family. The goal is to avoid problems rather than solve them.
- If your vision addresses a potential problem rather than an existing one, state it as such. For example: "This vision is intended to protect the relational integrity of our family. If this vision does not materialize, we have the potential of becoming a group of strangers living under the same roof, longing for the day when we will be free from one another's company."
- In many cases, a vision will address an existing problem that may not appear to be a problem to the casual observer.
- Remember, to the degree you enable people to see the world around them the way you see it, to that degree they will be willing to listen to your solution to the problem. As long as your audience is blind to the problem at hand, they will have little interest in hearing about your proposed solutions.

When casting the vision for why we needed to start a new church in the city of Atlanta—a city that is already full of churches—I presented the problem like this:

This city is quickly becoming a city of unchurched, undisciplined, biblically illiterate people—and there is a desperate need for churches geared to meet the spiritual needs of unchurched, undisciplined people. Churches that are a friendly rather than hostile environment for biblically challenged, skeptical, suspicious seekers. We have been commissioned to make disciples, and together, as a local church, we can do that far more effectively than each of us working on our own.

- State the existing or potential problem relateed to your various visions:

_____

_____

_____

_____

2. What is your proposed solution?

_____

_____

_____

_____

- It is only when the images which fill your mind are accurately conveyed to the minds of your audience that the vision has been cast. Take whatever time is necessary to develop a clear verbal picture.
- Begin by writing down a list of adjectives that describe what could and should be.
- Now begin forming sentences that describe your preferred future. To spark your own imagination, you may want to start with the phrase, I imagine...
- I imagine a family that...
- I imagine a company that...
- I imagine a church where...
- I imagine a marriage in which...

_____

_____

CHAPTER EIGHT

GOING PUBLIC, PART II

Visions are like lenses.
They focus unrefracted rays of light.
They enable everyone concerned with an enterprise
to see more clearly what is ahead of them.
THE LEADERSHIP CHALLENGE

A compelling vision will include these four components:

1. The problem
2. The solution
3. The reason something must be done
4. The reason something must be done *now*

We discussed the problem and the solution in chapter 7. Let's dive right into the third component.

3. THE REASON

The fact that the wall around Jerusalem had been torn down did not necessarily mean it should be rebuilt. The people's contentment with the current state of affairs proved that. Pointing out the problem and the solution was not enough. The people of Jerusalem needed incentive. They needed motivation. So Nehemiah followed up his one-two punch with a jab to their conscience.

> Come, let us rebuild the wall of Jerusalem *that we may no longer be a reproach.*" (Nehemiah 2:17b, emphasis mine)

This had to sting. Nehemiah softened the blow by including himself, "that *we* may no longer be a reproach." But any way you cut it, this was a blow to their pride. The term translated *reproach* means disgrace or embarrassment. Once again, Nehemiah was challenging the people to face up to reality. In essence he was saying, "We are an embarrassment! We are a disgrace. And we have allowed ourselves to continue in this state for over one hundred years! This is inexcusable."

Somehow, the people of Israel had been able to ignore what was evident to the surrounding nations. They had grown accustomed to their environment. Their national self-esteem had sunk to the point that they were content to live in a state of disgrace and dishonor. There was no national pride.

But it was worse than that. Nehemiah's words cut all the way through to their divine charter. They were not only an embarrassment and a reproach nationally, they were an embarrassment to God.

Israel was not just another nation. They had been commissioned by God to be a light to the nations. Their role was unique among nations. God had established Israel as the nation through which he would demonstrate his power, glory, and grace. He had chosen to reside and abide with them in a unique way by filling the ark of the covenant and the holy of holies with his glory.

Through miraculous military victories, God had proven over and over to the surrounding nations that Israel's God was the one true God. Israel was unique among the nations of the earth. And one day this nation, known for its prowess in battle, would produce the Prince of Peace; the Savior of mankind. And all the world would be blessed through Israel.

But nobody would have guessed any of that by looking at the condition of the capital city in Nehemiah's day. The temple was gone. The ark of the covenant was missing. Sacrifices had ceased. The glory was gone.

And gone as well were the confidence and courage of the nation's people.

Nehemiah knew the city was more than a reproach from a national standpoint. He understood that God's reputation and glory were at stake. And he knew God was not finished with his chosen people.

When he stood that day to call the people to action, he stood as a man who had the backing of the God of Abraham, Isaac, and Jacob. He cast his vision with the conviction of a man who knew God was on his side. Nehemiah knew his vision was, in fact, a vision originally cast to an old, childless man to whom God had promised children as numerous as the sand on the seashore. And just as God had fulfilled his promise to Abraham, so Nehemiah was confident that God would see his vision through to completion.

Nehemiah's vision wasn't so much about rebuilding a wall as it was about reestablishing a context for God to demonstrate his power and fulfill his promises to the nations. His vision went beyond simply coming to the aid of a nation in trouble. His vision intersected with the providential hand of God in history. Nehemiah's challenge to the people that day was a challenge to embrace their destiny as a people, the people through whom God would eventually introduce the Savior of the world.

All divinely inspired visions are in some way tied into God's master plan. Whether it is loving your spouse, raising your kids, witnessing to your neighbor, or starting a company. As a believer, there is a larger, more encompassing context for everything you do. For you are not your own. And your visions are not isolated islands of ideas.

Nehemiah recognized the link between his personal vision and God's master plan for the nation. We must do the same. For buried in that relationship is the divine mandate as to why you must follow through with the vision God has given you. What made Nehemiah's vision so compelling was the unique role Israel was destined to play in God's master plan. What makes your vision equally as compelling is the fact that your project is one small but vital part of what God is up to in history.

Now you may be tempted to think, "Wait a minute. Nehemiah was building the wall around the capital city of Israel. All I'm trying to do is get a company off the ground, raise my kids, keep my marriage together, maintain my witness in the marketplace. Is it really fair to compare my inconsequential visions to Nehemiah's?"

Well, I guess Billy Graham's parents could have made the same argument. After all, the only thing of any consequence his parents did was keep the family together, put food on the table—and raise Billy Graham.

Nehemiah's parents could have objected as well. "Who are we?" they could have asked. "We are nothing but transplanted Jews who have no purpose in life but to raise our children in the fear of the Lord in a culture that does not believe in our God." Fortunately, they were successful in what they set out to do. And there was a divine link. Like Billy Graham's parents, they had no idea what was in store for their son. But they kept the faith. And they were true to their vision of a son who would grow up as a devout worshiper of the Lord God.

Let's face it. You have no idea what God wants to do through you. Your seemingly small vision regarding your next-door neighbor, your children, your finances, your church, a potential ministry, may not be so small in the long run. You just don't know. But what you do know is there is a link between what you have been called to do and what God is up to in history. And the closer you can tie the two together the more compelling your vision will be.

Beyond the Bottom Line

I have the privilege of knowing Ron Blue. Besides being a highly accomplished writer and speaker, Ron is also the president and founder of Ronald Blue and Company (RBC). RBC is a financial estate and investment counseling firm that serves clients throughout the United States and Europe. Their services are based on biblical principles of financial management coupled with a thorough understanding of the technical aspects of financial planning. With over $1.5 billion in assets under management, RBC is a leader in the comprehensive financial planning industry.

Ron has a unique vision for RBC. He is committed to mentoring his clients in principles of good stewardship as well as sound financial planning. He envisions a day when the clients at RBC will collectively give one billion dollars a year to kingdom work. His is a vision clearly tied in with what God is up to in history.

Every CEO and company president has a vision of some kind. When presented with the opportunity, most can speak passionately about their respective companies. But there is something hollow in endless talk about customer service, market share, and quarterly earnings. Those things fail to capture an outsider's imagination.

But take that same corporate structure and tie it in directly with the great commission, and things come alive. RBC is not just about estate planning and returns on investment dollars. There is something much bigger at stake: It is the divine element that makes Ron's vision so compelling.

A clear explanation of the problem engages the mind. The solution will engage the imagination. But a compelling reason will engage the heart. The vision calls us to imagine what could be. The reason behind what *could be* moves us to believe that it *should be*. Once you cross this threshold, you are committed. There will be passion in your voice when you cast your vision.

Nehemiah believed with all his heart that the wall had to be rebuilt. Why? Because it was broken down? No. Because a broken-down wall around Jerusalem was a reproach upon God's people and God Himself.

When you finally zero in on *why* your vision must be accomplished, you will find yourself energized by the mere thought of what you have been called to do. *Why* translates into urgency and incentive. And when you speak of your vision, your conviction that this is something that should be done will make you persuasive in your communication. Why? Well, as the authors of *The Leadership Challenge* put it:

> When relating our hopes, dreams, and successes, we are always emotionally expressive. We lean forward in our chairs, our arms move about, our eyes light up, our voices sing with emotion, and smiles appear on our faces. We are enthusiastic, articulate, optimistic, and uplifting. In short, we are inspiring.[1]

When you think of visioncasting, you may picture a passionate speech delivered eloquently, forcefully, convincingly, and loud. But those ingredients are not necessary elements of effective visioncasting. The key ingredient is your conviction that this is something that must be done.

You cannot effectively cast your vision to anyone until you are convinced not only that it could be but that it should be. *Should be* comes as the result of discovering the *why* behind the *what* of your vision. And once the answer to *why* has gripped your heart, your words will have the potential to penetrate the hearts of your listeners.

Once you have made the connection between your vision and God's charge to you as a believer, your vision will transcend mere circumstances. You won't be launching a company, you will be financing the great commission. You won't simply be raising children, you will be influencing a generation. You won't be holding your marriage together, you will be reestablishing God's order in society. When we couple our personal visions with God's sovereign plan, we leverage the future.

So, how do you make the connection? How do you discover the divine connection between what you are up to as opposed to what God is doing? Run your vision through the grid of these two questions:

A. What Difference Will It Make?

What is there to gain? What is there to lose? What difference will it make if you are successful at accomplishing your vision? What difference will it make if you are not? This question surfaces what's really at stake.

- What difference will it make if I rebuild the wall around Jerusalem?
- What difference will it make if I get out of debt?
- What difference will it make if I transfer my Christian values and beliefs to my children?
- What difference will it make if I am successful in starting this new business or ministry endeavor?
- What difference will it make if I graduate from college?

B. Why Should I Attempt This?

This is a powerful question. It is a question you should ask of every goal you set. In forcing yourself to answer this question, you will discover a great deal about your values. Don't be content with your first answer. Ask *why* repeatedly.

As what's most important to you surfaces, one of two things will happen. Either you will realize your vision is, in fact, your vision, not God's; or you will hit upon a value that is important to your heavenly Father as well. That shared value will serve as the link between what you are attempting to accomplish and what God is up to on a universal scale.

In order to flesh this thing out, let's have an imaginary conversation with Nehemiah:

"Nehemiah, why should you rebuild the walls around Jerusalem?"

"Because they have been broken down."

"Why should you rebuild broken-down walls?"

"Because without walls the city is defenseless against her enemies."

"Why should a city that has been defenseless for over one hundred years be protected?"

"Because these are God's people."

"Why should God's people be protected?"

"Because God has a special assignment for his people."

Repeatedly asking *why* forces the dialogue to move from the realm of circumstance to one focused on values. This is not an easy process. At some point you may find yourself stumped. "I don't really know why I should…" At that point take some time to reflect. Wrestling with the question of *why* will always lead you back around to your core values. And in many cases it will lead you to some valuable insights about yourself as well as your vision.

Let's run another, more familiar scenario, through this grid.

"Young man, why should you marry Lisa?"

"Because we love each other."

"You didn't answer my question. Why should you marry her?"

"I want to be with her all the time and to have a family."

"You still didn't answer my question. Why should you marry her?"

"Because I don't believe it is right for us to live together and have children without first being married."

"Why is that not right?"

Let's hit *pause* for a moment. Do you see how the conversation is about to move from the level of circumstance to one of values and morality? It is at this juncture that the young man's vision for his life together with the woman he loves has the potential to intersect with God's divine plan for marriage. Let's continue.

"It is not right because…well, God says it is not right."

"Why should you do what God says?"

"Well, because he is God."

"You didn't answer my question."

"I want to do what God says."

"Why?"

"I believe God knows what's best for me."

Now we are in a discussion about values and beliefs. This young man's vision of his life together with his new wife has roots he may have otherwise been unaware of. Let's take it one step further.

"Why would God care about what's best for you?"

"He loves me."

"Why does he love you."

"I'm not sure. The Bible says he pretty much just decided to."

"So what have we learned?"

"I'm marrying Lisa because I believe God, who loves me, has a plan that is best for me, and by following his plan I have the best chances of having a successful relationship with Lisa. So my vision is a life together with Lisa lived in accordance with the values of principles in God's word."

Now, let's ask this fellow the first question we talked about.

"What difference will it make if you pursue this vision of life together with Lisa? What's really at stake?"

"Our peace. Possibly, our self-esteem. If we have children, their self-esteem and emotional health is at stake. Since people know we are Christians, our testimony is at stake. If our marriage fails, or if we skipped marriage and just moved in together, it would reflect poorly on God's kingdom. We would certainly not be very useful to him or the local church. In terms of what difference it could make, it could make a big difference with Lisa's brother who is not a Christian. We are hoping that he would see something in our relationship that would draw him to Christ."

Even with this imaginary dialogue you can see how these two questions can serve as a link between your personal vision and God's providential work in this world. As a believer, this is a vital link. Until you have made this critical connection, you are not ready to go public with your vision.

4. THE TIMING

The fourth and final element of visioncasting deals with the timing of the vision. Why should this vision be pursued *at this time?* Why should we do this now as opposed to later? What's the rush? Why all the urgency?

Nehemiah knew this was an especially critical element of his vision. I can just imagine a heckler in the back of the crowd calling out, "Hey buddy, what's the hurry? These walls have been down for over one hundred years. Relax! We'll get around to fixing them up."

Nehemiah addressed the issue of timing right up front. But you may miss it if your aren't looking carefully.

> And I told them how the hand of my God had been favorable to me, and also about the king's words which he had spoken to me. (Nehemiah 2:18a)

Did you catch it? Nehemiah's argument for the timing of the reconstruction was based upon God's sovereign engineering of circumstances. Apparently, he had filled them in on all the events leading up to his arrival in Jerusalem. He described the burden he felt when he first learned of the city's plight. He explained his frustration when he realized there was nothing he could do about it.

No doubt he walked them through his days and nights of travail for the remnant in Jerusalem. And then he gave them a blow-by-blow account of the day when the king noticed his sadness and asked the question that changed everything. Perhaps he told them about that anxious moment just before he told the king of the devastation in Jerusalem. And then he recounted the king's surprising reply.

Nehemiah's audience must have been spellbound as they listened to what could be nothing other than the hand of God at work on their behalf. For all they knew, God had abandoned them. To hear he had been working behind the scenes to enable them to restore their city was news they never expected to hear.

Nehemiah's story, not his presence, was the thing that convinced his audience the time to rebuild had finally arrived. It wasn't his vision that moved them to action. It was the news that God had acted on their behalf.

The walls had been in ruin for years. That was nothing new. But this was the first time in several generations the remnant had any evidence that God was looking upon them with favor. The fact that he was at work on their behalf awakened their dormant faith. News of his intervention sparked their interest and convinced them the time was right to begin reconstruction. As a result, they were eager to put their hands to the task.

Don't miss this. Nehemiah did not point to the broken-down walls as evidence that the time was right to rebuild. Instead he focused on God's intervention on behalf of the people. It bears repeating that the city had been a reproach since the day the walls were destroyed. That alone was not reason to begin rebuilding immediately. It was the fact that God had prepared the way that made the timing perfect.

As I have said over and over in the preceding chapters, a divinely authored vision will bear the thumbprint of God before, during, and after the work is completed. What he originates, he orchestrates. It will be evident at some level that this is his vision. It is that divine side of the equation that gives a vision its sense of urgency.

Once again I think of Joshua. Look at the relationship between the revelation of what God was up to in the land and Joshua's timing. These verses pick up right after the two spies returned from Jericho.

And they [the two spies] said to Joshua, "Surely the LORD has given all the land into our hands, and all the inhabitants of the land, moreover, have melted away before us." Then Joshua rose early in the morning; and he and all the sons of Israel set out from Shittim and came to the Jordan, and they lodged there before they crossed. (Joshua 2:24–3:1)

The land of Canaan had been sitting there uninvaded for years. What made the timing right for an invasion? What gave Joshua the confidence to lead the nation of Israel forward at that particular time? God was at work.

No doubt, these two spies, like the twelve spies Moses had sent into the land a generation earlier, came back with all kinds of good things to say about the land. It was everything they had imagined and more. But it was not the size of the fruit nor the beauty of the landscape that inspired them. It was the fear God had put into the hearts of the inhabitants of the land. The time was right to invade. For God was at work.

BUILDING BLOCK #8

CAST YOUR VISION TO THE APPROPRIATE PEOPLE AT THE APPROPRIATE TIME.

The fact that something needs to be done is not enough. People will give what they feel they can afford to meet a need. But they will give sacrificially toward a vision that bears the marks of God's involvement. There will always be needs. The list is endless. But when an opportunity comes along to invest our time and resources in something God is up to, it is amazing how much more of our time and treasure we are willing to invest.

I have an insatiable desire to be involved in something God is involved in. I am not alone in that quest. I meet people all the time who are more than willing to commit themselves to a project or task that is clearly a God thing.

Before you cast your vision, you must be able to answer the question, "Why now? Why should we throw our time and energy into this project now?"

If this is a vision God has placed in your heart, and if this is, in fact, the time to act on it, there should be something of a divine nature to point to—something that will indicate to people that God has gone before you to prepare the way. People want to be a part of something God is up to. They will join you in your vision if they are confident it is not simply *your* vision.

LET US ARISE!

When Nehemiah finished casting his vision to the people of Jerusalem, they were ready to go to work.

> Then they said, "Let us arise and build." So they put their hands to the good work. (Nehemiah 2:18b)

Don't you just hate that? It sounds so easy. It seems so unrealistic. It rarely works out like that in real life. Yet this is every visioncaster's dream. A team of committed, enthusiastic volunteers ready to roll up their sleeves and go to work.

Remember, this was not an overnight success story. This snapshot of success was years in the making. Nor does the story end here. After all, it is one thing to launch a vision. It is another thing to see it through to completion. And as we all know, the enthusiasm associated with the start of something never provides enough momentum to complete it.

At the same time, however, what we see here is the potential power of a well-cast vision. A carefully crafted vision has the ability to capture people's imaginations as well as their commitment. People will reprioritize their lives and lifestyles in order to be a part of a vision they feel called to.

Bill Hybles echoed these sentiments during a discussion on vision-casting and the church.

> It really is important to keep a vision in front of the collective body of Christ. And when people have a sense that they're on a journey, they're becoming—they're achieving—they're growing—they're developing into this bride of Christ. Radiant and beautiful and effective in the world, it really creates a sense of anticipation about being a part of a church as opposed to "Why are we showing up again?", "Why are we being asked to give more money?", and serve more and pray more? People don't ask the why questions when they have an exciting, God-honoring vision put out in front of them. They know why. Now the question is, to what extent can I give my life to that?[2]

People are looking for something to give their lives to. If God has given you a vision, he is going to raise up a team to work with you to that end. So prepare to cast your vision.

What is the problem?

What is the solution?

Why must something be done?

Why now?

Answering these four questions gives you the potential to engage people's minds, hearts, imaginations, and energy. When you can clearly verbalize the answer to these four questions, you are ready to go public with your vision.

"Public" may be your sixteen-year-old daughter or a conference room full of volunteers. The context doesn't matter. The principle is the same. Visioncasting has the potential to set a course for the people around you. And when they are convinced it is a God-honoring course, there will always be some who will ask, "To what extent can I give my life to that?"

VISIONEERING

PROJECT #8

Answer the following questions for each arena of vision

1. Why must I see this vision through to the end?

   • What difference will it make?

   • What is there to gain?

   • What is there to lose?

   • What's at stake?

   • Why should I attempt this?

2. Why must it be done now?

   • What do I stand to lose by waiting?

   • What evidence have I seen that God is involved?

CHAPTER NINE

THE POWER
OF VISION

A vision we give to others of who and what they could become has power
when it echoes what the spirit has already spoken into their souls.
LARRY CRABB

Treat people as if they were what they ought to be, and you help them become
what they are capable of becoming.
GOETHE

In this chapter we are going to depart from the storyline just a bit in order to explore one additional facet of visioncasting. Most of the visioncasting you do will have very little to do with what could be or should be as it relates to your life. The majority of the visions you cast will be centered on other people and their futures. Let me explain.

We are all visioncasters. We cast visions for people all the time. Chances are you cast a vision for someone today. It wasn't intentional. It probably wasn't life-changing. But along the way you made a comment to someone about what could or should be in his or her life. It may have been positive: "You will probably outsell everybody in this office." Or it may have been negative: "I don't think you were cut out for sales" (i.e. "You don't have a future in sales"). Affirming: "Honey, you can do anything you set your mind to." Or discouraging: "You will probably struggle with this the rest of your life."

Comments such as these shape one's picture of the future. Words point people in a direction. They plant mental seeds. Words can make or break a self-image. So, in a way, we are all visioncasters. Every relationship is a potential visioncasting opportunity.

The position we hold in people's lives determines the weight of our words and thus our potential to shape their future. Encouragement from Sandra means more than encouragement from a stranger. Every son knows the adrenaline rush associated with his father's recognition and approval. As a father, I am all too aware of my children's potential to hurt me. For unbeknownst to them, I long for their approval just as they crave mine.

PERSONAL VISIONCASTING

All of us have been impacted by the visions people intentionally or unintentionally cast for us. Understanding this simple concept will help you grasp your potential as a visioncaster in the lives of those around you. Just as people's words have set a course for your life, so you too have the potential to set or alter the course of another.

When I was in the eighth grade, I tried out for the eighth grade boys basketball team at my high school. I was one of about one hundred students who tried out that year. As you can imagine, it was a zoo. I don't know how the coaches ever managed to discover who had potential and who didn't. But after five rounds of cuts, I was still a potential candidate for the Tucker High School eighth grade boys basketball team.

The final cut happened on a Thursday night in December of 1972. When I think back to that pivotal night, I can almost smell that old Tucker High gymnasium. We were coming down to the final minutes of the tryout. At the end of the evening the head coach would read off the names of the guys who had made the team. If you didn't hear your name...

Anyway, we were scrimmaging. I was in the corner. Somebody passed the ball to me. I took a shot and missed everything. No rim. No net. No backboard. Nothing. The head coach was standing on the corner of the floor opposite me. He yelled across the court, "Stanley, you've got no backbone." He shook his head in disgust and walked over to the bench.

In a few minutes the scrimmage ended. The tryouts ended. And my chances for playing eighth grade basketball ended as well. But something else happened that night. That coach had cast a vision for me. His words, combined with the events of the evening, painted a picture of my future that took me years to overcome.

I believed him. I believed that in the arena of athletic competition I would never succeed. He told me what I could and should expect in the future in so far as competitive sports were concerned. He was an adult, a coach. His words cut deep. So I acted on them.

That was the last time I tried out for anything competitive. It wasn't until I was in my mid-twenties that I recognized what had happened and was able to move past it. Such are the power of words. Such is the power of visioncasting.

Jesus certainly understood this concept. Remember his first encounter with Peter? Peter wasn't Peter when he met Jesus. He was Simon. Simon Johnson to be precise (John 1:41–42). And then Jesus, in seeming total disregard for Simon's parents' choice of a name, decided to call him Peter. What was that all about?

Jesus was casting a vision. Jesus had a vision of what Peter could become. Jesus saw in Peter the potential for greatness. So he gave him a name that reflected his potential. Peter. The rock. From that day forward Peter carried a constant reminder of what Jesus saw in him. What he could be. What he should be. And in Peter's case, what he one day would be.

Then some time later, Jesus turned to Peter and filled in the blanks.

> I also say to you that you are Peter, and upon this rock I will build My church; and the gates of Hades will not overpower it. I will give you the keys of the kingdom of heaven; and whatever you bind on earth shall have been bound in heaven, and whatever you loose on earth shall have been loosed in heaven. (Matthew 16:18–19)

No doubt Peter's mind raced back to that first encounter when Jesus gave him his new name. It was more than a name change. It was a vision. In some yet-to-be-revealed way, he would serve as the foundation for something important, something still in the future.

And although there was no way Peter could comprehend the significance of Christ's words that day, he certainly walked away with a greater
sense of destiny. It was clear that God had something special in mind for
him.

If Peter knew his Old Testament, he knew he was not the first person
who was renamed in light of a divine purpose. Abraham was not always
Abraham. And for that matter, Sarah was not always Sarah, either. On the
day God instituted his covenant with Abraham, he changed his name to
signify the certainty of his future. His name change was part of the vision
he cast for Abraham and his descendants.

> Now when Abram was ninety-nine years old, the LORD appeared
> to Abram and said to him, "I am God Almighty; walk before me,
> and be blameless. I will establish My covenant between me and
> you, and I will multiply you exceedingly." Abram fell on his face,
> and God talked with him, saying, "As for me, behold, My
> covenant is with you, and you will be the father of a multitude of
> nations. No longer shall your name be called Abram, but your
> name shall be Abraham; for I will make you the father of a mul-
> titude of nations." (Genesis 17:1–5)

And regarding Abraham's wife,

> Then God said to Abraham, "As for Sarai your wife, you shall not
> call her name Sarai, but Sarah shall be her name. I will bless her,
> and indeed I will give you a son by her. Then I will bless her, and
> she shall be a mother of nations; kings of peoples will come from
> her." (vv. 15–16)

Abram means *exalted father.* Abraham means, *father of many.* Both
Sarah and Sarai mean *princess.* Renaming her was God's way of punctuat-
ing the appropriateness of her name. She would be the mother of kings.
From her womb would eventually come an entire dynasty.

God renamed Abraham and Sarah and Peter as a way of pointing
them in specific directions for their lives. Their names were a reflection of

what could be and what would be. In a similar way, our w
power to point people in a direction, to set their life's course
cially true of those who look to us for leadership.

Fortunately for me, that head coach was not the only auth
in my life whose words etched a picture on my heart.

MY EARLIEST VISION

In many ways I feel I am the product of a vision my father cast for me as
a child. Early on he would say to me, "Andy, God has something very special for your life. He is going to use you in a great way." His words found
their way into my heart.

During my junior high and high school days, those words would float
through my mind at what I considered the most inappropriate times.
"Andy, God has something very special for your life. He is going to use
you in a great way." His vision for my life probably did as much as anything to move me safely through the minefield of adolescence.

The following is a journal entry I made during the fall of my senior
year in high school. Keep in mind, I was in the twelfth grade when I wrote
these words.

September 29, 1975
I need to tell my boy at a young age that God told me he was
going to use my son in a great way. This greatly influenced my
life. Lord, I pray it will his.

My father's words served as guardrails at a vulnerable time in my
development. Time after time they kept me from veering off into moral
and relational ravines. As early as the twelfth grade I was able to step
back far enough to discern their impact. Like an arrow in the hands of a
skilled archer, he had aimed and released me with armor-piercing
momentum.

Vision is powerful. Particularly when it is cast by someone we look
up to and respect, someone we trust and are prone to emulate. Chances
are you either have or will have people in your life who feel that way
about you.

Neither of my parents ever pushed me toward ministry. But I believe their vision was the tool God used to draw me in that direction. Vision draws us. It draws us because it captures our imaginations. From there it has the potential to engage our hearts. And once our hearts have felt the energy that comes with a well-cast vision, we gain a sense of destiny.

This is what could be.

This is what should be.

By God's grace this is what will be.

Vision serves as intrinsic motivation. We move in a direction because we want to, not because we are told to. Instead of pushing and cajoling us into action, a vision draws and even enchants us.

Once an authority figure exits our life, his or her influence often disappears as well. But not so with the person wise enough to plant the seed of a positive vision in our hearts. Their influence is often felt for a lifetime. A carefully planted vision, like a seed, grows to take on a life and shape of its own. Long after the sower is gone, the seed continues to grow.

A WORD TO MOMS AND DADS

Moms, Dads, we are the premier visioncasters. We must paint a vividly clear picture in the minds and hearts of our children of what they can become in their character, conduct, and even their careers. We must pour into their spongelike souls a vision of what they could accomplish with their lives. After all, we see their potential far better than they do.

It is incumbent upon us as stewards of these precious lives to introduce them to their potential, to lift their eyes off of today's realities and focus them on tomorrow's possibilities. We must ask God to give us a clear vision for our children and cast it every opportunity we get.

The most significant visions are not cast by great orators from a stage. They are cast at the bedsides of our children. The greatest visioncasting opportunities happen between the hours of 7:30 and 9:30 P.M. Monday through Sunday. In these closing hours of the day we have a unique opportunity to plant the seeds of what could be and what should be. Take advantage of every opportunity you get.

Not long ago I was lying down with Andrew, my six-year-old, and Garrett, who just turned five, going through our nightly routine of verses, stories, and prayer. I don't know why I chose this particular night to introduce the subject of God's special plan for their lives, but I did. After our prayers I leaned down close to Andrew and said, "God has something special for your life, and I can't wait to find out what it is."

Without hesitating he asked, "What's yours?"

"What's my what?" I asked.

"What's God's special thing for your life?" he said.

I wasn't prepared for that. So I did what most dads do in a situation like that. I called a time out. "Andrew, it's late, but I will tell you all about that tomorrow night."

That began a whole new level of dialogue between my sons and me. As I have an opportunity to describe "God's special thing" in my life, I am finding opportunity after opportunity to point them toward a preferred future for their lives—what could be, what should be. My most significant visioncasting takes place on my knees with my face twelve inches away from the faces of my children.

About halfway through writing this book I began reading *Connecting* by Larry Crabb. Throughout the book he expands upon the power and importance of casting a vision for another person. The following two paragraphs really hit home about my role as a parent.

> What would it be like if we had a vision for each other, if we could see the lost glory in ourselves, our family, and our friends? What would the effect on your sons or daughters be if they realized that you were caught up with the possibilities of restored glory, of what they could become—not successful, talented, good looking, or rich but kind, strong and self-assured, fully alive.
>
> When people connect with each other on the basis of a vision for who they are and what they could become; when we see in others what little of Jesus has already begun to form beneath the insecurity, fear and pride; when we long beyond anything else to see that little bit of Jesus develop and mature; then something is released from within us that has the power to form more of Jesus within them. That power is the life of Christ, carried into another soul across the bridge of our vision for them, a life that touches the life in another with nourishing power. Vision for others both bridges the distance between two souls and triggers the release of the power within us.[1]

The New Testament casts a compelling vision for each of us who have trusted Christ as Savior. It is clear from even a casual reading of the text that God has no problem whatsoever seeing and relating to us as we will be, not as we are.

We are constantly referred to as saints. We are on our way to being conformed to the image of Christ. The apostle Paul goes so far as to say we are seated with Christ in heavenly places. Reread portions of the New Testament with this in mind. You will be amazed at how often we are addressed in light of what we are in the process of becoming and what we will one day be.

Check this out:

> Beloved, now we are children of God, and it has not appeared as yet what we will be. We know that when He appears, we will be like Him, because we will see Him just as He is. (1 John 3:2)

No doubt Jesus shocked his audience when he announced, "You are the salt of the earth....You are the light of the world" (Matthew 5:13–14). To which they probably responded, "We are? You've got to be kidding." At that moment they were no more "salt" and "light" than Peter was a "rock." But Jesus was comfortable speaking to their potential while overlooking their performance. He spoke to what they could be, what they should be, and for a handful, what they would become.

Apparently he was convinced this was the best approach to bringing about change in his audience. Clearly, he preferred this over concentrating on what people were doing wrong. In fact, the only group whose present performance he continually harped on was the group that was convinced it was doing a whole lot better than it really was.

JANE'S STORY

Think about this for a moment. What would happen if you were to begin speaking to people's potential rather than their performance? What if you made it a habit to dispense the same type of grace to others as has been poured out on you? What would happen if you intentionally laced your conversations with notions of what could be true of the people around you?

Jane McCall and I have been friends for eleven years. We have known each other longer than that. But our friendship didn't begin until a couple of years after we met. When I met Jane, she was a full-fledged street person. She had been a prescription drug addict for the previous twenty years. And now, at forty-one, she was a part of the government-sponsored methadone experiment. Methadone is a drug given primarily to heroine addicts to replace their drug of choice. To receive it legally, addicts had to report daily to a treatment center that administered the drug. Unfortunately, like heroine, methadone is highly addictive. So much so that it has its own black market.

Jane approached me after church one Sunday night and expressed a desire for help. I was twenty-seven years old at the time. I was fresh out of seminary. I knew a lot about the Bible but very little about helping anyone in Jane's condition. So I made all the classic mistakes. First, I believed everything she told me. That, of course, led to my next mistake: I gave her money on a regular basis.

Years later she would kid me, "Andy," she would say, "do you know how to tell when an addict is lying?"

"No, Jane, how do you know when an addict is lying?"

"His lips are moving."

For seven years I tracked with Jane as she was in and out of every hospital and rehabilitation program in the city. Just when I thought she was making progress, down she would go. And when I was ready to walk away, she would make up some incredible heartrending story, and I would feel sorry for her and jump back into the insanity.

On one occasion I helped Jane get a job at a local church. I thought she had kicked the drug thing once and for all. She was doing so well. Her boss was thrilled with her performance. And then she called me and said she had to talk to me immediately.

After a long drawn-out story she looked me straight in the eye and said, "Andy, I tested HIV positive. I feel like the best thing for me to do is to quit my job so as to protect you and the integrity of the church."

Of course my first thought was, "How heroic. How sensitive. God has done a miracle in Jane's heart." After all, this was the first job Jane had had in years. I knew she loved the environment she was in. And I was confident she enjoyed the people she worked around. For her to quit this job was a big sacrifice. Or so I thought.

Several weeks later, Jane admitted she had made the whole thing up. She had started using again, and it was interfering with her performance at work. Rather than tell me, she thought it would be better to make up the HIV story so she would have a good excuse for resigning. At that point, I resigned from Jane.

For a couple of months.

The one thing I did right with Jane was to take advantage of every opportunity I could to cast a vision of what God could do through her if she would put her addiction behind her once and for all. "Jane," I would say, "one day God is going to use you to reach people who would never listen to me." In the early years she would just shake her head. But as time went by she would bring it up. "Andy, do you really believe God could use me? Do you really believe anybody would ever listen to me?" For some reason, I really believed God wanted to use Jane. So I kept telling her. Eventually she began to believe me.

Somewhere along the way God birthed a vision in Jane. She began to see all the filth and sin and abuse as an opportunity. Her past, which had been a point of shame and embarrassment, took on a new meaning. What "could be" eventually blossomed into what "should be." And Jane embraced her potential with a vengeance.

Jane overcame her drug addiction. With that behind her, she tackled the deeper issues that had sent her scrambling as a teenager for something to mask her pain. It became evident early on in the process that recovery was not her ultimate destination. She believed God was going to use her, and she was preparing herself for whatever he had in mind.

She attended enough support groups, counseling sessions, AA, NA, and CA (Cocaine Anonymous) meetings to earn an honorary doctorate in addiction recovery, if there were such a thing. God used her extensive group experience to further define his vision for her life.

As she neared the end of the recovery process, she enrolled in a course designed to teach people how to lead support groups. Her instructor recognized Jane's eagerness to learn, and before long he allowed her to lead a group for sexually-abused women.

Jane was a fish in water. She loved those women in a way that only someone with Jane's background could love them. And they responded. Before long she had two groups. No case was too extreme. Nobody was unlovable. She saw potential in everyone who graced her presence.

From time to time Jane would invite me to sit in on her groups and answer theological questions or add a male perspective to the discussion. On one occasion Jane decided to focus the discussion on how to help husbands deal with their attitudes toward those who had abused their wives. So she invited the husbands to the meeting. She invited Sandra and me as well.

I have seen a lot of hurt. I have heard my share of heartrending stories. I have walked with people through just about every painful situation imaginable. In spite of that, I was still unprepared for the emotional intensity that permeated Jane's apartment that night. If you have ever sat in on a support group for sexually-abused women, you understand. If not, well, I don't know if there are adjectives to describe what we experienced. This was not my first meeting with Jane. But it was the first time spouses had been invited to the group. Their presence, comments, and insensitivity fueled a fire that was already raging out of control.

The meeting lasted about three hours. Sandra and I didn't hang around to socialize afterwards. As soon as we got in the car, we both broke down and started weeping. We didn't tear up—we wept. Never in our lives had we been in an environment of such intense emotional pain. It was more than either of us could bear. I had been invited to facilitate the discussion, but I was pretty much worthless.

Yet there in the middle of those precious ladies was Jane. God's appointed and anointed messenger. Delivering a message of hope and healing in a way that no one but Jane could deliver it. Pointing the way to what could be, what should be. Listening, loving, embracing, understanding, giving, sharing, refusing to give up on even the most difficult personalities.

What could be had come to be. Not because of any great effort on my part. Certainly not because of any skill or insight I possessed. But because the seed of vision had germinated, taken root, pushed to the surface, and blossomed. God had a plan for Jane. Jane recognized it and embraced it. And now she is a visioncaster. A visioncaster for a group whose hearts and hopes have been damaged almost beyond repair. A group who needs someone exactly like Jane to find the glowing embers of life and fan them into a preferred future.

When I think back to those early years with Jane, I am drawn once again to something Larry Crabb wrote describing the potential of helping a person lock in on what could be.

> Powerful relating consists of grasping a vision of what God has in mind for someone and the faith to believe that the vision could become a reality.2

WORD POWER

Words are powerful. They are life-shaping. We can use them for good or evil. To build or destroy. To point people in a God-honoring direction or to send them down a path of regret.

No doubt it was the potential of the spoken word that compelled the apostle Paul to write these words:

> Let no unwholesome word proceed from your mouth, but only such a word as is good for edification according to the need of the moment, so that it will give grace to those who hear. (Ephesians 4:29)

This from a man who was continually referring to unfaithful, antagonistic, immature church members as "saints." He practiced what he preached. He spoke to his audiences' potential, not their practice. Maybe it was the amazing metamorphosis in his own life that gave him the confidence to address these first-century believers for what they could be, should be, and by God's grace, would be.

Should we do any less? What kind of vision are you casting for the people around you? Dad, what kind of vision are you casting for your children? Mom, what kind of vision are you casting for your husband? Grandparent, what about those grandkids? Leader, what kind of personal visions are you casting for the people who have invested their time and talents in your vision?

In the next chapter we will refocus our attention on the development of your personal vision. As we continue our study, keep in mind that while you are the recipient of a divinely ordered vision, you will also be given opportunities to cast the Father's vision for those around you.

VISIONEERING
PROJECT #9
FOR PARENTS

1. What could be and should be as it relates to your children's character?

   List three character qualities you envision for your children.

   _____   _____   _____

2. Champion these characteristics by pointing out positive and negative illustrations as you run across them in stories, videos, or family experiences.
3. Include these characteristics in your prayers when you pray with your children.

   - "Lord, thank you that Shannon is becoming a lady who can be trusted in all situations."
   - "Lord, help Reggie and me to become men of character."
   - "Lord, thank you that Cindy is so sensitive and thoughtful."
   - "Lord, I know Andrew is going to do well in school; he is such a good listener."

4. When you see a natural inclination toward something good in your child, cast a vision for him or her around that natural bent.

   - For example, if you have a son who enjoys puzzles or problem-solving in general, you may say something like, "You know, Thomas, you are so good at figuring things out. Someday God may give you an opportunity to solve problems for other people."
   - If you have a daughter who exhibits gifts in the area of leadership you could encourage that in her by saying, "Christi, you are a good leader. People love to follow you. I can't wait to see how God is going to use that gift in the various stages of your life."

FOR LEADERS

Play to the strengths and potential of the people around you. Often people are not aware of their strengths. Our strengths are such a natural part of our makeup that we often don't recognize them. Here are two ways to do this.

1. When you give someone a new task or project, relate your confidence in his or her ability to perform in the future to something in them that facilitated his or her success in the past.

   - For example, "Jim, you did a great job recruiting volunteers for [whatever]. That's why I'm asking you to take on this new assignment. You are a natural when it comes to assembling the right team for a project. I imagine you will always do well working with people."

2. Look for opportunities to comment publicly and privately about the natural inclinations and abilities you see in the people around you. Then take it a step further by associating those inclinations and abilities to future success.

   - For example, "Didn't Carrie do a great job organizing the staff picnic? One thing I really appreciate about Carrie is that when you assign something to her, you can just forget it. You don't have to worry about it anymore. With the right support, I doubt there is any project she couldn't handle."

....

CHAPTER TEN

VISION HAS
ITS PRICE

*What I really lack is to be clear in my mind what I am to do,
not what I am to know…The thing is to understand myself,
to see what God really wishes me to do…to find the idea
for which I can live and die.*
SOREN KIERKEGAARD

Any vision worth pursuing will demand sacrifice and risk. You will be called upon to give up the actual good for the potential best. You will find it necessary to leave what is comfortable and familiar in order to embrace that which is uncomfortable and unfamiliar. And all the while, you will be haunted by the fear that this thing you are investing so much of yourself in may not work out at all.

There are so many unknowns associated with a vision. There are dozens of opportunities for things to go wrong. There is no guaranteed return on your investment. Sacrifice and risk-taking are unavoidable.

But to allow the cost and uncertainties to cause you to shrink back in your commitment or cause you to move out tenuously is to invite failure. Besides that, no one will follow you. Uncertainty in a leader is always magnified in the heart of the follower. John Maxwell says it this way: "People buy into the leader before they buy into the vision. People buy into the vision after the leader buys into it."[1]

Vision requires courage and confidence. It requires launching out as if you were absolutely assured of the outcome. Vision requires the commitment of a parachutist. You don't "sort of" parachute. You are either in the plane or in the air. You either do it or you don't. The tendency is to approach a vision the same way a first-time ice skater takes to the ice: cautiously, and never more than an arm's length from the railing.

BOTH FLIPPERS IN THE WATER

When I was nineteen I spent several weeks on a small out-island in the Bahamas. It was there that I was introduced to the joy of scuba diving. Michael Albury was my host. Michael was a resident of Man o' War Island. His life revolved around the water. And while I was there, I did everything in my power to try to keep up with him.

One afternoon he suggested we go scuba diving. In the safety and comfort of his living room that sounded like a good idea. But an hour later as we loaded the equipment on his boat I began to have second thoughts.

Michael invited another fellow and his girlfriend to accompany us. At the last minute the friend canceled out, but Shannon, his girlfriend, decided to come along anyway.

I was hoping we wouldn't go too far out. But of course, Michael wanted to show me the reef. After all, that was where all the "big fish" were. I had been around long enough to know the reef was also where the big sharks were.

After about an hour, we arrived at the designated spot. Michael was preparing our tanks and I was trying on flippers. That's when Shannon spoke up.

"Have you ever used tanks before?" she asked.

"No," I said. "Have you?"

"Not yet," she said, "but my boyfriend is giving me lessons."

"Lessons?"

"Yeah, we just finished going through the book."

"Book?" I asked. "Michael, what book? I haven't read any books."

She continued, "Next week we are going to do a practice dive on the beach."

"Practice dive? Beach? Hey, Michael, maybe we should do a practice dive on the—"

Before I could finish, he stuck the regulator in my mouth and told me to breathe normally. Right.

"Don't worry," he said, "I've never read the book, either."

Somehow I wasn't surprised. Before I knew it, I was standing on the side of the boat, looking like a Navy SEAL. Well, maybe not. Anyway, I was standing on the side of the boat looking down into what I was sure were shark-infested waters. Michael said, "Jump in. I'll be down in a minute."

That's when I learned you don't "sort of" scuba dive. You are either in the water or out. I had to decide. I had to commit. I didn't have the option to experiment. I couldn't keep one flipper on the boat and one in the water. It was all or nothing.

So I jumped. Michael was right. That was where all the big fish were.

Visions don't become reality until somebody is willing to jump in. Launching a vision always involves committing wholeheartedly to what could be. Goliath never would have been defeated had David not stepped out from the ranks of the Israelites to challenge the giant. Peter never would have known the thrill of coming to Jesus on the water had he not swung both legs over the side of the boat and stepped out into the deep. And the apostle Paul never would have known the joy of taking the gospel to the Gentile nations had he not packed his bags that first time and headed off into the unknown.

There is always risk. There is always a sacrifice. But it is an individual's willingness to break through the barriers imposed by risk and sacrifice that positions him or her to see what could be become a reality. He who shrinks back from the challenge spends his life wondering.

The men and women who gathered to listen to Nehemiah's vision for Israel certainly jumped in with both feet. Notice their response.

> I told them how the hand of my God had been favorable to me and also about the king's words which he had spoken to me. Then they said, "Let us arise and build." So they put their hands to the good work. (Nehemiah 2:18)

I love that last statement. "So they put their hands to the good work." In other words, they committed.

The way the story is depicted makes it sound as if the people in Jerusalem really didn't have anything better to do than rebuild the wall. You almost get the feeling they were standing around with their hands in their pockets until Nehemiah came along. But that was not the situation at all. This was an agricultural society. If you weren't working, you weren't eating. These folks were up to their eyeballs with things to do. Adding this project to their daily routine meant putting other things on hold. Translated, rebuilding the wall meant sacrifice and risk.

To complicate things even further, most of the people had moved out of the city into the areas surrounding Jerusalem. Rebuilding the wall meant leaving their homes, farms, ranches, and businesses and traveling into town to work. It meant putting life as they had come to know it on hold. It meant leaving their farms, cattle, and families unattended. Eventually they were asked to leave their homes altogether and move into the city to make the work more efficient. And they did so willingly. The vision of what could and should be compelled them to make the necessary sacrifice. "They put their hands to the good work."

As if the situation was not risky enough as it was, there was an additional complication to the work of rebuilding the city. Not everybody was excited about the prospects of Israel getting back on its feet economically and politically. Sanballat, governor of neighboring Samaria, was particularly disturbed that someone had come along to promote the welfare of Israel (2:10). He, along with the governors of other surrounding regions, had benefited financially as well as politically from Israel's weakened state. The last thing they wanted was Israel to flex her muscles and regain the clout she once carried in that region of the world.

So Sanballat and his allies began questioning Nehemiah's motives and intentions. They began circulating threatening rumors and letters. Their goal was to see to it that the wall was never completed.

Consequently, the men and women who were leaving their homes and farms to travel to Jerusalem to work on the wall did so at the risk of returning home to find their houses burned and their crops destroyed. Everything dear to them was at stake. Yet they put their hands to the good work. They were willing to make the necessary sacrifice. They acknowledged the risk and moved ahead with the project.

The people committed their time, talent, and treasure for an unspecified length of time to complete the task. And when they did, something unexpected happened. This disorganized, unmotivated, nationally uninspired remnant became a team. The moment they put their hands to the task they were transformed from a scattered self-serving flock into an army with a mission.

If God has birthed a vision in your heart, the day will come when you will be called upon to make a sacrifice to achieve it. And you will have to make the sacrifice with no guarantee of success.

I talk to people all the time who have what seem to be "God ideas" but who are unwilling to commit with both hands and feet. The conversations often begin with, "If I had a million dollars..."

A well-meaning lady once said to me, "You know, I am so burdened by the problems in the inner city. If I had a million dollars, I would love to go down there and start a school for underprivileged kids."

As sensitively as I knew how, I said, "I know people with far less than you have now who have started schools for inner-city kids. You don't need a million dollars to start a school." What she needed was the courage to act on her vision.

The difference between those with a burden for inner-city kids and those who actually do something is not resources. It is a willingness to take risks and make sacrifices. The people who make a difference in this world commit to what could be before they know where the money is coming from. Their vision is enough to cause them to jump in. Money usually follows vision. It rarely happens the other way around. Consequently, vision always involves sacrifice and risk-taking.

THE KAREN BENNETT STORY

On February 3, 1990, Karen Bennett and five of her friends left the suburbs and moved into an old abandoned nightclub in one of the most dangerous areas of Atlanta. For the previous six months they had conducted services on the streets for inner-city children. During those encounters God brought greater clarity to the vision he had birthed in Karen during her college days. In time it became apparent that she was to establish a unique ministry to the inner-city children of Atlanta.

Karen is a single, white female. At that time she was twenty-three years old. Not unlike other Atlanta singles, Karen was saving for her first

Gucci and driving a Honda. But the emptiness she saw in the eyes of those children was something she could not ignore. As her vision began to take shape, she became convinced that there should be a safe place for children in the middle of what was and continues to be a drug-infested war zone. So Karen and her friends decided to plant a children's church in the inner city. After allowing the idea to incubate for several months they began looking for a site.

> Month after month we kept going down there until we felt like it was time to have a church building for those kids. We started looking at old warehouses and old buildings in downtown Atlanta. Finally we found this one old nightclub that sits right in the middle of twenty-five major inner-city projects. I called the owner up and I said, "Well, how much do you want for this place?" He said he needed $2,000 a month rent.
>
> Well, he could've told me it was two million—I didn't have that type of money. I was on a church salary living in an apart-ment in the suburbs. But on the way home we each stopped by our bank and cleared out our checking and savings accounts. We looked for every nickel and dime we could find. That night we dumped it all into one pot; and between all six of us, we had $52.00.[2]

Karen contacted a couple of churches for support. They were sympa-thetic but unwilling to partner with her financially. Nobody was inter-ested in supporting a stand-alone, inner-city children's church. Whereas most single young ladies would have taken this as a signal to channel her energies elsewhere, Karen saw it as a test of her commitment to the vision. So she called a meeting.

> So it ended up that my staff and I got together that night and we just talked about it. It was one of those nights that we just had to be honest with ourselves. Is this what we were going to do? Or was this one of those things that we were just going to talk about until we were forty or fifty years old?

So we decided that we were going to take a chance, because every once in a while you've got to do that. The next day we went to our landlords and we handed in our notices to the leases on our apartments. We couldn't afford to have our nice apartments and have a church for those kids at the same time.[3]

Two weeks later, Karen and her unpaid staff moved into the night-club.

I remember that when we moved in, it was twenty or thirty degrees outside, and it was about twenty or thirty degrees inside. We forgot to check if the building had heat before we moved in. It didn't have heat and it didn't have air. It didn't have a toilet, a sink or a shower. It didn't have anything. We had to drive down to Hardees to use the bathroom.

Our new home came complete with cement floors and seventeen-inch sewer rats. We call them "gophers" up our way cause they "go for" you. We kept on trying to get the building upgraded, but nobody believed in us. Our parents thought we'd lost our minds. Sometimes you wonder if you've really heard from God or not.[4]

Karen and her "staff" continued working at their various places of employment. On payday they would deposit their paychecks into their ministry account. Then they would each take $20 a week for living expenses. On weekends they began going door-to-door in the projects inviting children to their Saturday services. They made four thousand personal visits every week. Over time they won the respect and trust of the parents in those communities. That is how the Metro Assembly got its start.

Today, Karen and her sixteen-member staff minister to over three thousand children every week in multiple weekend services. They sponsor a youth service that draws over two hundred teenagers. In 1994 they established a private school in the community. Tuition is twenty dollars per month. They have one hundred twenty-five students enrolled and over five hundred on a waiting list.

But Karen and her staff have paid a price for the success they are experiencing. Metro Assembly has been broken into over seventy times. Several years ago Karen was mugged. Three of their staff were beaten up by teenagers who attended one of their services. Most of the windows on their buses have been shot out. Ten of the children who attended their first church service have been murdered. The first funeral Karen performed was for one of her own staff members. Karen's response to all of this?

"If you decide that what God is asking you to do with your life is just too much on you and is just a little too inconvenient, then you will never see the miracles he has for you."5

A vision always requires somebody to go first. Karen's story illustrates this clearly. If you are consumed with a picture of what could be and should be in a particular area, chances are God is going to call you to make the first move. This is especially true if the success of your vision depends upon the willingness of others to join you. You cannot lead people any further than you are willing to go yourself. You cannot cast a compelling vision for people if you have not demonstrated your willingness to make sacrifices and take risks.

BUILDING BLOCK #9

DON'T EXPECT OTHERS TO TAKE GREATER RISKS OR MAKE GREATER SACRIFICES THAN YOU HAVE.

One reason Nehemiah's vision was so compelling was the sacrifices and risks he had taken to come as far as he had. He had gone to a great deal of trouble to give the people of Jerusalem an opportunity to rebuild the walls. He had walked away from his cushy palace job and traveled hundreds of miles in the hopes that a group of people he had never met would join him in a project that had little chance of success.

One thing about Nehemiah, he was committed. Both flippers were in the water. He wasn't asking anyone to do something he had not demonstrated a willingness to do himself.

LEADING BY EXAMPLE

In February of 1997 our church needed to raise a million dollars in a four-month period in order to begin construction on our first building. Several things were working against us. To begin with, North Point Community Church was just sixteen months old at the time. We were still dealing with the enormous cost involved in starting a new church. Second, we had a young congregation. Almost half of our regular attenders were single adults. To complicate things even further, we had just closed on a piece of property two months earlier. I had really pushed our folks to give sacrificially. Now we were facing yet another seemingly unrealistic deadline.

As I prayed about what approach to take in presenting the need, I felt impressed to follow Nehemiah's example. Nehemiah divided the work of rebuilding the wall into forty sections. Then he assigned people to each section.

I broke our financial goal down into bite-sized pieces and made assignments. There was one big difference. Nehemiah assigned specific portions of the wall to specific people. I simply presented the various amounts that would need to be given and left it up to our people to sign on to a particular portion of the goal.

I said we needed 500 people to give $500, 250 to give $1,000, 50 to give $5,000, and 10 to give $25,000. I had no idea who would be responsible for what. I just laid it out there and trusted God to prompt people to commit to a particular portion of our wall.

Before I made the presentation, however, I had to settle something in my heart. I was about to ask our congregation to make a financial sacrifice in order to launch our building program. But up until that time I had not given sacrificially to further the ministry of our church. In terms of my personal financial support, I had simply transferred my normal giving patterns to our new church. I was taught as a child to give ten percent off the top. That's what I had always done. So, from the very beginning I gave ten percent of everything I made to the church. But that was not sacrificial.

As I prepared to present the giving assignments to our congregation, I knew God wanted me to do more. As the leader, I had to lead the way. If I was expecting our people to give sacrificially, I had to do the same. So I prayed the prayer God always seems to answer in the clearest way, "Lord, how much do you want Sandra and me to give?"

Almost immediately, an idea popped into my mind. It wasn't a voice. It certainly wasn't an emotion. It was strong impression. The kind I have learned to take seriously while at the same time moving cautiously. Like many Christians I struggle with discerning God's will when it comes to issues not directly addressed in Scripture. So I spent a couple of days thinking and praying about it.

HAPPY VALENTINE'S

The longer I prayed, the more convinced I became. I was supposed to contribute to the building fund by not taking my salary from the church during the four months we were raising the money. That was challenging to say the least. It would certainly mean a sacrifice. But that wasn't all. I felt equally impressed to announce my decision to our congregation. That seemed a bit extreme. I never felt it was anyone else's business how much I gave. Besides that, Jesus wasn't too keen on the religious leaders who flaunted their giving habits. But in this particular case I felt it was my duty as the leader to demonstrate my willingness to put my money where my vision was.

This was a decision that would affect my entire family, so I knew I would need to check it out with Sandra. I have a tremendous respect for her discernment. If she was okay with it, I knew it was probably the thing to do.

This whole ordeal took place in February. As it turned out, the first opportunity I had to run this by her was on Valentine's Day. So there we were, sitting in a nice restaurant, celebrating our love for one another. And I dropped the good news. "Sandra," I said, "I've got an idea. I think we are supposed to go without salary for four months while we raise the million dollars for the building. And I think I am supposed to tell the whole church what we are doing. What do you think?"

I will never, and I mean never, forget the next thing that came out of her mouth.

She smiled and said, "It is those kinds of things that make me love you even more."

We had a happy Valentine's Day.

AUTHENTIC VISIONCASTING

There is something inauthentic about a man or woman who casts a vision for which he or she is not willing to personally sacrifice. It is hypocritical to ask others to take risks we are not willing to take ourselves. If God has birthed a vision in you, it is only a matter of time until you will come upon the precipice of sacrifice. What you do at that juncture will in all likelihood determine the future success or failure of your vision. It will certainly determine your capacity to garner the support of others.

In that moment you will be forced to decide if what could be, really should be. If you move forward, the vision will become a part of you. If you cross the line of sacrifice, your potential to lead others across will soar. But if you retreat...If you retreat, you will always wonder.

Unlike my situation, you probably won't need help discerning what kind of sacrifice your vision requires of you. Usually that is evident. You won't need discernment, you will need courage. Courage to commit. Courage to invest what you deem most valuable in a dream that may net little or no return.

I don't know what would have happened if Sandra and I had backed away from the challenge to give sacrificially. Maybe nothing. But I have a feeling that if we had flinched, what took place would not have happened. Not because God needed me. Not because I am of such consequence that God could not work things out in spite of me. God can do whatever he wants. The reason I believe so much hinged on our willingness to give is because of a pattern that stands unbroken throughout history.

For reasons known only to him, God has chosen to work through men and women who are willing to make sacrifices for the sake of the "thing" he has placed in their hearts to do. His choicest vehicles are those men and women who courageously lay the things that represent safety and security at his feet for the sake of what could be and should be. In a small way, that is what we did. And at some point, you will be required to do the same.

Search the Scriptures. Search the pages of church history. You won't find an example of anyone God used in even a small way who did not make some kind of sacrifice in order to pursue the vision. Sacrifice and risk are always part of the equation.

I would be naïve to say I understand completely why God operates this way. But one thing I do know. When a man or woman is willing to give up something valuable for a God-ordained vision, God looks upon it as worship. To worship is to ascribe worth to something. Theologically speaking, worship is recognizing and responding appropriately to the greatness of God.

When we sacrifice in order to do the thing God has put in our hearts to do, we are recognizing and responding to his greatness. We are in effect saying, "Father, this vision is worth whatever sacrifice I need to make. You are worthy of my allegiance."

Sandra's affirmation made me feel much better about sharing our contribution to the building program with our congregation. But by Sunday, I was having second thoughts: *What if people think I'm bragging? What if people feel manipulated? How are we ever going to recover financially?*

I don't know when I have ever been so nervous before a message. But when I stood to speak, I knew I was doing exactly what I was supposed to do. The following is an excerpt from the sermon that night.

As I studied for tonight's message, God convicted me of two things. First, as your leader, it is my responsibility to challenge you to go where you have never gone before. And frankly, I have a tendency to hold back. Partly because of my personality. Partly out of a fear of being misunderstood. And partly out of sensitivity to those who are putting their toes back into the religious waters for the first time and who are expecting a pitch for money.

The second thing I have been convicted of is that as your leader, I must lead the way in both sacrifice and risk. Both my feet must be planted squarely in the vision. I've got to let go of the side of the pool and wade out into the deep water and ask you to follow me.

When we as a body are willing to commit wholeheartedly to this vision, I believe God is going to do something special. Nehemiah was specific in his instruction to the people regarding the rebuilding of the wall. I need to be specific as well. The time has come for us to begin our building. The time has come for us to put our hands to the good work.

At that point I presented the giving assignments I outlined earlier in this chapter.

Most of us give out of savings, and I assumed I would do the same. But God wants us to wade way out. I felt it was important to let you know how critical this juncture is for us as a church. We cannot give as we have given in the past. The time has come for us to fully embrace the vision God has given us by giving sacrificially.

I went on to share my decision not to take any salary for the next four months. That was one of the most difficult things I have ever done as a pastor. I was visibly uncomfortable. Not because of the decision. But because of the awkwardness of telling everybody. And yet I knew in my heart that as a leader, as the primary guardian of the vision, that was what I had to do.

That was a turning point for our congregation. They put their hands to the good work. Our members quickly embraced the giving assignments. People began to give sacrificially. Several couples gave their tax refund checks. Others postponed trips and gave the money they had been saving. I received dozens of letters from members telling me how God had used the message that evening to pry open their hands and their hearts.

In four months, we raised $1,046,000.00. But more importantly, this exercise of faith sparked a season of spiritual renewal for our congregation. As Nehemiah was about to discover, sacrifice for the sake of a God-ordained vision paves the way for spiritual renewal. Spiritual renewal often begins with physical sacrifice.

When you give sacrificially or in some other way abandon your comfort zone in order to pursue a God-ordained vision, something happens on the inside. At that point you become a follower as well as a leader. Through sacrifice we submit ourselves to the thing God wants to do. We sign on in a tangible way to his agenda at the expense of our own. The net result is that we submit ourselves to God. That simple act of humility almost always sparks renewal.

When the inhabitants of Jerusalem rolled up their sleeves and went to work on the wall, God went to work on their hearts. Rebuilding the wall was the beginning of a spiritual breakthrough in Israel. By taking hold of the vision, they were forced to loosen their grip on their treasure, time, and self-reliance. God took advantage of the opportunity.

TREASURE HUNT

The reason physical sacrifice often results in spiritual renewal goes back to a principle Jesus taught in the gospel of Matthew. As your treasure goes, so goes your heart. Jesus said it this way: "For where your treasure is, there your heart will be also" (Matthew 6:21).

Your heart and your treasure are linked. If you want to know what you are really committed to, look at your checkbook and credit card statements. There is your heart, plain and simple. There is no clearer reflection of your priorities and values. The way you handle your money is an indicator of where your heart is.

Nehemiah knew that if the people commited their financial resources to God's kingdom, their hearts would eventually follow. When you sacrifice monetarily for the sake of a God-ordained vision, it is like handing your heavenly Father the key to your heart. For the most part, our wallets are the path to our heart. Why? Because for most of us, our money serves as the basis of our security.

Your vision has not truly captured your heart until it captures your wallet. For this reason, at some point along the way, God is going to call upon you to make a financial sacrifice for the thing he has put in your heart to do. He knows that when you commit your treasure to the vision, your heart will follow. When you take those first sacrificial steps to act on your vision, your heart moves with you and attaches itself to the vision.

When we loosen our hands from around our treasure, he loosens the world's death grip from our hearts. When you apply your hands to a divinely ordered vision, God begins a reordering of your heart as well.

Those initial steps of faith seal your commitment. What was once an idea becomes a passion. What filled your head grips your heart. From that point on you will pursue your vision with a deeper commitment than you thought possible.

Physical or financial sacrifice introduces a heightened sense of excitement and anticipation. When you sacrifice for the sake of a divinely inspired vision, you are in with both flippers. You are out of the plane and in the sky. You are committed.

Once you have crossed the line of sacrifice, you have cast your lot with the heavenly Father in a tangible way. In that moment you will become increasingly aware of your dependence upon him. If he doesn't show up, you are in trouble. In a very real way, your fate is in his hands. And as the people of Israel were about to discover, physical sacrifice serves as an invitation for divine intervention. An invitation our heavenly Father is eager to accept.

VISIONEERING
PROJECT #10

1. What will you need to give up in order to pursue your vision? What will your vision cost you?

   Short term _____

   _____

   Long term _____

   _____

2. What is your hesitation? What do you feel when you think about taking the next step? What is the worst thing that could happen? Is it worth the risk?

3. Are you asking or expecting people to commit to something at a level you yourself have not yet committed?

4. If the risk you are taking has the potential to jeopardize the livelihood of other people, make sure you involve them in the decision-making process. How could you do this?

CHAPTER ELEVEN

WARDING OFF
CRITICISM

I f you didn't already know, you will soon discover that:

- Visions are easy to criticize.
- Visions attract criticism.
- Visions are difficult to defend against criticism.
- Visions often die at the hands of the critics.

Chances are, if you have shared your vision with anyone, you are painfully aware of the truth of those four statements. Visions involve two elements that often cause them to draw negative attention: change and gaps.

CHANGE

Whenever you attempt to bring about change, it plays on the insecurities of those who have grown accustomed to the way things are and have always been. In this way, a vision is often seen as a threat. Consequently, it is not uncommon for the negative emotions a vision stirs up in people to be unleashed in the form of criticism. What you are convinced "should be" will be perceived by others as the very thing that "should not be."

To make matters worse, the critics appear to be armed with the "facts." Often they have history and experience on their side. And understandably so. A vision is about the future, not the past. A vision has no history. And yet history and experience are what give birth to a vision. It is past experience that makes the visionary discontent with the way things are. It is from an understanding of history that a picture of what could be and should be takes shape. It is unfortunate that the fertile soil of history and experience is the very soil often used to bury a vision. The birthplace of a vision can become its burial ground as well.

GAPS

Visions are easy to criticize because of their inherent gaps. The very nature of a vision is that there is far more solid information on the *what* side of the equation than on the *how* side. There are holes in the plan. As long as someone simply wants clarification on what you want to see happen, you are in good shape. But once he begins questioning how you plan to pull it off, things get a little thin. But again, that is the nature of a vision. At least initially.

These gaps in the plan make visions easy targets for criticism. Ask enough "But what about…?" questions and you can dismantle just about any vision. The newer the vision, the more susceptible it is to the damaging, discouraging effects of this line of questioning.

It is important to remember that it is the nature of a vision to have gaps. If there were no gaps, somebody else would have already delivered the goods. For this reason, every successful inventor, leader, and explorer faces criticism. You are in good company.

A CITY WORTH FIGHTING FOR

Nehemiah and his crew certainly faced their share of criticism. His vision did not go unnoticed by the rulers of the regions around Jerusalem. As we pointed out earlier, the idea of Jerusalem becoming a walled city again sent a chill through the hearts of the governors nearby. They knew Israel's history almost as well as they knew their own. For Israel to get back on her feet economically and militarily meant the end to their control in that region.

Sanballat, the governor of Samaria, had the most to lose. He wielded the lion's share of the power. The other governors, including previous governors in Jerusalem, took their cues from him. The fact that the Jews would begin rebuilding the wall without consulting him was infuriating. He was losing control.

Notice his response:

> Now it came about that when Sanballat heard that we were rebuilding the wall, he became furious and very angry and mocked the Jews. He spoke in the presence of his brothers and the wealthy men of Samaria and said, "What are these feeble Jews doing? Are they going to restore it for themselves? Can they offer sacrifices? Can they finish in a day? Can they revive the stones from the dusty rubble even the burned ones?" Now Tobiah the Ammonite was near him and he said, "Even what they are building—if a fox should jump on it, he would break their stone wall down!" (4:1–3)

Sanballat was thorough in his criticism. He left no stone unturned in his search for reasons why the wall would never be completed. He criticized the character of the builders. He questioned their ability. He challenged their commitment to finish what they started. And to top it off, he questioned the feasibility of the project to begin with. Even if they had the commitment and ability to build, it was doubtful as to whether or not the wall could be rebuilt.

Then his sidekick, Tobiah, chimed in. He described Nehemiah's entire work force as incompetent. Even if they were able to finish the wall, the weight of a fox would cause it to crumble.

Sanballat leveled his criticism with a specific purpose in mind. He wanted to discourage the workers to the point of quitting. So he saw to it that his opinions on the project were repeated throughout the region. Before long, word began to circulate among the workers. But the people were working with "all their heart" (4:6b, NIV). They were not discouraged. So Sanballat came up with another plan.

Now when Sanballat, Tobiah, the Arabs, the Ammonites and the

Ashdodites heard that the repair of the walls of Jerusalem went on, and that the breaches began to be closed, they were very angry. All of them conspired together to come and fight against Jerusalem and to cause a disturbance in it. (vv. 7–8)

If words weren't enough to halt the workers, Sanballat and his cronies would stop the work by force. He called together the rulers of the provinces to the east (Ammonites), west (Ashdodites), and south (Arabs) of Jerusalem. They would attack the city from all sides. Jerusalem wouldn't stand a chance against the combined forces of their armies. There would be no wall.

Soon word began filtering into Jerusalem that their neighbors were preparing for war.

The Jews who lived near them came and told us ten times, "They will come up against us from every place where you may turn." (v. 12)

Notice, this time it was other Jews warning the builders against continuing the wall. Jews living to the north of the city reported that Sanballat's army was approaching their northern border. Jews living to the east reported that the Ammonites were approaching from the east. The city was surrounded.

The message was clear, "Give up or face the threat of death."

To make things worse, the obstacles to rebuilding the wall were beginning to look insurmountable. There was more rubbish than they had anticipated having to deal with. They were tired. The thrill of a new project had worn off. Like children on a long road trip, they were starting to complain, "Are we there yet?"

It was more than they could handle. Their families were at risk. Their own people were encouraging them to abandon the work. The combination of fear and discouragement pushed them over the edge. So they walked off the job. They quit. They were no longer willing to put their hands to the good work.

Who could blame them? Think about it. When you weigh the risk of what they were facing against the rewards of finishing the wall, why stick with it?

There was really only one good reason. Vision.

We can all identify with the way Nehemiah's team must have felt. If you are pursuing a vision of any magnitude, you have been criticized. Perhaps your vision reminds someone of what they are not. But at the same time it reminds them of what they could and should be. And the only thing they know to do is criticize.

NEW BELIEVER BLUES

This is one reason new believers often face so much rejection from their non-Christian friends immediately following their conversion. The new believer catches a vision of what could and should be for his or her life and it reflects poorly on those who are content with the way things are. So they do what they can to discourage progress. They criticize the decision.

When someone catches a vision for bettering himself educationally or financially, his vision is often met with criticism from the people closest to him. Why? Because those who have no vision for their own academic pursuits or financial freedom feel threatened by those who have decided to get up and do something with themselves. Their insecurities about their own lack of education surface or they are forced to take a painful look at where they are financially as opposed to where they could be.

Maybe your vision is causing someone around you to feel as if he or she is losing control. This is why unbelieving spouses are sometimes critical of their believing partners. I've seen parents criticize their own children as a result of this same dynamic. Your vision may play to the insecurity of those who are an authority over you. So they open fire in an attempt to bring you back down to their level.

Perhaps your vision is drawing criticism because of the gaps. A God-ordained vision always has more questions than answers. So the people around you are questioning your vision to death. They don't come right out and criticize you, they just ask you a lot of *how* questions. Either way, the message is the same, "Don't bother, it will never happen."

DEATH OF A VISION

Regardless of what's driving your critics, if you let them get to you, your candle will go out. You will lose heart. You will give up. What could be and should be will never be. At least not as a result of your labor. And when your dream dies, a part of you dies as well.

I have seen it dozens of times. A person will have a mental picture of what he wants his future to look like. And someone comes along and convinces him to ditch his dream and move on with his life.

- Stephanie wants to marry a Christian who will provide spiritual leadership in the home. So she passes up opportunities to go out with non-Christian guys. But her "friends" eventually douse her flame with statements such as, "There aren't any guys out there like that. You are wasting your life away." After a while, Stephanie decides her friends are probably right. Maybe her standards are too high. So she gives up on her vision.
- Ben wants to see his daughter come to faith in Christ and return to a lifestyle in keeping with biblical principles. But his "friends" are constantly saying, "Leave her alone. Kids are different today. That worked for you. She's got to make her own way in this world." It makes sense to Ben. And his vision dies.
- Jim and Linda are buried under a pile of debt because of a series of poor decisions early in their marriage. As a result of something they read, they catch a vision for debt-free living. Then they make the mistake of sharing their vision with Linda's parents. "That's unrealistic," they say. "Everybody has debt. Besides, by the time you get out of debt, you will be so old you won't be able to enjoy it." Jim and Linda walk away discouraged. A day or two later, they abandon their plan.
- Tracy has an idea for a new business. Before long she is gripped by the possibilities and potential. It is more than an idea, it is a vision. She feels confident this is the direction God is leading her. But the folks at the office analyze her plan to death. "Tracy, where are you going to get the financing? Nobody is going to lend you money on an idea like that." Sure enough, the first and only bank she talks to turns her down. And the vision is extinguished.
- As a Christian single, Chris was always appalled by the adultery in his office. It appeared nobody was faithful to his wife. And it didn't seem to bother any of them. When Chris got married, he vowed to be different. He envisioned a lifetime of faithfulness to Jenny. But the guys in the office had a different agenda for Chris. They were determined to bring him down to their level. Eventually Chris believed

the lie. Nobody is faithful anymore. At a conference in Detroit, Chris gave up on his vision. What he didn't realize was that in doing so, he extinguished Jenny's vision as well.

- Pete, a college freshman, shows up for classes with a vision for making a difference for Christ on his campus. He envisions starting a Bible study for the guys on his hall. Three weeks into the fall semester he is sitting alone in his dorm wondering why everyone is avoiding him. His roommate sticks his head in the door and says, "Give it up, Pete. I know you mean well. But nobody's interested in all that Jesus stuff right now. Come on, let's go grab a beer." Pete grabs his jacket and follows his roommate into the night. And the vision is snuffed out.

Whether it comes in the form of a direct statement or packaged in a subtle smile, criticism can be devastating to a vision. If you internalize it, eventually you will get discouraged and give up. And understandably so. In most cases, circumstances support the point of view of our critics.

So how should we respond?

If you are a believer, you have a unique opportunity when it comes to responding to criticism. As we have already discussed, any God-ordained vision will have its roots in God's overarching vision for this world. As long as your vision is in some way tied to what God is up to, you have an incredible option when it comes to responding to criticism.

Your first response may be, "Well, that counts me out. I'm trying to get a business off the ground. What does that have to do with 'God's overarching vision for the world'? Besides, the criticism I receive has nothing to do with anything spiritual."

Well, before you close the book, I want you to think about something for a moment: God does not compartmentalize our lives. From God's perspective there are no spiritual versus nonspiritual components of your life. He makes no distinction. There is no secular division of your life. You are a spiritual being. Therefore everything you are involved in has spiritual overtones. He sees you holistically.

The apostle Paul described it this way:

Or do you not know that your body is a temple of the Holy Spirit who is in you, whom you have from God, and that you are not your own? For you have been bought with a price: therefore glorify God in your body. (1 Corinthians 6:19–20)

The Christians in the city of Corinth believed there was a division between the soul and the body. They thought they could sin with their bodies and it had no impact on their souls. Paul pointed out that no such division existed.

When Christ purchased you at Calvary, he purchased all of you: body, soul, and spirit. There is no division. You are to "glorify God" through your actions, regardless of where they take place and what role you are in at the time. You are to glorify God as a spouse, parent, friend, employee, boss, and citizen. There is no distinction. What you do at the office is no more or less spiritual than what you do at church or at home.

Consequently, there is a spiritual element to your vision regardless of which category of life it emanates from. There are no secular pursuits. Your vision does not exist apart from your responsibility to glorify God. The challenge is to discover the link.

The question becomes, how can my heavenly Father be glorified through this vision? This is a question God is eager to answer. My experience has been that the men and women who ask it sincerely, discover the link quickly.

There's another way of looking at this. As a father, I don't compartmentalize my children's lives. I care about every facet of everything they do. Why? Because they are my children. My relationship to them determines my interest level. My love for them makes everything they do important to me.

You have a heavenly Father who feels the same way about you. Only more so. You are his child regardless of which particular role you are playing at the time. He loves you as a professional just as much as he loves you as a homemaker or a citizen. Your vision for the different roles you play is of keen interest to him. After all, you are his child.

Consequently, when your vision is on the verge of being snuffed out by the criticism of others, your Father is interested. It concerns him. In this way, your response to criticism is a spiritual matter. And your heavenly Father is more than willing to get involved in the conflict.

NEHEMIAH'S RESPONSE TO CRITICISM

Nehemiah had no problem believing God was interested in the success of his mission. This was clearly a spiritual endeavor. The fact that his work revolved primarily around brick, mortar, and trash detail did not distract him from the spiritual dimension of his vision. He was able to see through the details to the root of what his vision was all about.

His response to the criticism and threats of the leaders around him provides us with an excellent model for dealing with criticism. Nehemiah did three things:

1. He prayed.
2. He remembered the source of his vision.
3. He revised his plan.

PRAY

Twice in this episode Nehemiah prays. A portion of his first prayer is actually recorded for us. There are two things that stand out about this prayer. To begin with, it stands in stark contrast with the verse right before it. And second...Well, just read it, and you will pick up on the other unique quality of Nehemiah's prayer.

> Hear, O our God, how we are despised! Return their reproach on their own heads and give them up for plunder in a land of captivity. Do not forgive their iniquity and let not their sin be blotted out before You, for they have demoralized the builders. (Nehemiah 4:4–5)

I'm thinking that mercy was way down on Nehemiah's gift list. This prayer is so strong and so...well...*mean* that several commentators have felt the need to defend Nehemiah. They read between the lines and assume Nehemiah understood Sanballat to be taking aim at God with his criticisms. They interpret this prayer as Nehemiah's way of taking up for God. The attitude being, "How dare they stand in your way, God. You ought to..." And thus the strong language. They say, in effect, that Nehemiah was coming to God's defense.

That may be the case, but I think Nehemiah was just ticked off. He was tired. The builders were tired. And now this! He was not in the mood for mercy. He wanted justice! Mostly, he wanted Sanballat and his crew out of his face. I'm not sure I would have the guts to pray like that. But I have sure felt that way when criticized. After all, criticism enters through the door of our emotions.

Was this an appropriate prayer? Sure it was. He was expressing how he felt to his Father. Did God grant his request? I don't know.

Don't miss this. In a high-stakes, emotionally charged environment, Nehemiah's immediate response was prayer. That is almost unbelievable. In both instances where prayer is mentioned, it immediately follows a reference to the criticism Nehemiah was facing. Look at the contrast between Nehemiah's prayer and the verse preceding it.

Now Tobiah the Ammonite was near him [Sanballat] and he said, "Even what they are building—if a fox should jump on it, he would break their stone wall down!" (v. 3)

Now read Nehemiah's response again.

Hear, O our God, how we are despised! Return their reproach on their own heads and give them up for plunder in a land of captivity. Do not forgive their iniquity and let not their sin be blotted out before You, for they have demoralized the builders. (vv. 4–5)

There is no transition. Nehemiah moves from the criticism right into the prayer. Prayer was his initial response to his critics. This explains his hostile tone. Nehemiah didn't take any time to cool down. He didn't collect his thoughts. He immediately passed along everything he was thinking and feeling directly to the only One who could do anything about it. He didn't sugarcoat it. He didn't spiritualize it. He just unloaded.

Then he went back to work! Check out the next verse:

So we built the wall and the whole wall was joined together to half its height, for the people had a mind to work. (v. 6)

By responding this way Nehemiah avoided a common mistake associated with criticism. He didn't allow his enemies to become the focus of his attention.

Our natural response to criticism is to defend ourselves. This is especially true when our vision is under attack. We are tempted to begin a dialogue with our critics or with those who are parroting their criticism. Consequently, we waste energy and thought trying to answer questions for people who are often not really interested in answers. Without realizing it, our focus begins to shift. Instead of being vision centered, we slowly become critic centered.

Nehemiah was able to remain vision-centered in spite of the criticism he and his team received. He continued to channel his thoughts and energy in the direction of his vision.

Criticism strikes an emotional chord in us. That emotion must go somewhere. To reflect it back on our critics is to play their game. To bottle it up inside can result in depression or ulcers. Another option is to dump it out on someone completely unrelated to the situation: spouse, friends, employees, your children. That only complicates things.

The only healthy and profitable thing to do is to pour out your heart to your heavenly Father. R-rated words and all. After all, he knows what's in your heart anyway. And hey, he's been around. He can handle a little venting. He is honored when we take our deepest frustrations and hurts to him. To do so is an expression of trust. That kind of honest communication is necessary if you are going to develop intimacy with the Father.

If you wonder whether or not it is appropriate to express what you are feeling to God, read through the book of Psalms. David sure didn't hold anything back. He was quick to pass along exactly what he was feeling.

> There is nothing reliable in what they say; their inward part is destruction itself. Their throat is an open grave; they flatter with their tongue. Hold them guilty, O God; by their own devices let them fall! In the multitude of their transgressions thrust them out, for they are rebellious against you. (Psalm 5:9–10)

Try working this next one in next time you are called upon to pray in church:

> Let evil recoil on those who slander me; in your faithfulness destroy them. (Psalm 54:5, NIV)

How would you respond if somebody in your Sunday school class or prayer group prayed with that kind of vengeance? You would probably recommend he get counseling. You would caution the preschool director against using him. He would be blacklisted from every committee in the church.

But wait! These words were written by the "man after God's own heart." The same man whose word pictures give life to our favorite hymns and choruses. Praying with that tone may unnerve the average Christian, but it doesn't seem to bother God.

Prayer puts criticism in its proper context. When you evaluate the words of the critic in light of your finite resources, sketchy plans, and naïveté, it can be overwhelming. But when criticism is held up against the backdrop of the Father's infinite resources and omniscience, it loses its power. Your anxiety level will decrease. Your passion will be rekindled. And you will find the strength to once again put your hands to the good work.

Prayer enables you to evaluate criticism from God's perspective. With the proper perspective you will be in a better position to respond appropriately to your critics. Having vented to the One who knows your heart, you will find it easier to address your critics with grace.

When somebody criticizes your vision, channel your emotion to your heavenly Father.

REMEMBER

Not only did Nehemiah pray, he remembered. He remembered who it was that brought him to Jerusalem to begin with. He remembered God's intervention with King Artaxerxes. He remembered what could and should be true of Israel politically and spiritually. Those memories gave Nehemiah the courage to press on in spite of the criticism and threats.

These weren't memories that just popped into Nehemiah's head. The text implies Nehemiah intentionally thought back over the events leading up to that present moment. He reflected on God's faithfulness. He rehearsed in his mind the pivotal points at which God had intervened on his behalf and on behalf of the nation. By looking back, he found the energy to move forward.

Then once again, Nehemiah exhibited his skills as a leader by calling the people of Jerusalem to remember. Notice what he directed them to remember.

> When I saw their fear, I rose and spoke to the nobles, the officials and the rest of the people: "Do not be afraid of them; *remember* the Lord who is great and awesome, and fight for your brothers, your sons, your daughters, your wives and your houses." (Nehemiah 4:14, emphasis mine)

Nehemiah dealt with the present by focusing the worker's attention on God's faithfulness in the past and a vision for the future. In essence he was saying, "Don't focus on the men who at this moment seem to wield power. Instead, think back to the greatness of the God who called you. Think ahead to what could be if we persevere."

Nehemiah's mention of brothers, sons, and daughters was a reference to Israel's future. He was reminding the people of what was truly at stake.

If you are like me, whenever you, or your vision, is criticized, the tendency is to begin second-guessing yourself.

- Maybe they're right.
- Maybe it is impossible.
- Maybe I don't have what it takes.
- Maybe I am just wasting my time.
- Maybe nobody will come along.

The obstacles of the present can easily overwhelm your commitment to what could and should be in the future. As long as you respond to criticism by evaluating *your* potential, you will be tempted to give up. But when you respond by remembering who it is who has called you, when you "remember the Lord who is great and awesome," it is a different story.

Notice that Nehemiah didn't defend himself or try to counter the criticisms leveled against him. The truth was, some of Sanballat's observations were valid.

It was true that the workers were not skilled builders. They were not the most committed bunch of folks, either. They actually walked off the job at one point. Furthermore, there were some sections of the wall that could not be rebuilt. Sanballat was not completely wrong in his assessment of the project or the workers.

But Nehemiah wasn't in this because he was convinced the people had the character, competency, and commitment to pull it off. He wasn't in it because he was convinced the wall could be rebuilt to its original specifications.

He was participating in this project because this was what God had put in his heart to do. Of course it was impossible. Most divinely originated visions are impossible. Nehemiah's critics had some valid points. But the critics weren't factoring in God. Nehemiah believed God was with him. So he called the people to remember.

Valid Criticism

Chances are, some of the criticisms of your vision are valid, too. If you are honest, you have no defense. After all, it is true:

- You don't have the necessary experience.
- You don't have the financial resources to see your vision through to completion.
- You don't have the necessary skills.
- You have no formal education in this particular field.
- People have tried this before with no success.

But so what? When God gives you a vision or points you in a direction, the issue is not your ability or the feasibility of the project. The issue is will you follow through with what you know to do? Will you do what you can do and trust God to do what only he can do? For Nehemiah, that meant going back to work. So he did.

What does following through and trusting God mean for you and your vision?

On my desk at work I have a card that reads, "Lord, you got me into this; I'm trusting you to see me through it." Every time we hit a snag at church, that little phrase runs through my mind. I find myself constantly saying, "Lord, this church was your idea, not mine. So I'm looking for you to do what only you can do."

As long as I keep that thought on the front burner, I don't feel the pressure of all the unanswered questions and unraised money. But the moment I assume responsibility for things I have no control over, I want to crawl in bed and pull the covers over my head.

As you face the inevitable criticism that comes with a God-given vision, take time to remember the Lord who is great and awesome. Think back to the time when he first birthed this vision in your heart. Reflect on the ways he intervened early on in the process. Reread those portions of Scripture he used to guide you originally. Remember the Lord who is great and awesome.

REVISE THE PLAN

In addition to praying and remembering, Nehemiah responded strategically.

> But we prayed to our God, and because of them we set up a guard against them day and night. (4:9)

I love that verse. There is a principle here every leader should take to heart. Nehemiah understood the delicate balance between walking by faith and leading strategically. His trust was in God. But at the same time he didn't abandon his responsibility to do what he could to further the vision. So he revised his plan.

> From that day on, half of my servants carried on the work while half of them held the spears, the shields, the bows and the breastplates; and the captains were behind the whole house of Judah. Those who were rebuilding the wall and those who carried burdens took their load with one hand doing the work and the other holding a weapon. As for the builders, each wore his sword girded at his side as he built, while the trumpeter stood near me. (vv. 16–18)

Posting a guard did not demonstrate a lack of faith. Bearing arms while they worked didn't make the people in Jerusalem any less dependent upon God. Nehemiah was not under the impression that these measures would assure success in the event of a sudden attack. He was all too aware of the odds. If Sanballat and his crew decided to invade Jerusalem, Nehemiah knew they wouldn't stand a chance of defending themselves without God's intervention. But it was a responsible step nonetheless. He did what he knew to do and trusted God for the rest.

Nehemiah's willingness to adjust his plan illustrates an important maxim for anyone who has a vision:

BUILDING BLOCK #10

DON'T CONFUSE YOUR PLANS WITH GOD'S VISION.

Don't rush by this one. When we lose sight of the distinction between our plans and the vision we are pursuing, we set ourselves up for a large dose of discouragement. I have seen people abandon their vision because their plan failed. Failed plans should not be interpreted as a failed vision.

Here's the distinction:

- A vision is what could and should be.
- A plan is a guess as to the best way to accomplish the vision.

Granted, your guess may be an educated, informed, prayerfully considered, experience-laden guess. But it is a guess just the same. And let's face it, you are capable of guessing wrong. And when you do, you will experience some measure of failure. But that is never a good reason to abandon the vision. It is simply a signal to abandon the plan.

Sam Walton, founder of Wal-Mart, was clearly a visionary. Throughout his career he stayed committed to his original vision of providing value to his customers in order to make their lives better. But he was notorious for changing plans and abandoning strategies. Jim Walton, Sam's son, addressed this unexplored side of his father's business savvy.

We all snickered at some writers who viewed Dad as a grand strategist who intuitively developed complex plans and implemented them with precision. Dad thrived on change, and no decision was ever sacred.[1]

It is easy to lose sight of the vision when your plans don't work out. Failed plans always have a backlash of negative emotion. If internalized and personalized, these emotions have the potential of convincing you that you—not just your plans—are a failure. After all, it was your plan.

To make matters worse, everyone who knew what you were trying to do probably knows the plan failed. In most cases those who are watching from the outside will find it impossible to distinguish between the plan and the vision. They see them as one and the same. The death of one is the death of the other.

Those who are partnering with you may have an equally difficult time recognizing the difference between plans and vision. For that reason, when a plan fails, the vision must be recast. Recasting the vision allows those around you to transfer their focus from the failed plan back to the original vision.

Nehemiah's challenge to "remember the Lord who is great and awesome" was his way of recasting the vision. Apparently the workers had walked off the job by this time. After all, the plan wasn't working. They were about to be overrun. Nehemiah knew he had to get their eyes off the immediate plan and back on to why they had decided to rebuild the wall in the first place.

Once he did that, he revised the plan, and the people went back to work. Check out the results:

> When our enemies heard that it was known to us, and that God had frustrated their plan, then all of us returned to the wall, each one to his work. (v. 15)

Apparently Sanballat and company were counting heavily on the advantage of a surprise attack. When they lost the element of surprise, they backed off. They weren't really up for battle, either. It was mostly saber rattling. An attempt to frighten and demoralize the workers.

By switching to plan B, Nehemiah called their bluff. More importantly, his revised plan gave the people in Jerusalem the incentive they needed to go back to work on the wall.

REFINING AND REVISING

I have never met anyone or heard of anyone who accomplished anything significant for the kingdom who didn't have to revise plans multiple times before the vision became a reality.

VISIONS ARE REFINED—THEY DON'T CHANGE;
PLANS ARE REVISED—THEY RARELY STAY THE SAME.

Be stubborn about the vision. Be flexible with your plan. Strategies and timelines are always up for grabs. And besides, in the process of revising your plans, God may choose to refine your vision.

Several years ago our church was in the process of raising money for an additional piece of property. I had come up with what I thought was a great plan for raising the money. I ran it by a couple of folks who thought it was a good plan as well. So I presented it to the congregation. Everybody seemed to be on board. But the deadline came and went, and we had only raised half the amount needed.

Several well-meaning people asked if I thought this was God saying we shouldn't move forward with the purchase. Their assumption being that since the plan didn't work and the money didn't come in, God's "hand" must not be on the project.

I could see their point. I certainly didn't want to lead the church in the wrong direction. For a couple of days I had second thoughts about the whole project. But thanks to the counsel of a couple of men, both older and wiser, I concluded we just hadn't planned well. The problem was the plan, not the vision.

Looking back, I am so glad we didn't abandon the vision. To have done so would have been a big mistake both financially and strategically. Remember, your initial plans are just that: *yours* and *initial* (meaning suitable for refining).

Don't be afraid to learn from your critics. All of us resist the notion of "giving in" to our critics. You will feel you are giving in when you revise your plan in response to something your critics say. It will feel as if you are allowing them to determine your agenda. But that is not the case at all.

The software package I am using to write this manuscript has gone through thousands of revisions through the years. Many of those revisions were in response to criticisms the company received regarding the product. This latest version is the culmination of three years of development, twenty-five thousand hours of customer research, and over one million feature requests on the company's wish line. They claim this is the most researched and customer-tested release to date.

Now why would a company who has been writing word processing software since the mid-seventies spend so much time gathering complaints and suggestions from people who use—and refuse to use—their product? Why would they let a group of outsiders influence their agenda to that extent? Are they just a bunch of wimps? Don't they know what they are doing? Of course they do. And that is precisely why they value the criticisms brought against them by users and non-users alike. It is why Microsoft is a household name.

Microsoft's vision to develop the world's leading word processing software is the very thing that drives them to find out what the critics are saying. It was their commitment to the vision that gave them the incentive to listen to and to even seek out the opinions of their critics. As a user or non-user of their software, you have the potential to influence their product. *But not their vision.* Complaints, bugs, or lost market share may compel them to revise their product (i.e. their plan), but not their vision.

Think about how foolish it would have been for Microsoft to ignore their critics. Instead, they incorporated what they learned from their critics into their plan. That's what vision is all about.

There are times when every visionary must swallow his pride and revise his plan. Don't let the source of a good idea keep you from letting it better reach your goal. Nehemiah was forced to play Sanballat's game to some extent. Arming the workers and posting guards delayed the completion of the wall. But in the end, it worked to Nehemiah's advantage.

Eventually, your vision will attract criticism. After all, you are introducing change. Your plan is full of gaps. You know what could and should be, but you aren't as clear on how it's going to happen. Visions do not come with instructions. Passion, yes. Instructions, no.

If you are not prepared, your vision could die at the hands of well-meaning (or mean-spirited) critics. Yours would not be the first. But it need not be that way. Channel your emotion to your heavenly Father.

Remember who it is who called you and why. If necessary, revise your plans. Then look for him to orchestrate that which he originated.

RESPOND TO CRITICISM WITH PRAYER, REMEMBRANCE, AND IF NECESSARY, A REVISION OF THE PLAN.

VISIONEERING
PROJECT #11

1. When your vision is criticized, what is your normal response? Where do you channel your emotion?

2. What are the primary criticisms brought against your vision?

3. Which of these criticisms do you consider valid?

4. Do you need to revise your plans in light of these criticisms? If so, how?

5. What helpful information can you glean from your critics?

6. How have those who are partnering with you been affected by the criticism?

7. Is it time to recast your vision to those who may have been affected?

....

CHAPTER TWELVE

ALIGNMENT

Some single mind must be master, else there will be no agreement in anything.
ABRAHAM LINCOLN

I f you are the Lone Ranger type, this chapter may not be of much use. However, you may want to dog-ear the corner of this page because chances are you will not be able to deliver your vision alone. And once you have identified your supporting cast, the information in this chapter may come in handy.

From time to time every driver notices his car pulling slightly to the left or right. Take your hands off the wheel for even a moment, and your vehicle begins to veer off to one side or the other. This is one of the first indications that your car's front end is out of alignment.

In the world of automobiles, "alignment" is a catchall word describing a combination of different relative positions of a wheel and tire. In order for a car to roll and steer easily, predictably, and efficiently, various parts must be "in alignment." When the front end of a car is out of alignment, it means parts engineered and assembled to work together are actually working against each other. If not corrected, misalignment can result in the need for major repairs and can even cause a breakdown.

But that raises a question. How do parts that were engineered to work together get to the point where they start working against each other? There are two things that can cause a front end to get out of alignment: normal use or a bad jolt.

What's true of your car is also true of the team you have assembled to deliver your vision. Time (normal usage) and a bad jolt will do more to destroy a team's alignment than anything else. And wouldn't you know it, Nehemiah was forced to deal with both.

NORMAL WEAR AND TEAR

The work on the wall was taking its toll on the workers. To begin with, they were running out of food. Natural conditions had produced a famine in that region (5:3). In addition, many of the workers had neglected preparing and planting their fields in order to attend to their assignments on the wall.

As it turned out, there was extra grain available, but only a handful of the workers had the money to pay for it. In some cases this was because they had taken time away from their businesses in order to work on the wall. Understandably, there was a growing sense of resentment toward the entire project.

For some, the only way to deal with the financial pressures was to mortgage their farms and in some cases their homes in order to buy food for their families. This met the need for the short term. But bottom line, the wall project was a threat to their livelihoods.

To make matters worse, they were still obligated to Persia for a hefty amount of taxes (5:4). They were forced to borrow the necessary funds to pay their taxes. Once their land was mortgaged, they had no choice but to mortgage themselves and their children. In ancient times family members were actually used as collateral. If a man could not repay a loan, his wife and children could be sold as slaves.

As the workers came to grips with the gravity of their situation, they lost interest in rebuilding the wall. Who could blame them? They were falling hopelessly behind financially. If things continued, they would be incapable of paying off their debts and regaining possession of their homes and land. Their minds were divided. Their loyalties were divided. At that moment the felt need was in the realm of family and finances not national security or patriotism.

But that wasn't the worst of it.

In the midst of all of this, Nehemiah discovered some nobles and city officials who were actually profiting from the crisis in Jerusalem. These were the fortunate ones with the extra grain to sell and money to lend. They were taking advantage of the people's misfortune by loaning money at exorbitant interest rates and selling grain at inflated prices. They were holding the mortgages for homes, land, and farms. Most disgusting of all, they were accepting their own countrymen and their families as collateral! In other words, they were allowing their neighbors to borrow themselves into slavery.

The nobles and officials had an agenda other than the completion of the wall. In fact, they were doing fine before Nehemiah showed up and started all this wall business. They weren't convinced Jerusalem's new independence was going to benefit them anyway. Chances were it would diminish their influence.

What they were doing was a direct violation of the Law. The law of Moses forbade charging interest of another Jew. And the Law forbade permanent slavery for unpaid debts. Besides, everything they were doing was simply unethical in light of the sacrifice the workers had made.

But these were men who had never moved beyond a what's-in-this-for-me mentality. And sooner or later, that attitude always exposes itself.

Whatever alignment was left in the wake of the famine was gone now. When the people realized what was happening, and the extent to which it was happening, they were ready to declare war on the upper class. The working class was no longer worried about the enemy lurking outside the city. Their biggest threat was their Jewish brothers. This was a big bump. A jolt.

And the vision? Well, nobody was very concerned about the vision. They were losing everything and everybody dear to them. What good was a wall if you had nothing to defend? Nehemiah had a colossal alignment problem on his hands. Everybody was pulling in a different direction.

ALIGNING YOUR TEAM

Regardless of how effectively you cast your vision initially, eventually a team member or two will work his way out of alignment. He will develop an agenda that is off-center to the vision. Instead of working with the rest of your team, he will be pulling ever so slightly in a different direction. This usually transpires well into the implementation stage of a vision.

Worse yet, someone may develop a competing agenda. Instead of a slight pull, he may be pulling directly against you. When a team loses its alignment, it is far less efficient. More energy is expended and less progress is made. There is extra wear and tear on team members. It makes for an unpleasant ride. And the longer you ignore the problem, the more costly it becomes

Like an automobile, if the situation goes unchecked, eventually there will be a breakdown. What begins as a slight irritation can develop into an expensive problem. Team members who are out of alignment can bring the progress of a family or organization to a screeching halt.

What causes teams to lose their alignment? Time (usage) and bumps.

TIME

Over time, people get distracted. They lose their passion. They get bored. They develop their own agendas. All of these things cause them to pull to the left or right of center.

It isn't necessarily anybody's fault when this happens. It is just a fact of team life. It is unrealistic to think the people you gather around you will feel as passionate about the vision as you do. And it is unrealistic to think they will stay as focused as you will. The daily cares of life demand people's attention. And with their attention go their time and passion.

In spite of that, you still need a measure of alignment among team members if you are going to deliver on your vision. You cannot accomplish what God has put in your heart with a team of people who have lost their focus.

BUMPS

The other thing that causes teams to lose alignment is an unexpected event. A crisis, for instance. Whereas time and usage will gradually pull a team out of alignment, a crisis can do so overnight.

On several occasions, I have watched parents allow a rebellious child to become the focus of their family life. Meanwhile, the compliant children get neglected. Before long, the "good kids" start pulling against Mom and Dad in order to regain the attention and affection they once enjoyed. Without a conscious decision on Mom and Dad's part, the vision shifts from raising morally and socially responsible children to "fix Sally." Almost overnight, things are out of alignment. Family members are working toward different ends.

Most business owners have experienced the organizational and economic blow to alignment caused by a slump in sales or the loss of a major account. The mood around the office can change instantly. Instead of working to further the vision of the company, employees begin working to secure their employment. They quit taking risks. They become obsessed with getting the credit due them. Power struggles ensue. Or they assume they see the handwriting on the wall and begin looking for a way out. Either way, the vision suffers. Team members are pulling against each other in conflicting directions. Things are out of alignment.

In this situation, it is tempting for a manager or business owner to become problem centered instead of vision centered. It is natural to respond to the declining culture by addressing and readdressing the problems. But like the parents in the preceding illustration, managers and owners have the potential to cause further misalignment in the company.

Granted, a crisis demands attention. But an alignment problem worsens when the crisis continues to be the point of focus to the neglect of the vision. Imagine a hospital that focused all of its personnel and financial resources on emergency room situations. Imagine the chaos in maternity, neurology, and oncology. Certainly hospitals must deal with emergencies. But their vision goes beyond what happens in the ER.

Chances are, you will hit some bumps along the way. They will demand some attention. But be careful not to allow the pursuit of your vision to be replaced with crisis management.

Another environment that clearly illustrates the importance of proper relational and organizational alignment is marriage. Every individual contemplating marriage has a mental picture of what could be and should be in a family. You have a vision. Your vision or picture becomes an agenda. Once you are married you begin working toward the goal of arranging reality to match the picture.

There is nothing wrong with that, per se. Where it becomes problematic is when two people have different pictures, different visions.

Once they say I do, each begins working toward a slightly different goal. If their pictures are not in alignment, their visions will be in conflict. What could be and perhaps should be, won't be—in either case. What begins as a slight irritant, if not dealt with, often results in a major breakdown.

Visions thrive in an environment of unity. They die in an environment of disunity. No matter what kind of organization you are in—business, school, church, family—when personal goals and agendas conflict with an agreed-upon corporate vision, the corporate vision suffers. Conflicting agendas within an organization will eventually pull people's attention away from the vision, the common goal, and onto smaller, more personal concerns. If these conflicts go unresolved, they can bring progress to a grinding halt. And they can make for a miserable working or living environment.

BUILDING BLOCK #13

VISIONS THRIVE IN AN ENVIRONMENT OF UNITY; THEY DIE IN AN ENVIRONMENT OF DIVISION.

You may know this all too well. Perhaps you have a boss who gives lip service to the corporate mission statement but who works behind the scenes to make sure nobody looks better than he does. You may be married to someone who has agreed in theory to establishing a certain environment in the home. But in practice he seems to be working toward something entirely different. Something that centers around his wants and wishes rather than what's best for the entire family.

You may be dating someone who is quick to affirm the values and standards you want for your life. But in the day-to-day reality, he or she pulls in another direction.

Or maybe you are in an environment like Nehemiah. One where a person or group is taking personal advantage of your genuine commitment to a vision, goal, or ideal.

When individuals function from the standpoint of self-promotion and self-protection, alignment evaporates. Whether it's a family, church, or business, when team members are out of alignment, inefficiency rules. You begin measuring gallons to the mile versus miles to the gallon.

LOCATING THE PROBLEM

When team or family members lose sight of (or simply abandon) the agreed-upon vision, several things will surface in their behavior.

1. They will attempt to control rather than serve.

Their controlling tendencies may be disguised by a desire to lead or even serve. But in time their need to control will surface. What services they do perform will have strings attached.

2. They will manipulate people and circumstances to further their own agendas.

They may even use the vision to leverage their plans.

3. They will exhibit an unwillingness to resolve their differences face-to-face.

They are often content to let gossip take the place of confrontation. They opt to talk about you rather than to you. They would rather sit on their hurt feelings than go to the person who hurt them or forgive and move on. They use their hurt to justify their self-centered agenda. After all, nobody really understands them.

4. They exhibit an unwillingness to believe the best about other teammates.

On a healthy team, team members believe the best about one another. Everybody is innocent until proven guilty. When team members begin working on secondary agendas, they become suspicious of everybody else. Why? Because they read their own impure motive into everybody else's actions.

5. They view team members' failures as their own personal successes.

They evaluate the success of other team members in relationship to their own successes and failures rather than the success of the team. Consequently, they have a difficult time sincerely rejoicing over the success of others.

One night Sandra and I were out having dinner when I noticed two couples from church sitting across the restaurant. Naturally, I went over to speak to them.

"I'm glad to see you," one fellow said. "We have a situation we need to talk to you about."

"What is it?" I asked.

"We need a bigger room for our Sunday school class. But Reggie tells us there isn't one available."

Reggie was our minister to married adults at the time. He was responsible for facilitating our married adult Sunday school program. That included space allocation. Nobody knew more about who was where and what was available than Reggie. In fact, he had just done a masterful job moving our married adults into a new education facility.

"Well," I said, "If Reggie says there isn't another room available, I guess there isn't another room." At this point I wasn't quite sure what the point of the conversation was. But I found out pretty quickly.

"So who do we need to talk to?"

I still didn't get it. "What do you mean?"

"Who is over Reggie?"

Finally I started catching on. "Nolen is over Reggie. But if Reggie says there aren't any rooms available, it won't do any good to talk to Nolen."

"Should I just call and make an appointment or is this something you could mention to him?"

I couldn't believe what I was hearing. These were two couples in leadership roles who had lost sight of the big picture in a big way. Their personal class agenda was pulling against our vision for the church. I stood there wondering how this room dilemma had been communicated to their class. Considering the size and popularity of the class, this had the potential of being a big bump.

I wasn't sure what to say. However, I was sure I should *not* say what initially came to mind. I closed the conversation and went back to my table. I was really disappointed. I called Reggie the next day and gave him a heads-up. I knew we hadn't heard the end of this. And sure enough we hadn't.

Things were eventually resolved. But not without some hurt feelings and some reorganization. The whole event was a big reminder of how quickly good people can lose sight of a vision. In this case I'm sure both of these couples would be quick to defend their commitment to our vision. But as often happens, something got lost in the application.

A TIME TO ACT

The front end of your car will never work itself back into alignment. Generally speaking, people don't either. In both cases, outside intervention is necessary. And the sooner the better. But dealing with alignment problems is much like stopping to sharpen a saw. On one hand, you know the work will go faster and easier if you stop to sharpen your blade. On the other hand, you hate to take time away from working. But in the long run, sharpening your saw is the thing to do.

Nehemiah knew he could not ignore the problems plaguing the workers. To do so would only contribute to the problem. But neither could he afford to lose sight of the vision. God had not called him to Jerusalem to fix the economy. He had been commissioned to rebuild the wall. However, he was wise enough to know the two were linked. The sooner he addressed the economic crisis, the sooner the workers would be able to devote their energy to rebuilding the wall.

There was something else driving Nehemiah. As I mentioned earlier, what the nobles and city officials were doing was illegal. The Law forbade a Jew from making another Jew a slave (Leviticus 25:39–42). An Israelite who could not pay his debts could be hired as a servant, but he or she could not to be sold as a slave. Selling a Jewish brother to Gentiles as a slave was clearly forbidden as well (Exodus 21:8). But the nobles and officials were auctioning their Jewish brothers and their families to the highest bidder.

Especially irritating was the fact that Nehemiah had just spent a good bit of time and money buying back Jews who had been sold as slaves to Gentiles. Now these nobles and officials were reselling them. This meant that Nehemiah was going to have to buy them back again. All this at a time when money was scarce to begin with.

Nehemiah knew that ignoring God's law made them an unblessable people. God was not going to honor their efforts so long as they showed such blatant disregard for his law. Yet they needed God's hand of protection and provision like never before. Too much was at stake to allow things to continue as they were. So Nehemiah took action. He called a public meeting.

> Then I was very angry when I had heard their outcry and these words. I consulted with myself and contended with the nobles

and the rulers and said to them, "You are exacting usury, each from his brother!" Therefore, I held a great assembly against them. (Nehemiah 5:6–7)

It is interesting that Nehemiah took the time to call a meeting in the midst of everything that was going on. This underscores his understanding of how important it was to deal with these kinds of issues head on. As unrelated as it must have seemed at the time, this was an investment in the vision. This wasn't about settling a civil dispute. The vision was at stake. Alignment was crucial to getting the wall rebuilt.

I said to them, "We according to our ability have redeemed our Jewish brothers who were sold to the nations; now would you even sell your brothers that they may be sold to us?" Then they were silent and could not find a word to say. Again I said, "The thing which you are doing is not good; should you not walk in the fear of our God because of the reproach of the nations, our enemies?" (vv. 8–9)

Did you see how he tied this issue back into the larger scheme of things? Remember, the reason for rebuilding the wall was to reestablish Jerusalem as a light to the unbelieving Gentile nations. This civil disturbance had the same connotations as the broken-down walls. Nehemiah was quick to address the current crisis in light of God's vision for Israel.

"And likewise I, my brothers and my servants are lending them money and grain. Please, let us leave off this usury. Please, give back to them this very day their fields, their vineyards, their olive groves and their houses, also the hundredth part of the money and of the grain, the new wine and the oil that you are exacting from them."

Then they said, "We will give it back and will require nothing from them; we will do exactly as you say." So I called the priests and took an oath from them that they would do according to this promise.

I also shook out the front of my garment and said, "Thus may

God shake out every man from his house and from his possessions who does not fulfill this promise; even thus may he be
shaken out and emptied." And all the assembly said, "Amen!"
And they praised the LORD. Then the people did according to
this promise. (vv. 10–13)

Granted, it is pretty much a storybook ending. It appears all the loose
ends were sewn up tight as a result of Nehemiah's strong words. But as we
will see, alignment is not something a leader addresses once. Remember,
normal wear and tear eventually pulls the most committed team out of
alignment. And Nehemiah's team was no different. But for the time being,
this particular crisis was resolved, and the people went back to work.

TAKE ACTION

It is okay to have problems. It is not okay to ignore them. Alignment
problems are a fact of life for organizations and families. How big they
become will be determined by your willingness to address them.

My tendency is to wait and see if things will work themselves out. In
most cases I just don't want to take the time to get involved. There are
always too many "important" things to do. But things rarely work themselves out. The longer I wait, the more complicated things become.

When it appears things have worked themselves out, it is usually a
case of a problem going underground. And the next time it surfaces, there
are more people involved and more issues to resolve.

If God has birthed a vision in your heart, there is too much at stake
to allow alignment issues to go uncorrected. Pick up the phone and make
that call. Write that letter. Make that appointment. Take action.

Explain how the particular issue you are addressing impacts the original vision. It is this relationship, between the crisis and the vision, that
gives a sense of urgency to your words. Otherwise, you could be accused
of blowing things out of proportion.

And along the way, model the behavior that is conducive to alignment
among team members.

- Lead, don't control.
- Be a man or woman of integrity.

- Resolve your differences face-to-face.
- Believe the best about other team members.

To do otherwise is to contribute to the discord in your family or organization—discord that could ultimately derail your vision. If those four things are true of you, you will have the moral authority to confront abuses in these areas when they surface in team members. In addition, you will be a better leader, husband, wife, employer, or whatever other role God has chosen for you at this time. And most importantly, you will be blessable.

VISIONEERING
PROJECT #12

1. Are there alignment issues among team members that need to be addressed?

2. What's keeping you from confronting the issues?

3. What is the worst thing that could happen as a result of a confrontation?

4. How does the misalignment among team members relate to the overall vision?

5. How might the vision be negatively impacted if the alignment issue is not addressed?

6. How has your leadership or behavior contributed to the alignment problems among team members?

7. What steps do you need to take to address your contribution to the problem?

....

CHAPTER THIRTEEN

MORAL
AUTHORITY

Example is not the main thing in influencing others, it is the only thing.
ALBERT SCHWEITZER

When I was twenty years old, I went to work as an intern for the youth minister at my dad's church. This was my first official ministry position. I knew absolutely nothing about youth ministry. However, I knew a great deal about being a youth. And that's probably why Sid hired me.

After a few weeks of following Sid around, trying to figure out exactly what an intern was supposed to do, he sat me down for a heart-to-heart.

"Andy," he said, "you are a leader. I need you to lead."

Lead? How could I lead? I didn't know anything about youth ministry. "But you are the youth minister," I said.

I'll never forget his response.

"Andy, there is a difference between having position and having influence. I have a position. But you have influence with the students. They will obey me because of my position. But they will follow you because of your influence. Now I need you to use your influence and lead. Don't be afraid. Lead."

Your influence is far more critical to the success of your vision than your position. Generally speaking, it is not men and women of position that give birth to and deliver great visions. A visionary often has nothing to leverage other than his influence. It is the influence of the visionary, regardless of how limited it may be, that serves as his platform and podium. Influence is often the only vehicle available for moving others to act. In many cases, influence is enough.

Influence is a funny thing. It's hard to define. It's hard to describe. But you know when somebody has it. And you know when somebody doesn't. No doubt you are aware of the people who influence you. But you may not be sure why they have so much leverage in your life.

Visionaries must be influencers if they are going to see their visions through from start to finish. You must be able to move people from where they are to where you believe they could and should be. Position is optional. Influence is essential.

Often the passion that accompanies a clear vision from God is all it takes to elevate a visionary's influence. That was certainly the case with Nehemiah. He was merely the cupbearer to the king. But once his burden for Jerusalem began to burn in his soul, he became an influencer. He influenced a king. And he went on to influence a disorganized, hapless group of strangers in Jerusalem.

There are other dynamics that elevate a man or woman's influence within a particular sphere. Some are apparent: wealth, rank, communication skills, education, accomplishment, performance. But there are people who have none of those things who still wield great influence. Again, influence is a tricky thing. You know it when you see it. But it is not always clear why certain people have it.

As adults, the people who influence our lives often have little authority in the traditional sense. They rarely carry a symbol of power. They don't have to. Something about their lives gives them authority that translates into influence. We find ourselves drawn to them. We want to be like them. They almost demand our respect. Not because of their position. It is something else.

But what? What is it about the people we allow to influence us that opens us up to their influence?

THE ESSENTIAL INGREDIENT

If God has birthed a vision in your heart, chances are you have begun to exploit the arenas in which you believe you have influenc in order to gain and maintain the influence required to deliver on vision, there is one quality that is a must. Without this, whatever influence you perceive you have will eventually evaporate.

Every great leader, every successful father and mother, anybody who has ever received and followed through successfully with a God-given vision has possessed a form of authority that rests not on position or accomplishment, but on an inner conviction and the willingness to bring his or her life into alignment with that conviction. It is the alignment between a person's convictions and his behavior that makes his life persuasive. Herein is the key to sustained influence.

The phrase that best captures this dynamic is moral authority. To gain and maintain your influence you must have moral authority. Moral authority is the critical, nonnegotiable, can't-be-without ingredient of sustained influence. Without moral authority, your influence will be limited and short-lived.

Moral authority is the credibility you earn by walking your talk. It is the relationship other people see between what you say and what you do, between what you claim to be and what you are. A person with moral authority is beyond reproach. That is, when you look for a discrepancy between what he says he believes and what he does, you come up empty. There is alignment between conviction and action, belief and behavior.

Nothing compensates for a lack of moral authority. No amount of communication skills, wealth, accomplishment, education, talent, or position can make up for a lack of moral authority. We all know plenty of people who have those qualities but who exercise no influence over us whatsoever. Why? Because there is a contradiction between what they claim to be and what we perceive them to be.

We will not allow ourselves to be influenced by those who lack moral authority in our eyes. Inconsistency between what is said and what is done inflicts a mortal wound on a leader's influence.

For this reason, moral authority is a fragile thing. It takes a lifetime to earn. But it can be lost in a moment. And once it is lost, it is almost impossible to restore.

If others are aware of a discrepancy between what you say you believe and what you do, or between what you do and what you want them to do, you will have little moral authority. If people recognize alignment between your beliefs, actions, and expectations, you will have moral authority. It is all about walking your talk.

As a visionary, the one thing you can control and must protect at all costs is your moral authority. Moral authority makes you a leader worth following. Moral authority positions you to influence people at the deepest level: heart, mind, and conscience. For this reason, your moral authority will enable you to maintain your influence with those who feel called to follow you.

Family is a realm in which the significance of moral authority is easily evaluated and understood. Think for a moment about your parents. Were they (or are they) leaders worth following? Do thoughts of Mom and Dad elicit feelings of respect?

If so, it is because you perceive consistency or alignment between what they say and what they do. Your respect for them is not determined by their financial, academic, or social accomplishments alone. In fact, you may hold them in high regard in spite of their financial, academic or social standing. They have moral authority.

If, on the other hand, you have little respect for Mom and/or Dad, your feelings probably stem from what you perceive to be an inconsistency between what they said and did, what they claimed to be and what they truly were. And all the financial, academic, and social accolades in the world cannot compensate for the inconsistency.

Think for a moment. Isn't it true that as their inconsistencies became more and more apparent, you found yourself less and less open to their influence? As they lost their moral authority, they lost their influence. On the other hand, parents who maintain their moral authority are able to maintain their influence throughout their children's lives. Such is the power and potential of moral authority.

This same dynamic is at work in every marriage. As a husband, my ability to influence Sandra hinges on my competency and my moral authority. And the same is true of her influence over me. By being competent in an area, she can trust I know what I am talking about. But my moral authority, the alignment between what I say and do, is what enables her to trust my motive. My moral authority determines whether or not she believes I have her best interests in mind.

All the ability, talent, and charisma in the world cannot take the place of moral authority. What you have seen happen in your own family, good or bad, has the potential to be repeated in your relationship with those who have chosen to partner with you in your vision.

NEHEMIAH'S BIG DECISION

The last time we looked in on Nehemiah he had just successfully navigated the inhabitants of Jerusalem through a complex civil and economic crisis. As you recall, things climaxed in a heated confrontation between Nehemiah and the city officials.

Nehemiah challenged the most powerful people in his community about using their wealth to take advantage of the workers. When Nehemiah was finished with them, they tucked their tails between their legs, apologized, returned what they had taken, and went away. As he tells it, "Then they were silent and could not find a word to say" (5:8b).

As I mentioned in the previous chapter, the outcome of Nehemiah's confrontation seems a little unrealistic. How is it that these powerful, wealthy nobles and city officials immediately backed down and agreed to mend their ways after one confrontation with Nehemiah? Surely there was more to it than that. Real life doesn't work that way.

Actually, there was more to it than that. In the verses following Nehemiah's clash with the nobles, we discover something about Nehemiah that positioned him to win the showdown with such ease. Nehemiah had moral authority. Moral authority that was twelve years in the making.

When Nehemiah arrived in Jerusalem he was one in a long line of governors assigned by the Persian government to oversee that territory. Previous governors had used the position to enrich themselves at the expense of the people. With their appointment came the right to levy taxes at their discretion. In addition, they had a right to a portion of everything that was harvested by the farmers in their region.

Nehemiah wisely chose to forgo those privileges. By doing so, he set himself apart from his predecessors. But more importantly, he demonstrated his heartfelt commitment to the project and to the people of Jerusalem. Nobody could accuse him of being in this for personal gain.

He was there to restore Jerusalem to a place of honor and influence among the nations. He was there to fulfill God's vision for his nation.

> Moreover, from the day that I was appointed to be their governor in the land of Judah, from the twentieth year to the thirty-second year of King Artaxerxes, for twelve years, neither I nor my kinsmen have eaten the governor's food allowance.
>
> But the former governors who were before me laid burdens on the people and took from them bread and wine besides forty shekels of silver; even their servants domineered the people. But I did not do so because of the fear of God. I also applied myself to the work on this wall; we did not buy any land, and all my servants were gathered there for the work.
>
> Moreover, there were at my table one hundred and fifty Jews and officials, besides those who came to us from the nations that were around us. Now that which was prepared for each day was one ox and six choice sheep, also birds were prepared for me; and once in ten days all sorts of wine were furnished in abundance. Yet for all this I did not demand the governor's food allowance, because the servitude was heavy on this people. Remember me, O my God, for good, according to all that I have done for this people. (5:14–19)

It is easy to see why Nehemiah's words carried such weight with the nobles and officials. No wonder they backed down. They must have been humiliated. Think about it. Nehemiah actually had the right to take advantage of the people in Jerusalem. His position entitled him to exploit those he led. Besides that, every governor before him had done so. Yet he went out of his way not to place a hardship on the people.

The nobles and city officials had no right to do what they were doing. They were actually breaking the Law. And by breaking the Law they had placed a hardship on, of all people, Nehemiah. For if you will remember, he had to take his own money and buy back the Jews the nobles and city officials had sold into slavery. Can you imagine how embarrassing it would be to face Nehemiah having done what they had done? His lifestyle shamed them.

Take note. It was not Nehemiah's position that gave him the leverage with the nobles and city officials. It was his moral authority. He had walked his talk since the day he arrived and announced his intention to rebuild the wall. There was alignment between his beliefs and behavior. He lived a life in keeping with his vision.

THE SOURCE

Moral authority is not a method. It is not a way to get things done. It is not a means to a prearranged end. Genuine moral authority is not something a leader sets out to develop in order to become a better leader or to gain influence with people. Leaders and influencers who are driven purely by a desire to be leaders and influencers rarely maintain their moral authority. Why? Because great leadership is rooted in something other than a desire to be a great leader. Influence is rooted in something other than a desire to be an influencer.

Nehemiah's decision to forfeit his right to the governor's allotment of food was not driven by a conscious desire on his part to bolster his moral authority among the people. And he certainly could not have anticipated his confrontation with the nobles and city officials. His decision stemmed from his reverence for God and his commitment to the vision: "But out of reverence for God I did not act like that. Instead, I devoted myself to the work on this wall" (vv. 15b–16a, NIV).

Nehemiah did not consciously choose to forgo his rights as governor to gain influence with the people in Jerusalem. He did what he did in order to maintain a blameless walk before God. After all, God had not sent him to Jerusalem to become a wealthy landowner. God had not worked on his behalf so he could become a governor. His appointment as governor was simply a means to an end. He was there to rebuild the wall and to remove the reproach from the city.

Nehemiah was on a mission from God. In light of that, it would have been counterproductive for him to have levied additional taxes on the people. They were burdened and distracted enough as it was. Claiming what was "rightfully" his would have interfered with the reconstruction.

For Nehemiah, gaining and maintaining moral authority was not a leadership ploy. It was a natural expression of his devotion to God. It was the logical choice in light of what he felt called to do.

Moral authority is a reflection of a man or woman's commitment to something outside the realm of influence and leadership. Moral authority is the result of a commitment to do what's right. Regardless. Men and women who maintain their moral authority are not playing to the crowd. They are not driven by a desire to gain influence. Their number one concern is doing the right thing—even if doing the right thing appears to jeopardize their influence.

But it goes further than that. Here is where so many people with "God" ideas veer off course. As a leader, you must be willing to do the right thing even if it jeopardizes your vision.

You probably need to let that sink in for a minute.

The day will come when you will be faced with a set of circumstances that on the surface will seem to dictate that you compromise ethically or even morally for the sake of seeing your vision through to completion.

Chances are, when it happens, you will be so far down the road with your vision that the temptation to compromise will be almost unbearable. Those who have journeyed with you will urge you to press on at any cost.

The Scriptures are full of examples. Abraham finally had a son and God said, "Sacrifice him." Abraham's dilemma was not unlike the one you will eventually face. Do I obey God, or do I do what appears to best serve the completion of the vision?

How about David standing in the shadows of the cave in Engeddi watching Saul relieve himself? God had promised him the throne. To the casual observer it seemed the only way to attain the throne would be to kill the king. His closest friends urged him to do so. It looked like it would only be a matter of time before Saul and his troops tracked David down and killed him. But it was against the law of God to kill the king.

So David stood there peering through the darkness pondering the question every visionary will face along the way: Is my ultimate allegiance to God or to the vision?

The point is, you must maintain your moral authority at all costs. Even if it costs you your vision. You must be willing to abandon your vision if that is what's necessary to maintain your moral authority. Vision is important. But maintaining one's moral authority must take priority over the pursuit of a vision.

Just as God intervened on behalf of Abraham and David, if your vision is truly a "God thing," he will intervene for you.

SHORTCUTS

In addition to the temptation to breach your integrity, you will be tempted to take shortcuts. On the surface, these shortcuts appear to be a way of speeding up the vision. They are a way of getting things done or moving things along. After all, God doesn't want us to sit around and wait for things to fall into place, does he?

Moral and ethical compromises of any kind lead to the loss of moral authority.

Nehemiah faced an ethical dilemma. He was aware of the injustices being inflicted upon the people by the nobles and city officials. But he was also aware that this same group had the potential to have him run out of town. Their wealth gave them leverage with the people. They had the power to bring the reconstruction project to a halt.

But right is right and wrong is wrong. And Nehemiah could not in good conscience ignore what these officials were doing to the people. The vision was important. But he could not turn his back on injustice for the sake of getting the wall rebuilt. He took a risk by confronting the leaders the way he did. But to ignore what they were doing, to pretend everything was fine, would have been a compromise of integrity. So he put the vision on hold in order to address an issue of right and wrong.

BUILDING BLOCK #14

ABANDON THE VISION BEFORE YOU ABANDON YOUR MORAL AUTHORITY.

When you face your moral or ethical fork in the road, here is the question to ponder: Would God lead me to embrace a vision that would force me to do something he forbids?

Of course not.

Maintain your moral authority at all costs. As a visionary, it is your primary point of leverage. Without it, you are no longer a leader worth following.

Your ability to gain and maintain moral authority with the people who are partnering with you will have far more to do with the condition of your heart than your commitment to lead. Moral authority is rooted in a desire to please God rather than man. Moral authority is the overflow of character, not leadership ability.

Obey God at all costs. Hold your vision in an open hand. And watch for him to intervene.

MOTHER TERESA

In our generation, no one has demonstrated the power of moral authority more than Mother Teresa. She embodied her vision. She never required anyone to do anything she had not already done herself. Skeptics threw rocks at her theology but never her character. And for that reason, the stone throwers always came off looking rather foolish.

Her vision was to establish an order of nuns whose sole purpose was to care for those who live in conditions unworthy of human dignity. In 1948 she cast her vision to the Vatican and two years later the Missionaries of Charity was officially sanctioned by the Church. Their charge was to seek out and care for the poor, abandoned, sick, and dying.

Consistent with her vision, Mother Teresa chose the streets of Calcutta as her parish. It was there that she unintentionally carved for herself a reputation that would win the respect of the world.

In 1952 she and her Missionaries of Charity received permission from officials in Calcutta to use a section of an abandoned temple for their first enterprise: a home for the dying. Mother Teresa referred to it as Nirmal Hriday. Here, the poor of Calcutta, who often died alone in the streets, could find comfort and cleanliness in their final hours.

It didn't take long for word to spread that a group of Catholic missionaries had taken up residence in the neighborhood. Hindu priests were uncomfortable with a missionary organization so close to their temple. They petitioned city authorities to relocate the hospice.

On one occasion, priests from the KaliGhat Temple led a large delegation to the Nirmal Hriday and demanded that the missionaries leave immediately. It is reported that Mother Teresa came out and personally addressed the crowd with these words, "If you want to kill me, here I am! You can merrily behead me. But do not disturb my poor patients."[1]

Eventually, an opportunity arose for the Missionaries of Charity to demonstrate the sincerity of their call and the purity of their motives to those who eyed them suspiciously. It was an opportunity most would have missed.

It came to Mother Teresa's attention that one of the Hindu priests was in the advanced stages of tuberculosis. Because his illness was untreatable, he had been denied a bed in the city hospital.[2]

In an unprecedented gesture of kindness and grace, Mother Teresa brought the dying priest to Nirmal Hriday. There, she personally cared for him until the day he died. The Missionaries of Charity then carried the priest's body back to the temple for Hindu rights.

This event captured the hearts of the people of Calcutta. Mother Teresa's willingness to live out her message broke down the theological and cultural walls that separated her from the people she had come to serve.

Throughout her life, Mother Teresa's primary credential was her moral authority. But that was enough to procure for her both audience and influence with the most powerful people in the world. But even when she found herself thrust into the unfamiliar and oftentimes hostile halls of power, Mother Teresa maintained the courage of her convictions. Her words were always consistent with the life she lived and the theology she held so dear.

Peggy Noonan, former special assistant to President Reagan, was an eyewitness of what was probably the most significant public demonstration of Mother Teresa's commitment to consistency of belief, word, and deed.

On February 3, 1994, Mother Teresa came to Washington and gave a speech that left the entire audience dazzled and part of it dismayed, including a United States senator who turned to his wife after Mother Teresa concluded and said, "Is my jaw up yet?"

It was the annual National Prayer Breakfast at the Hilton Hotel and three thousand people were there, including most of official Washington....By tradition the president of the United States and the first lady always attend, and on this day in 1994 Bill and Hillary Clinton were up there on the dais, as were the vice president and Mrs. Gore and a dozen other important people, senators, and Supreme Court justices...As she stepped up onto a little platform that had been placed beneath the podium there was great applause. She nodded at it. Then she took her speech in her hand and began to read from it in a soft singsong voice....

The audience was composed of liberal Democrats, conservative Republicans, and moderates of all persuasion. Perhaps half were Christian members of the prayer breakfast movement, some quite seriously devout and some less so—there's a bit of this-world networking that goes on. The other half was a mix: Muslims, Jews, searchers, agnostics and atheists, reporters and bureaucrats, waiters and diplomats. A good-natured and attentive mix. And they all loved her. But as the speech continued it became more pointed.

"I can never forget the experience I had in the sitting room where they kept all these old parents of sons and daughters who had just put them into an institution and forgotten them, maybe. I saw that in that home, these old people had everything—good food, comfortable place, television, everything—but everyone was looking toward the door. And I did not see a single one with a smile on their face. I turned to a sister and I asked, 'Why do these people who have every comfort here, they are looking toward the door? Why are they not smiling? I'm so used to seeing the smiles on our people. Even the dying ones smile.'

"And Sister said, 'This is the way it is nearly every day. They are expecting, they are hoping that the son or the daughter will come to visit them. They are hurt because they are forgotten.'

She continued, "But I feel that the greatest destroyer of peace today is abortion, because Jesus said, 'If you receive a little child, you receive me.' So every abortion is the denial of receiving Jesus, the neglect of receiving Jesus."

Well, silence. Cool deep silence in the cool round cavern for just about 1.3 seconds. And then applause started on the right hand side of the room, and spread, and deepened, and now the room was swept with people applauding, and they would not stop for what I believe was five or six minutes.

But not everyone applauded. The president and first lady,

seated within a few feet of Mother Teresa on the dais, were not applauding. Nor were the vice president and Mrs. Gore. They looked like seated statues at Madame Tussaud's. They glistened in the lights and moved not a muscle, looking at the speaker in a determinedly semi-pleasant way....

Now, Mother Teresa is not perhaps schooled in the ways of world capitals and perhaps did not know that having said her piece and won the moment she was supposed to go back to the airier, less dramatic assertions on which we all agree. Instead she said this:

"(Abortion) is really a war against the child, and I hate the killing of the innocent child, murder by the mother herself. And if we accept that the mother can kill even her own child, how can we tell other people not to kill one another?...Any country that accepts abortion is not teaching its people to love one another but to use any violence to get what they want. This is why the greatest destroyer of love and peace is abortion."

Mother Teresa now spoke of fighting abortion with adoption, of telling hospitals and police stations and frightened young girls, "Please don't kill the child. I want the child. Give me the child. I'm willing to accept any child who would be aborted and to give that child to a married couple who will love the child and be loved by the child."

Perhaps she didn't know, or care, that her words were, as they say, not "healing" but "divisive," dividing not only Protestant from Catholic but Catholic from Catholic. It was all so unhappily unadorned, explicit, impolitic. And it was wonderful, like a big fresh drink of water, bracing in its directness and its uncompromising tone....

And Mother Teresa seemed neither to notice nor to care. She finished her speech to a standing ovation and left as she had entered, silently, through a parted curtain, in a flash of blue and white....She could do this, of course, because she had a natural and unknown authority.[3]

I love that story. I love the mental image it evokes. Imagine it. A tiny, slightly stooped woman standing on a box so as to allow her to be seen over the lectern addressing some of the most powerful men and women in the world. And packed into that aging frame was enough moral authority to lay low anyone who dared raise a finger in opposition. Such is the power of moral authority.

As Christians, it is imperative that we develop and maintain our moral authority. We have been called to be influencers. And the world is watching. Christ didn't commission us to become authorities so we could tell people how they ought to live. He called us to be influencers by the way we live, so people would want what we have.

THE RECIPE

Developing and maintaining moral authority requires three things: character, sacrifice, and time.

CHARACTER

Character is simply the will to do what is right, as God defines right. Nehemiah did not require the food allotment that was legally his because it was not the right thing to do under the circumstances. He confronted the city officials and nobles because it was his responsibility as the governor to protect the people. Nehemiah was first and foremost committed to doing the right thing. His commitment to rebuild the wall was secondary to his commitment to do the right thing.

The issue here is surrender. To be a man or woman of character requires you to surrender to God's standards, values, and principles. Character requires you to continue in a state of surrender when God's law makes sense and when it doesn't. It assumes you will abide by his Word when it benefits you and when it sets you back. Men and women of character do the right thing even when doing right delays or dismantles their visions.

On my first date with Sandra we ran out of things to talk about after thirty minutes. She is quiet by nature, and I was nervous. After a few agonizing moments of silence I blurted out, "So, have you done any modeling?"

I have no idea where that question came from. I could just picture Sandra getting back to her dorm that night, waking up her roommate and saying, "You've got to hear this one." I couldn't even make eye contact. For all I knew, the girls in her dorm probably kept a list of tacky pickup lines. She was going to win some sort of prize at my expense. People would be walking up to me for months whispering, "So, have you ever done any modeling?"

To my surprise she said, "Yes, a little."

The tone of her voice told me there was a story. And her body language let me know this was a sensitive subject. But since we didn't have anything else to talk about, I pressed on.

"Really, tell me about it."

Soon after Sandra moved to Atlanta to attend Georgia Tech she was given an opportunity to do some modeling for the Atlanta Apparel Mart. That led to another opportunity and then another. Before long modeling became a part-time job. Besides being a good source of income, it was a lot of fun. And of course, it was very flattering.

A company in Atlanta was putting on a big costume party. Sandra and two other girls were invited to model costumes for the ladies who had been invited to attend the party. Each girl had several outfits to show to the mostly female audience.

Her first costume was something along the lines of an evening gown. But when she returned to her dressing room to change into the second outfit, she was shocked. Her second costume was…Well, it wasn't anything she wanted to be seen in. She took a look at the next one and it wasn't any better.

The way she tells it, she changed back into her own clothes, found the fellow in charge and informed him she could not go out on the runway dressed "like that." He was incensed. They were right in the middle of the show! And besides, it was "just a bunch of women."

Sandra didn't budge. She simply gathered her things and left.

Needless to say, I was impressed. Here was a woman who walked her talk in the most difficult of environments, even when it meant walking away from an opportunity that was profitable.

That is the essence of character. She did what was right regardless of the cost. What she didn't know was that her decision that afternoon would give her moral authority with hundreds of teenage girls in the years that followed. And someday it will give her moral authority with our daughter, Allie.

SACRIFICE

As we discussed earlier, a vision, by its very nature, requires resources that are not readily available. The man or woman who champions a vision must step up to the plate and demonstrate a willingness to sacrifice in order to deliver. Sacrifice is the clearest demonstration of your commitment to what could be.

Generally speaking, people will not invest more in a vision than the one who originally cast the vision. In order to get others to give sacrificially, you must lead the way.

When you make a genuine sacrifice for the sake of your vision two things happen:

1. The people around you catch a glimpse of what's in your heart.
2. You catch a glimpse of what's in there as well.

When you sacrifice for the sake of your vision, it is like letting go of the side of the rink and skating out into the center of the ice. You know you are committed. And those around you are assured of your commitment as well.

Untested devotion does little to move the hearts of others. But once you demonstrate your commitment by personal sacrifice for the sake of the cause, your potential for influence escalates considerably. Sacrifice penetrates the superficial, self-protecting resistance posed by those who are looking for excuses not to pitch in and support you. Sacrifice will often silence your critics.

Lane Jones, one of our pastors, told me about an incident that took place in a college speech class which illustrates the power of linking sacrifice with conviction.

Our assignment was to prepare a speech to persuade. The topics ran the gamut from selling products to defending Christianity. One of the girls in the class was a little older than the rest of us, probably 23 or 24. I knew her to be a Christian from other comments she had made in the class, and so it was no surprise when she chose to speak on the merits of the pro-life position.

I remember the tension. Much of her argument was from a

religious perspective. And as you would imagine, the class was very diverse in moral and religious persuasion. She went through the normal arguments against abortion. Then, having made all of her theoretical points (some that had already been made in other speeches—abortion was big that quarter), she finished by challenging the "accepted" exceptions of rape, incest, and endangerment of the mother's life. She said she didn't even agree with abortion in these extreme cases.

At that point, even the other pro-life advocates in the class were getting uncomfortable. And I imagine the pro-choice people were thinking they had an easy target.

But after she finished making her points she concluded by sharing how her own world had been shattered a couple of years earlier when she had been raped. The rape resulted in a pregnancy. She then produced a 5x7 picture of a small child of obvious mixed racial makeup and introduced him by name.

She said her son was the joy of her life and she couldn't imagine life without him. Then she reiterated her position that she believed that abortion under any circumstances was unacceptable.

As she finished I remember the silence that followed. Most of the other "controversial" speeches had been followed by more debate and partisan attacks. But not this time. There was nothing to debate. There was nothing theoretical about her position.

My professor made his way back up to the front of the class. Paused. And then made this comment. "The most powerful argument a speaker can make is one from personal experience." I was reminded once again of the truth that an audience can disagree with a position, but they can't disagree with the reality of a conviction lived out.[3]

When you make a personal sacrifice for something you believe in, it gives you moral authority.

The pro-choice people in Lane's class may not have been convinced by the girl's story. But in the face of that kind of moral authority they knew better than to raise mere intellectual objections. They may have questioned her views, but not her integrity or authenticity.

There is something compelling in the words of men and women who have sacrificed for what they believe in. And the critic who responds with mere intellectual arguments generally comes off looking shallow and desperate.

TIME

Moral authority is not achieved overnight. It is not something you can manufacture at will. Moral authority is developed through a proper response to circumstances, circumstances over which you have no control.

You can involve yourself in exercises and disciplines that will strengthen your character. But moral authority can only be achieved when your character is put to the test. Your response to these unexpected tests will determine your moral authority.

Nehemiah was a man of character before he chose not to take advantage of his position as governor of Judah. But his decision to forgo his allotment of food gave him moral authority. Sandra was a woman of character before she refused to model the costumes that afternoon. But it was her decision to walk out that gave her moral authority with the teenagers she discipled later on.

Experience is a necessary component of moral authority. Therefore moral authority requires time. In Mother Teresa's case, it took a lifetime to develop the moral authority to make her address at the National Prayer Breakfast. Her moral authority didn't hang on one significant incident from her life. It was supported by years of selfless service to the poor of Calcutta.

There will be dozens of opportunities to demonstrate your commitment to walk your talk. Each time you publicly demonstrate alignment between the two, you become more credible, more believable. Your message becomes more compelling.

While you have control over your response to these opportunities, you cannot mark their arrival on a calendar. So you must be careful how you live. Every day represents another potential opportunity to develop or destroy your moral authority.

HANDLE WITH CARE

When I was a teenager, there was a fellow in his thirties who agreed to disciple me and several of my friends. I'll refer to him as Jim. Jim was an excellent Bible teacher. Hundreds of young people would gather every week to hear him teach. So we were honored that he was willing to spend time with a small group of us.

In addition to meeting with us at his home for discipleship and prayer, Jim took us camping and rafting. On our last camping trip together something happened that disappointed me so deeply I dropped out of his group and could not even bring myself to attend his Bible study from that point on. I didn't know what to call it at the time, but Jim made a decision that caused him to lose his moral authority with me.

We were camping in the north Georgia mountains. There were five of us. Jim, me, and three of my buddies. Jim owned some property that was part of a new golf and residential resort. There were no houses at that time, just raw, wooded land. The only real sign of civilization was a club-house, a swimming pond, and a man-made creek that was designed to function as a water slide. This water slide was made out of smooth stone. And the water actually ran out of the pond like a creek.

As you might imagine, the water slide was where we spent most of the afternoon. But we were not alone. Dozens of other families were there as well. Consequently, the line got longer and longer as the day wore on. Jim was not the most patient fellow in the world. Everybody knew that. And I suppose it was his impatience, combined with his love for adventure, that prompted the incident that followed.

Unlike modern water slides, there was really no way to close this one. After all, it was a creek. So, at six o'clock, they put a big sign on a chain that said, CLOSED. For most people that was all that was needed.

At about five, Jim gathered us up and said. "Look guys, they close the water slide at six o'clock. Let's go eat, and then we will come back after it's closed and play until dark."

I was shocked. Not at the idea of sneaking back to the water slide after it was closed. In fact, I'm sure I would have suggested doing that whether Jim was in on it or not. I was certainly not above bending a few rules for the sake of a good time.

What shocked me was the fact that Jim, our leader, would suggest such a thing. I couldn't believe it. I was so crushed that after dinner I didn't go with them. I chose to swim alone in the pond.

Looking back as a forty-year-old man, I believe I judged Jim too harshly. But as a sixteen-year-old, I expected more from my spiritual leaders. From that point on, it was hard for me to listen to Jim speak. His talk didn't match his walk. At the time I didn't completely understand the dynamics of what had happened, but in effect, Jim had lost his moral authority with me. And he never knew it. His character had been tested, and he had made the wrong decision.

Moral authority is a fragile thing. It can be lost in a single decision.

LOST AND FOUND

Whenever I speak on the subject of moral authority, I am asked whether it can be reestablished once it has been lost. I believe in many cases it can. But the price is high. Gaining forgiveness from people is one thing. Regaining your moral authority is something else altogether. Many stop with forgiveness and do not go the distance necessary to regain their moral authority. Let me explain.

Remember Zacchaeus? The wee little man? What if after his encounter with Jesus he had gathered the people he had wronged together and made the following remarks: "I have good news! I have met Jesus and received forgiveness of all my sins. I realize I have abused my rights as a tax collector, and consequently, many of you have been penalized financially. I want you to know how sorry I am. Please forgive me. I promise to be more careful from this point on."

How would you have reacted to a speech like that from a man who had enriched himself by overtaxing you? Would you forgive him? Maybe. Would you invite him over for dinner? Probably not. Would you take your family to hear him give his testimony at the synagogue the following Sabbath? I don't think so.

Even after a sincere apology, Zacchaeus would have had no moral authority. There were no actions to back up his words. Worse than that, for years his actions portrayed a heart of greed and deceit.

But imagine what the people in his community thought when he announced he was going to give half of his possessions to the poor (Luke 19:8)! Half. Not a tenth. Half. The religious leaders didn't even do that. Nobody did that.

But that was just the beginning. In addition, he would pay back everyone he had overtaxed. But he wouldn't stop there. He would pay each person he had cheated four times the amount he had taken illegally.

Zacchaeus went way beyond what was fair and equitable. He went way beyond matters pertaining to forgiveness. He made restitution. And nobody expected restitution of that magnitude. He went beyond what most people would consider reasonable. But when all was said and done, I imagine Zacchaeus had moral authority. People took his faith seriously. When he spoke about meeting Jesus, people listened.

Granted, Zacchaeus didn't lose his moral authority. He never had any to begin with. But I think you see the point. For anybody to take him seriously, he had to do more than merely ask for forgiveness. That was not enough.

If you have lost your moral authority, regaining it is going to cost you. Words alone won't get the job done. Rebuilding your moral authority will require the same three ingredients outlined in the previous section. But for you it will require more time and more sacrifice.

You must take full responsibility for your actions and the consequences of your actions. It is the second part of that equation that trips people up. Being sorry in your heart may gain you favor with God but not with man. To regain your moral authority you must take responsibility for the practical ramifications of your actions. That may mean restitution. It will most certainly mean some sort of sacrifice.

People with moral authority don't go unnoticed. Mom, Dad, maintain it with your kids at all costs. Leaders, live in such a way that your life punctuates your words and beliefs. There will always be people who won't believe what you believe. But don't give them grounds to doubt that you believe what you claim to believe. Our lives will always speak louder than our words. Like Nehemiah, let's make sure they are saying the same thing.

All great leaders, all successful fathers and mothers, all visionaries who ever received and followed through successfully with a God-given vision had credibility and influence because they walked their talk. Their lives were persuasive. They had moral authority.

VISIONEERING
PROJECT #13

1. Are there inconsistencies between what you say and what you do as it relates to your vision?

2. In light of your strengths and weaknesses, where is the greatest potential for inconsistency?

I am constantly encouraging the people of our church to invest in the lives of unbelievers with the goal of inviting them to an event where they will hear a clear gospel presentation. We refer to this as our "Invest and Invite Evangelism Strategy."

A potential inconsistency for me is to become so absorbed with "church people" that I don't invest in the lives of the unchurched. If that were to happen, I would lose my moral authority to champion that part of our vision.

3. Is there an arena in which you have lost or damaged your moral authority?

Think through the various roles and relationships in your life:

• What about your moral authority with your spouse?
• What about your moral authority with your children?

- What about your moral authority with the people you work with?
- What about your moral authority with those who have come alongside you to support your vision?

4. What steps do you need to take to rebuild your moral authority?

....

CHAPTER FOURTEEN

DISTRACTIONS

I am doing a great work and I cannot come down.
NEHEMIAH

Each year I perform about seven weddings. Before I agree to marry a couple, I ask them to commit to meet with me at least four times for pre-marital counseling. In most cases they are eager to do so. Through the years I have learned it is wise to begin the counseling as soon as possible. Why? Because as the wedding date gets closer, a couple thinks less about marriage and more about the wedding. This is especially true of brides. And understandably so. Planning a wedding is no casual endeavor. The responsibility for planning the wedding day generally falls on the shoulders of the bride. Consequently, she feels most of the pressure leading up to the big day.

As understandable as that dynamic may be, it is an unfortunate one. The wedding often distracts a couple's attention away from the main thing: marriage. To a couple anticipating life together, marriage is a vision. They both move toward the wedding day with a mental image of what could be and should be. They each have expectations. Often they envision a relationship quite different from what their parents experienced. In many instances, they know more of what they don't want than what they do. Marriage is, in every sense of the word, a vision.

Unfortunately, most couples spend far more time preparing for the wedding than they do the marriage. Yet if you were to ask the average engaged couple which is more important, the wedding or the marriage, they would all agree that marriage is what really matters.

I have never seen an ugly wedding. I have seen plenty of ugly marriages.

On more than one occasion I have suggested to couples that they postpone their wedding. In all but one instance, the objections cited by the couple were wedding related.

"But the invitations have already been printed!"

"But we have relatives and friends who have adjusted their vacation schedules to be here on that date."

"It's too late for that. Everything is planned."

No one has ever argued with me based on my evaluation of the relationship. They always assure me they can work their problems out after they are married. Wedding plans are always the issue. Couples feel it is too late to call it off. An event—the wedding—becomes the driving force in the decision-making process rather than the original vision—a life of happiness together.

I love what my dad told my sister just before walking her down the aisle. Keep in mind, he was actually going to perform the ceremony as well. He said, "Becky, if you are standing at the altar and change your mind about this whole thing, just wink. I'll pass out on the floor and bring the entire ceremony to a halt!"

Life is full of distractions. Visions are often lost among the many lights on the horizon of life. Important things are sacrificed for urgent things. What could be is often lost in the flurry of what is. What should be gets buried under what must be. After all, weddings are urgent. Marriages are…Well, they are marriages.

Regardless of the nature of your vision or visions, if you are not careful, you will get distracted. The daily grind of life is hard on visions. Life is now. Bills are now. Crisis is now. Vision is later. It is easy to lose sight of the main thing, to sacrifice the best for the sake of the good. All of us run the risk of allowing secondary issues to rob us of the joy of seeing our visions through to completion. Distractions can slowly kill a vision.

In this chapter we are going to talk about three specific types of distractions: opportunities, criticism, and fear. These were the three types of distraction Nehemiah faced as he worked to complete the wall around Jerusalem. These are three primary distractions all men or women with visions face as they endeavor to make what could and should be a reality.

A SINISTER INVITATION

Last time we checked in with Nehemiah he was dealing with yet another round of civil unrest. Once he got that all worked out, everybody went back to work on the wall. A few days later they finished the majority of the reconstruction. All that remained was replacing the doors in the gate (6:1).

Just as things were looking up, Nehemiah's enemies on the outside began stirring up trouble again. Sanballat and his friends realized Nehemiah was only days away from completing the project. They were amazed and angry. Their military threats had been to no avail. And apparently they were unable to muster the courage to actually attack the workers. So they came up with yet another plan.

Instead of trying to distract or intimidate the workers, they decided to focus their attention on Nehemiah. If they could distract the leader, they knew it would impede the progress of the entire project.

> Now when it was reported to Sanballat, Tobiah, to Geshem the Arab and to the rest of our enemies that I had rebuilt the wall, and that no breach remained in it, although at that time I had not set up the doors in the gates, then Sanballat and Geshem sent a message to me, saying, "Come, let us meet together at Chephirim in the plain of Ono." (Nehemiah 6:1–2a)

Sanballat and company invited Nehemiah to a meeting. Their plan was to pull him off the project, get him away from his supporters, and then kill him. Nehemiah didn't know the full extent of their plan initially. All he knew was they wanted to have a meeting. For all he knew, they wanted to work out a peace agreement of some kind. It was apparent to everyone in the area that this project was going to be completed. It would make sense that the provinces surrounding Jerusalem would begin normalizing relations with Jerusalem now that they were gaining status in the area. But look at Nehemiah's response.

But they were planning to harm me. So I sent messengers to them, saying, "I am doing a great work and I cannot come down. Why should the work stop while I leave it and come down to you?" They sent messages to me four times in this manner, and I answered them in the same way. (vv. 2b–4)

I love his reply: "I am doing a great work and I cannot come down."

Now, Mr. or Ms. Reader, I want you to do something a little out of the ordinary. I want you to read that statement again, out loud. Ready? Go.

I am doing a great work and I cannot come down.

Now read it out loud again. But this time, emphasize the word "great."

I am doing a great *work and I cannot come down.*

Nehemiah knew what he was about was a God thing. It was an important thing. He was doing a *great* work. He didn't have time for a meeting. He would not allow himself to be distracted from his *great* work. He would stay focused. He was not going to let up. He would be relentless about this thing God had called him to do.

Taking time to meet with Sanballat was not a "bad" thing. Making peace with an enemy is normally considered a good idea. But God had called Nehemiah to rebuild the wall. He viewed this opportunity as a distraction. And it is a good thing. Sanballat had no intention of making peace.

DISTRACTION #1: OPPORTUNITIES

Every day of your life, every day of my life, opportunities come along that have the potential to distract us from the main things that God has called us to do. Entertainment opportunities, athletic opportunities, financial opportunities, relational opportunities, religious opportunities, investment opportunities, career opportunities, business opportunities, vacation opportunities. The list is endless.

In my world, the opportunities with the greatest potential to distract me are almost always good opportunities. Things I can easily justify: planning meetings, counseling, speaking engagements, community functions, conferences. I could be out six nights a week taking advantage of "good" opportunities. Like you, I could be even busier than I already am, making even less progress toward accomplishing the few things I know God has set before me to do.

To accomplish the important things you must learn to say no to some good things. More often than not, it is good things that have the greatest potential to distract you from the best things, the vision things. If Nehemiah had accepted Sanballat's invitation, his enemies would have killed him. In the same way there are appointments, hobbies, relationships, and invitations that, if taken advantage of, will kill your chances of accomplishing your vision.

GRANT'S STORY

I have a good friend whom I'll refer to as Grant. I consider him a mentor as well as a friend. Grant is fifty-six. When he was in his early twenties, he went to work for a fellow in the outdoor advertising business. Grant is the kind of guy who could sell just about anything to anybody. So he did quite well in that job. But there was a problem.

The fellow he worked for expected his employees to work six days a week. The owner lived for his business, and he figured everybody else ought to as well. If you weren't in the office Monday through Saturday, there was something wrong. You weren't a company man. As an incentive, the owner promised the inner circle of employees a significant cut of the profits if he ever sold the company, which he eventually did.

Now Grant didn't mind working hard. And he certainly didn't mind being well compensated for his labor. But he and his wife had a vision for their family that went beyond owning a big house and a couple of new cars. And working every Saturday pretty much eliminated any hopes they had of creating the family environment they were envisioning. So Grant decided to forgo this "excellent" opportunity.

When Grant turned in his resignation, his boss asked him what he was going to do. Grant told him he didn't know. And he didn't. But he knew one thing: Whatever he did next would support rather than compete with his vision of what could be and should be regarding his family.

Grant went on to begin his own outdoor company in a different part of the country. God blessed his courage and commitment. His businesses have thrived. But more importantly, he and his wife saw their vision for their children become a reality.

As I mentioned, his former employer did finally sell his company. The men who stayed with him all those years received a big check. But most of them had lost their families along the way. A couple of them went bankrupt a few years after they received their compensation.

The owner of the company paid a price relationally as well. His children are grown and gone. His interaction with them is infrequent and superficial.

A POSITIVE TREND

I am meeting more and more men and women who are choosing to forgo "good" career opportunities for the sake of their families. That's a wonderful trend. In many cases I have watched as God has blessed these families financially as well as relationally.

Don't allow "good" opportunities to rob you of your family vision. When you tuck your children in at night, just whisper to yourself, "I am doing a great work, I cannot come down." Men, when you are tempted to pick up the phone and tell your wife you will be home late from work (again), just look over at her picture on your credenza and whisper, "I am doing a great work, I cannot come down." Then stand up, grab your keys, and head for the car.

Ladies, as you struggle with the temptation to squeeze one more "good" activity into a schedule that is bursting at the seams, think about your family and whisper to yourself, "I am doing a great work, I cannot come down." Don't allow yourself to get distracted by events, organizations, hobbies, and activities that do nothing to further the vision God gave you when you said "I do" and when he blessed you with children.

If you are single, don't get distracted from your vision of what could be and should be relationally. Allowing God to shape your character while you wait for him to bring the right person into your life is a great work. Guard your purity and integrity at all costs. You are too busy to come down.

It is not just family that gets sacrificed on the altar of opportunity. I know people who have a vision of being out of debt but who are continually distracted by the allurement of more stuff. I have seen lake houses distract men and women from their vision for ministry. Many Christians catch a vision for reaching their unbelieving friends and neighbors and then allow hobbies and various forms of entertainment to distract them.

For every vision, there are dozens of potential distractions. Be careful that you don't let good opportunities rob you of the joy of seeing your vision become a reality. Work hard to distinguish between the good things and the main things, good opportunities and the thing to which you feel called.

DISTRACTION #2: CRITICISM

The second distraction Nehemiah faced was criticism. Surely Nehemiah was growing accustomed to this by now. But these criticisms weren't aimed at the workers or the feasibility of the project. These criticisms were directed at him.

His criticism came in the form of false accusations. Sanballat sent Nehemiah the same invitation five times. The first four times Nehemiah responded the same way, "I am doing a great work and I cannot come down." The fifth time, however, Sanballat sent more than an invitation.

> Then Sanballat sent his servant to me in the same manner a fifth time with an open letter in his hand. In it was written, "It is reported among the nations, and Gashmu says, that you and the Jews are planning to rebel; therefore you are rebuilding the wall. And you are to be their king, according to these reports. You have also appointed prophets to proclaim in Jerusalem concerning you, 'A king is in Judah!' And now it will be reported to the king according to these reports. So come now, let us take counsel together." (vv. 5–7)

In those days, letters were written on papyrus or leather. The custom was to roll the writing material, tie it with a string, and seal it with clay. But this letter was open (v. 5). Sanballat purposefully neglected to seal the letter so as to make its contents known to everyone who handled it. His goal, of course, was to spread the rumor that Nehemiah was trying to establish himself as the king of Judah.

Nothing could have been further from the truth. But people usually aren't interested in the truth. If word got out that Nehemiah was laying the groundwork to declare himself king, he would face opposition from all sides. For one thing, his own people were not interested in breaking off ties with the Persian government. For another, if that rumor ever reached the ears of King Artaxerxes, he knew he would find himself back in Susa with a rope around his neck. Either way, Sanballat would be happy. He wanted Nehemiah out of the way. It didn't matter to him who did his dirty work.

Nehemiah could have easily justified going on the defensive. A lot was at stake. Kings weren't very patient with governors who allowed their political aspirations to go to their heads. Besides that, the workers in Jerusalem were itching for an excuse to quit. But once again Nehemiah stayed focused on the task at hand. He didn't take time off to defend himself. He wasn't worried about what might be. He continued to work toward what could and should be.

Here is how Nehemiah responded.

> Then I sent a message to him saying, "Such things as you are saying have not been done, but you are inventing them in your own mind." (v. 8)

He knew what Sanballat and Company were up to.

> For all of them were trying to frighten us, thinking, "They will become discouraged with the work and it will not be done." (v. 9a)

Instead of chasing rumors, Nehemiah turned his attention to the One who had led him into this thing in the first place. "But now, O God, strengthen my hands" (v. 9b).

As we've noted, nothing brings out the critics like a vision. If you are passionate about something that is yet to be, eventually someone will criticize you and question your motives.

People will not understand the intensity of your focus. In our society we are not accustomed to leaders passing up good opportunities for the sake of something that is yet to be. There is a general distrust of those who are trying to do anything new or innovative, especially if they claim to be doing it for a reason other than personal gain.

MISDIRECTED ARROWS

What makes this so painful is that men and women with a vision are often accused of trying to do the very opposite of what their vision is about. Think about Nehemiah's situation. Here's a guy who walked away from a very influential position at the king's right hand. Upon arriving in Jerusalem he refused to exploit his position as governor. He wouldn't even accept the allotment of food set aside for him. Then he finds himself accused of being power hungry.

This is a pattern I see over and over. It is a dynamic that makes the pain of criticism more acute. Consequently, it is difficult to ignore. It becomes an emotional issue. After all, you are not just being accused. You are being accused of the very thing you are striving not to do. That hurts.

Here's the danger to your vision. Anger is a form of focus. Anger is distracting. The emotions dredged up by the words of your critics have the potential to distract you from the vision God has placed before you. Think about it. What could have been more irritating to Nehemiah than to be accused of being on some sort of power trip? Sanballat hit the bull's-eye. Add to that the fact that he posted these accusations on the ancient equivalent of the Internet. Nehemiah must have been furious.

But instead of grabbing his sword and marching off to find Sanballat, Nehemiah once again channeled his frustration to God, "O God, strengthen my hands." Paraphrased, "God, you take care of my reputation. In the meantime, I'll continue doing what you brought me here to do."

Don't be distracted by criticism. Take your frustrations and anger to the One who got you into this thing to begin with. Time will tell who is right. The worst thing you can do is allow your anger to shift your focus. I have wasted a lot of valuable "vision time" trying to answer my critics and track down the source of rumors. Pour out your heart to the Father, and then get back to work.

DIRTY LENSES

There is another dynamic at work. Not only will you be accused of the very thing you are trying not to do, you will probably be accused of whatever it is your accusers are guilty of.

Sanballat is a prime example. He was the one who was power hungry. The reason he was so miffed by Nehemiah's success was that his own power was being threatened. He did what so many critics do: He assumed of Nehemiah what was true of himself. Surely Nehemiah had his own interests in mind. Why else would he be so committed to rebuilding the wall?

People with impure motives question the motives of those around them. It's called projection. Since their actions are laced with their own selfish ambitions, they assume everyone else's are, as well. These folks will examine your zeal through their self-serving lenses and assume the worst. You can't convince them otherwise. There is no use trying. Again, pour out your frustration to the Father and keep working.

The less abstract your vision, the more criticism you are likely to receive. When you begin acting on your preferred future, look out.

"All you do is work."

"Why won't you go?"

"Why wouldn't you stay?"

"You're so religious."

"Sure, family is important, but come on! It's just one night."

"You're no fun anymore."

"How much do you plan to make on this thing?"

"I know someone who tried that once."

People need an explanation for the unusual behavior of the man or woman with a vision. Unfortunately, they are often unwilling to accept the truth. So they write it off as something else. If you decide to make your family the priority over business and begin to cut back your hours, you may be accused of not having what it takes to cut it in the marketplace. I know single men who have been accused of being gay because they have decided to remain sexually pure until they're married. Stay-at-home moms are often accused of doing so because they lack any marketable skills.

There are always going to be accusations when you are focused on accomplishing a vision. Men and women with a vision stand out. That makes people uncomfortable. The current of society always moves in the direction of conformity.

THE SOLUTION

The best way to silence your critics is to see your vision through to completion.

Allow me to jump ahead in our story for a moment. Notice the change in Nehemiah's critics once the wall around Jerusalem was completed.

So the wall was completed on the twenty-fifth of the month *i*
in fifty-two days. When all our enemies heard of it, and a/
nations surrounding us saw it, they lost their confidence; foi .._,
recognized that this work had been accomplished with the help
of our God. (vv. 15–16)

You've got to love that. Nehemiah's critics lost their self-confidence
because they realized God was involved. Nothing silences critics like a
vision that's brought to completion.

If God is the source of your vision, the day will come when even your
harshest critics will have a difficult time explaining away what he has
done through you. It is hard to argue with success. It is even more difficult to argue with divine success.

Don't allow criticism to distract you. If need be, vent to the Father,
and then channel your excess energy back into the thing he has commissioned you to do. You are not accountable to your critics, though they will
do everything in their power to make you think you are. You are accountable to the One who has invited you to partner with him to create what
could and should be.

The apostle Paul encouraged the believers in Thessolonica to maintain their vision of Christlike conduct with these words. "Faithful is He
who calls you, and He also will bring it to pass" (1 Thessalonians 5:24).

The same can be said of every divinely inspired vision. What God has
determined to be, will be. Our responsibility is to remain faithful.

DISTRACTION #3: FEAR

Nehemiah faced a third potential distraction. In addition to opportunities
and criticism, he was placed in a potentially life-threatening situation.
Once again, Sanballat was at work behind the scenes. The idea this time
was to frighten Nehemiah into doing something that would discredit him
in the eyes of the people of Jerusalem.

Sanballat realized they were not going to get Nehemiah to come out
to them, so they found somebody on the inside to set him up.

When I entered the house of Shemaiah the son of Delaiah, son of
Mehetabel, who was confined at home, he said, "Let us meet

together in the house of God, within the temple, and let us close the doors of the temple, for they are coming to kill you, and they are coming to kill you at night." (Nehemiah 6:10)

Shemaiah, a Jew living in Jerusalem, invited Nehemiah to his house for a meeting. When Nehemiah arrived, Shemaiah fabricated a story about a plot on Nehemiah's life. According to the story, Sanballat was planning to send an assassin into the city to murder Nehemiah in his sleep. Nehemiah's only hope, according to Shemaiah, was to run to the temple and cling to the altar.

This was a pretty ingenious plot. You see, only priests were allowed into the area of the temple that housed the altar. Nehemiah was not a priest. To violate the temple in this way would discredit him among the Jews.

There was an exception to this rule. According to the Law, there were certain circumstances in which a person other than a priest could go into the temple for refuge. If someone accidentally killed another person and the victim had a relative who was likely to take revenge, he was allowed to enter the temple and cling to the altar for refuge. The assailant would be safe there until a judge could hear the case (Numbers 35:6–15).

So there were opportunities for people to go into the temple for asylum. But this clearly was not one of those occasions. Shemaiah was trying to trick Nehemiah into making a decision that would discredit him in front of all the people in Israel. To run to the temple for refuge would not only be a violation of the Law, it would undermine his authority as a leader. Word would get out that the governor was hiding in the temple from a would-be assassin. That wouldn't exactly instill confidence in the workers. Not to mention the fact that there was no assassin.

Once again, Nehemiah refused to be distracted from the work. His response tells us something about how he viewed himself in relation to his vision.

But I said, "Should a man like me flee? And could one such as I go into the temple to save his life? I will not go in." (v. 11)

Had Nehemiah been in this thing simply for his own interest, he would have had every reason to run. But Nehemiah had not only embraced this vision, the vision had embraced him. Compared to the great work to which he had been called, the threat of assassination seemed trivial. This was another way of saying, "I am doing a great work. I cannot come down even to protect my life. There is something bigger at stake than my safety."

Nehemiah understood the magnitude and significance of his vision. "Should a man like me, a man who has been given this sacred responsibility—this divine assignment—abandon the task to save his own life?" Nehemiah recognized he was a part of something bigger than himself. He knew he was expendable. So he refused to run.

Nehemiah probably suspected from the outset that this was another of Sanballat's attempts to distract him from the work. And at some point his suspicions were confirmed.

> Then I perceived that surely God had not sent him, but he uttered his prophecy against me because Tobiah and Sanballat had hired him. He was hired for this reason, that I might become frightened and act accordingly and sin, so that they might have an evil report in order that they could reproach me. (vv. 12–13)

Every vision involves elements of the unknown. In the early stages, there is more unknown than known. The unknown is fertile ground for fear. Consequently, everybody with a vision must face and work through some "what if" scenarios.

"He is not exactly what I'm looking for, but *what if* nobody else comes along?"

"I really need to quit, but *what if* I can't find another job?"

"I know I need to say no, but *what if* it costs me my bonus?"

"I know God wants me to initiate this relationship, but *what if* they reject me?"

"I need to raise some capital, but *what if* I can't find any investors?"

Then there's the big one. The "what if" that buries more visions than any other: *What if I fail?*

Like anger, fear is a form of focus. We can get so focused on what might be that we lose sight of what could and should be. Fear can cause us to begin evaluating our situation based on what bad thing might happen rather than what good thing we want to see happen.

If we give in, we begin shrinking back from the vision. We come down off the wall, away from our great thing, and run for the safety of the altar.

Don't allow fear of the unknown to cause you to miss out on what God wants to do through you. Don't allow fear to rob you of your vision for your marriage, your finances, your relationships, your career or ministry. Don't allow fear to distract you from what you believe could and should be. Don't allow what could take place to cause you to back down from pursuing what ought to take place.

In light of what God has called you to do, should a man or woman in your position retreat? When you think of the potential good that could come from your vision, should someone in your position run away in fear of what might happen? I don't think so. And in your heart, you probably don't think so, either.

A SCHOOL TOO FAR

In high school I was a below-average student. After my first semester of college I received a letter from the Dean of Students informing me I was being put on academic warning. If I didn't pull my GPA up to a 2.5 by the next semester, I would be put on academic probation. So I buckled down and began to study. But after my second semester I received another letter informing me I had been placed on academic probation. One more bad semester and I would be out.

Fortunately, my third semester went better. This had more to do with the number of hours I took than my academic prowess. Either way, I was able to stay in school. It took me five years to finish college. I took summer courses throughout. All that to say, I'm not the smartest guy in the world. Grades never came easy. I can remember being in study groups and thinking, "How do these guys pick it up so quickly?"

When I decided to go to graduate school to prepare for ministry, I was encouraged to apply to Dallas Theological Seminary. In my heart, that's where I wanted to go. The curriculum was perfectly suited for the things I was interested in. Some of my favorite preachers and writers had attended there. Even my parents were encouraging me in that direction.

But there were two problems: First, it was a four-year program, as opposed to the traditional three-year seminary degree. Four more years of school seemed unthinkable. Second, DTS had a reputation for being very tough academically. They required three years of Greek and two years of Hebrew. Most seminaries required half of that. The grading system was like nothing I had ever seen. They required prospective students to take the GRE. I knew that would be a disaster (which it was...both times!). If I did manage to get in, I was sure I wouldn't be able to cut it academically.

So I did what any coward would do. I threw away my DTS application and applied at two other schools. Bottom line, I was scared and intimidated. DTS was so far out of the question that the summer before I was to begin school, I flew out to Texas to check out a school in Fort Worth. I actually drove to Dallas to see the city and never bothered to find DTS.

Two months before school was to begin, my dad called me from out of town to inform me that he had been praying for me regarding my choice of seminaries. That was a strange thing for him to be praying about, considering I had made up my mind weeks prior to this conversation. I already had a roommate and a class schedule. Why was he still praying about my decision? The decision had been made.

But as I sat there on the edge of my bed thinking through our conversation, it occurred to me that my choice of schools was based more on my fear of what might happen in Dallas than it was a desire to go to the other school. That was no way to make a decision. The next morning, I called DTS and asked for an application.

As I moved through the admissions process, it became clear to me that DTS was where I was supposed to be. I was still afraid. But I had a vision for the kind of ministry I wanted to be involved in. DTS would equip me to follow through with that vision. So I went. It was even more demanding than I imagined. But it was where I was supposed to be. God was gracious. I graduated on time. But once again, I was there every summer trying to keep pace with the grueling academic schedule.

Don't allow fear of the unknown to deter you from what God has put in your heart to do. Worse than failure is living with the regret of never having stepped out in faith to pursue your vision. Besides, a person to whom God has entrusted such an important vision has no need to retreat in fear.

BUILDING BLOCK #15

DON'T GET DISTRACTED.

Don't get distracted. Don't let good opportunities or criticism or fear derail your pursuit of the vision. Keep your eyes focused on the finish line.

At the end of this chapter there is a place to list the opportunities that consistently distract you from the thing or things God has put in your heart to do. I hope you will take a minute and do some real soul-searching. You don't want to wake up one day and realize you have *spent* your time rather than *invested* it.

When distractions come, remember these three things:

- You are doing a great work, you don't have time to come down.
- Success will silence your critics.
- The significance of your calling rules out the option of retreat.

Some time ago, I shared this principle with the congregation of North Point. Afterwards I received the following e-mail from one of our leaders. Vicky is an extraordinarily talented actress. For the time being, however, she has chosen to put her career ambitions on hold in order to be a stay-at-home mom. Her husband, Paul, is a freelance sportscaster and television personality.

> Dear Andy,
>
> I wanted to let you know what happened to me a few days after your encouraging sermon. I had read an audition with Paul over the phone, as he sometimes does on a voice-over audition. After the audition he said, "They will probably cast *you*. You are really good at this."
>
> A week later, I happened to return a call to this same agent on Paul's behalf, and the lady I talked to commented on how great she thought my reading was. Her coworker had remarked that she didn't realize Paul's wife did voice-over work, and she said if I ever wanted to do any work to call her.
>
> How flattering for this housewife who never ventures beyond

the Christian elementary school where I substitute for little pay and work many other hours as a volunteer with kids that I love. I know the difference in earnings only too well. And in Atlanta there are many opportunities to pursue voice-over work.

I thanked her, and said maybe when Lindsay was older, but that right now I couldn't consider it. There was no struggle to say this. I hung up the phone, smiled, and said aloud: "I am doing a great work, and I cannot come down."

Thanks for encouraging the ladies who might have really struggled to say this. It's what I hope a lot of mothers will realize, and your sermon was encouraging to all of us. As a follow-up, when I told Lindsay about this, she squeezed my hand for a long time. She knows that we give up things so that I can be a stay-at-home mom.

But the best part came on Mother's Day. I always insist that she make, rather than buy, a card for me because she makes these incredible cards. This one was no exception. On the front cover was a sketch of two hands reaching toward each other. The words written across the sketch were: "I am doing a great work..." The back cover was similar, but in this sketch the hands were touching, and the words read: "...and I cannot come down."

That was all the confirmation I will ever need.

Thanks,

Vicky

VISIONEERING
PROJECT #14

1. What opportunities consistently distract you from your vision(s)?

2. What do you plan to do about it?

3. How do you respond when people criticize your vision? How do you respond when people question your motives?

4. Within the context of your vision, what is your greatest fear?

5. Within the context of your vision, what is the worst thing that could happen?

6. Imagine for a moment that you failed miserably at what you are attempting to do. What would the consequences be?

CHAPTER FIFTEEN

....

THE INEXPLICABLE

LIFE

Empty nets lying there at the water's edge,
Told a story that few could believe and none could explain....
STEPHEN CURTIS CHAPMAN

As I write this chapter, Sandra and I are in the process of teaching Garrett, our five-year-old, how to read. I'm not convinced five-year-olds need to know how to read. But Garrett has assured us it is time for him to read. After all, his older brother can read. So we harnessed the power of sibling rivalry and hit the books.

The other day I came home, and he was anxious to read for me. We went upstairs, sat down on the floor, and he began.

A man gave an old coat to an old goat. That old goat said, "I will eat this old coat." So he did. "That was fun," he said. "I ate the old coat and now I am cold." And now the old goat is sad.

It took Garrett about three minutes to get through those three lines. It seemed like thirty minutes to me. When he finished, I asked him a few questions about what he had read to check his comprehension. The conversation went something like this.

"Garrett, what did the old man give to the goat?"

"What man?"

"The man in the story. The man in the story gave something to an old goat. What did he give him?"

"I don't know."

"He have him a coat. The old man gave the goat a coat. What did the goat do with the coat?"

"Wear it?"

"No, he ate it."

"That's funny, Daddy."

Early on, it became evident that Garrett and I have two different agendas. I want Garrett to read and comprehend. Garrett just wants to sound out the words right. The whole process brought back unpleasant elementary school memories for me. I can still remember being called upon to read in front of the class. Like Garrett, my goal was simply to get through the assigned pages without saying any of the words wrong.

Everyone at Henderson Mill Elementary knew there were dire consequences for misreading in front of the class. You see, there was a fellow in my grade who went by the name of Mary Jane. I never knew his real name. Actually, I never thought to ask. But I knew the saga of how he acquired his nickname.

When he was in the first grade he was reading a story in front of the class. He came to a passage that read, "'Hello,' she said. 'My name is Mary Jane.'" Unfortunately, he missed the "she said" part. He read, "Hello, my name is Mary Jane." That was all it took. From that point on, he was Mary Jane. Needless to say, comprehension was not the first order of the day at Henderson Mill Elementary School. We just wanted to say the words right.

But while we were hyperfocused on sounding out the words correctly, something was taking place behind the scenes. Slowly but surely we were learning to comprehend. This, of course, was the goal of our teachers and parents. They knew that once we were able to comprehend what we were reading, a new world would be opened to us. So they were not content to merely let us get by with sounding out the words correctly. They inched us closer and closer to comprehension. In the end, their agenda won out.

A DEEPER CURRENT

While you are busy about the process of pursuing your vision, something is going on behind the scenes that you are probably not aware of. It's something you cannot see. It may not become apparent until your work is accomplished. While you are consumed with the nuts and bolts of your vision, God is at work on a parallel plan that will ultimately complement and give deeper significance to the vision or visions that absorb your attention.

We are like Garrett in that we are focused on the task at hand. But like a parent teaching his child to read, our heavenly Father has a broader and more significant agenda in mind. These are not competing agendas. On the contrary, as we will discover, one is a necessary precursor to the other. The visions we are so intent on seeing through to completion actually pave the way for something much greater.

Nehemiah certainly knew what it was like to be consumed by the details of a vision. After a while he must have felt like Bill Murray in *Groundhog Day*. Every day must have looked and felt like the day before. More rocks to move. More debris to clear. More civil unrest to deal with. It would have been easy to get lost in the daily routine of rebuilding the wall. But God was working in the background accomplishing things he was not even aware of.

To understand God's parallel agenda in Nehemiah's day we need to take a quick look at God's purpose for establishing the nation of Israel to begin with.

A LIGHT TO THE NATIONS

God's ultimate intention for Israel was to establish her as a light to the surrounding nations. The prophet Isaiah said it this way:

> I will also make you a light of the nations so that My salvation may reach to the end of the earth. (Isaiah 49:6b)

The idea was that pagan nations would see God's activity in the life of Israel and conclude, "Israel's God is God!" Israel was to be a lighthouse. A beacon. They were to serve as a constant reminder of God's greatness and power. God desired to manifest his character through Israel to all those who came into contact with the nation or even heard about it. In this way, Israel would bring glory to God and salvation to the surrounding nations.

We see this happening throughout the Old Testament, beginning with Moses leading the people of Israel out of Egypt and continuing right up to the days of Nehemiah. Over and over God made his presence known to the rest of the world through Israel.

This explains some of the rather odd narratives we find scattered throughout the Old Testament. For instance, the plagues in Egypt. What was that all about? When you read that story, it seems like a lot of stalling. God knew what it would take to change Pharaoh's mind. Why didn't he just start with the tenth plague and be done with it?

God had an agenda beyond simply delivering his people from bondage. He wanted to teach the people of Egypt a lesson. Humanly speaking, Egypt was the most powerful nation in the world at that time. Pharaoh considered himself a god. There was no better place in all the earth for God to begin demonstrating his power through his chosen people than Egypt.

Icon by icon, idol by idol, Israel's God unraveled Egypt's entire religious system. Each of the plagues was directed at something the Egyptians considered sacred. For instance, they worshipped the Nile. God turned it to blood (Exodus 7:20). They worshiped the sun. God brought three days of darkness over much of Egypt (10:22). God's precision was daunting. Their entire assemblage of gods was no match for the God of Israel.

When the people of Egypt awoke in the night to find their firstborns slain by an angel of death, they had no recourse but to admit Israel's God was the true God. And Pharaoh succumbed to the pressure to let Moses' people go.

The ancient world was saturated with pagan religions and cults. Every nation had its own god (or gods). The power of these gods was determined on the battlefield. It was not unusual for an army to carry an idol or icon of their god into battle. A victory for the army was a victory for their god and vice versa. When two armies met for battle, the assumption was that the army with the most powerful god had the advantage.

It was in this highly superstitious and militaristic climate that God set out to make himself known. So throughout Israel's history we find God intervening militarily in ways that humbled and astounded her enemies.

Why would God ask Joshua to march around Jericho rather than attack the city head on? Because God was after more than simply the destruction of a Canaanite city. He had a point to make. He wanted the surrounding nations to be awed, not by Israel's military prowess, but by her God.

Why command Gideon to reduce his army to a handful of soldiers before allowing them to charge into the Midianite camp (Judges 7)? The same reason. Why have a shepherd boy with a sling slay a seasoned warrior (1 Samuel 17)? Why instruct Jehoshaphat to put the choir in front of the army as they marched into battle (2 Chronicles 20:21)? In every case, God was up to something behind the scenes. He was using Israel as a mirror to reflect his glory and might.

From time to time the mirror was tarnished. Israel would forget the source of her strength and glory. She would lose sight of her sacred charter and embrace the idolatry of her neighbors.

Like a good father, God was quick to discipline his people. Discipline generally came in the form of foreign invasion. With the threat of military and political chaos looming on the horizon, Israel's kings would often repent, and God would flex his muscles once again and save the nation. It was as if God were saying, "People are watching. I can't let you get by with disobedience. My reputation is at stake. This isn't just about you. It is about me!"

Eventually, Israel's leaders refused to soften their hearts toward God. Nebuchadnezzar invaded, destroyed the infrastructure of the nation, and marched the best and brightest of the leadership off to Babylon. Through captivity and the loss of her independence, God disciplined the nation of Israel for her idolatry and general unfaithfulness. As you may have guessed, it was this captivity that set the stage for Nehemiah's return to Jerusalem years later.

While Nehemiah was busy about the task of rebuilding the walls, God was setting the stage once again to demonstrate his power to the nations. Notice the response of Israel's neighbors when the wall was finally completed.

So the wall was completed on the twenty-fifth of the month Elul, in fifty-two days. When all our enemies heard of it, and all the nations surrounding us saw it, they lost their confidence; for they recognized that this work had been accomplished with the help of our God. (Nehemiah 6:15–16)

The phrase "lost their confidence" literally means they "fell much in their own eyes." In other words, their high opinion of themselves received a serious setback.

This was the same group that had been so cocky before. This was the group that had accused the builders of not having what it took to get the job done. They had been so intimidating, so threatening. But all that came to an abrupt halt once the doors were put in place. And notice who got the credit. Not Nehemiah. Not the builders. "They recognized that this work had been accomplished with the help of our God."

With God's help, Nehemiah and his crew did in fifty-two days what some said couldn't be done at all. And that, of course, was the point God had planned to make all along. Once again, Israel's neighbors were confronted with the power and presence of Israel's God.

As I mentioned earlier, the most encouraging thing about this story is that there are no overt miracles. God clearly intervened. But nothing supernatural took place. No parting seas. No earthquakes. No plagues. Just hard work, good leadership, and the touch of God.

YOUR OPPORTUNITY

While you are consumed by the details involved in pursuing God's vision for your life—being a good parent and faithful spouse, remaining pure, looking for Mr. or Mrs. Right, becoming Mr. or Mrs. Right, building a business or ministry—God is up to something you may have been unaware of. What was once true of Israel is now true of you.

In the New Testament an important transition took place. God transferred the responsibility of being a light to the nations from Israel to the church and to individual believers.

Jesus explained it this way:

You are the light of the world. A city set on a hill cannot be hidden; nor does anyone light a lamp and put it under a basket, but on the lampstand, and it gives light to all who are in the house. Let your light shine before men in such a way that they may see your good works, and glorify your Father who is in heaven. (Matthew 5:14–16)

Whereas the focus was once on Israel and her military victories, it is now on our lifestyles and personal character. As we slosh through the brick and mortar phase of pursuing our vision, we are to live lives that reflect the character of Christ. We are to conduct ourselves in such a way that causes people to take notice. And upon further examination, to draw the conclusion that there is something divine about our lives. In short, we are to live inexplicable lives.

BUILDING BLOCK #16

THERE IS DIVINE POTENTIAL IN ALL YOU ENVISION TO DO.

God's ultimate plan for your life reaches beyond the visions he's given you for your family, business, ministry, and finances. He has positioned you in your culture as a singular point of light. A beacon in a world that desperately needs to see something divine, something that is clearly not of this world.

Above and beyond the achievements associated with your vision, he wants to draw people to himself. Our visions are means to a greater end. Namely, the glory of God and the salvation of men and women. This is his ultimate objective, his ultimate desire.

I'm afraid the majority of believers have never seen this important relationship. Consequently, our churches are filled with men and women who compartmentalize their lives. They differentiate between the religious and the secular. The religious being all those duties that have to do with God; the secular being their other pursuits.

To make matters worse, they underestimate God's interest in their secular pursuits—after all, there wasn't anything very "religious" about rebuilding the walls around Jerusalem—and they overestimate his interest in their religious ones.

The truth is, our secular pursuits have more kingdom potential than our religious ones. For it is in the realm of our secular pursuits that secular people are watching. The marketplace, the club, and the salon are the environments that so desperately need a brush with the divine. It is there that God desires to demonstrate his power through those who are willing to be used in such a way. It is in the context of those arenas that the "awe factor" is potentially the greatest.

For that reason, men and women who understand this broader

potential for their visions see no distinction between the religious and the secular. Both their sacred and secular duties are played out on the same stage with the same goal in mind. They see themselves as lights at all times in all contexts. For those unique individuals, every role, relationship, and responsibility carries divine potential.

These are the unique few who have not substituted gimmicks and tradition for the real thing. I'm afraid too many of us are content to set ourselves apart by bumper stickers and schedules. I've yet to hear a story of a Christian motorist being flagged down by another driver who was pierced to the heart by the sight of a fish on the back of a car. And our Sunday morning routines certainly haven't left the world standing in awe of our God.

STANDING OUT

In Nehemiah's day the completion of the wall highlighted God's presence and power. The question we must consider as we pursue the various visions God has set before us is this: What about my vision has the potential to point to the presence and power of God? To borrow Nehemiah's words, what would have to happen for people to realize this work has been done with the help of God?

I have been privileged to know dozens of men and women who understand the relationship between the visions God has given them and what he ultimately wants to do through them. Of the people I am thinking about right now, not one of them is a professional minister. However, all of them view themselves as ministers.

In examining their lives I have noticed three things that consistently attract the attention of those who stand outside the faith and watch them. I'm sure there are more. But here are three that are hard to miss and almost impossible to ignore. These are the marks of an unexplainable life.

1. PEACE

Peace is a rare commodity. People spend a lot of time and money trying to artificially manufacture it. Chemically induced peace is big business. Genuine peace stands out. It pricks people's curiosity. It elicits questions.

"How could you just sit there and take it?"

"Doesn't that scare you?"

"Don't you hate him?"

"You forgave her?"

"Aren't you worried?"

"Do you realize what's at stake?"

"Aren't you going to sue?"

"How do you sleep at night?"

"Are you always this calm?"

Gill and Jimmy

A friend asked me to have lunch with him and a fellow he had been shar-ing Christ with for nine years. Nine years! Anyway, during the course of our conversation I asked Gill (the unbeliever) what it was that kept him in this nine-year dialogue with Jimmy. I'm thinking, after nine years he ought to be ready to tell this guy to shove off.

He laughed. "That's simple," he said. "He's got something I want. He doesn't worry."

Peace is one part of the light we have been called to set out on the hill in our secular environments. From God's perspective, the peace you maintain as you pursue your vision may be more important than the ful-fillment of your vision. That's convicting to me. So often I allow the details and pressures of life to rob me of my peace and joy.

But what if my peace and joy are not merely for my benefit? What if peace and joy are the beacons God wants to use to cause those I come into contact with to pause and wonder? What if my peace and joy are the elements that make my faith authentic for someone? And what if the pur-pose of those dark circumstances is to give my peace and joy an oppor-tunity to shine brighter than normal and attract more attention than in the wrinkle-free days when everything goes right?

Do you know why peace shines so brightly in this world? Because everybody you come into contact with entered adulthood with a picture of what they hoped the future would be like. The emotional aspect of their picture included peace. They didn't think of it in those terms. They labeled it happiness. More than anything, they wanted to be happy.

Now, years into the pursuit, life isn't what they intended it to be. They have accumulated a good portion of the stuff they set out for. But relationally, things aren't right. And emotionally they are empty. They aren't happy. They don't have peace. They can't lie in bed at night, stare up at the ceiling, and breathe a sigh of relief. Everything isn't okay on the inside, but they don't know what to do about it.

When they finally meet someone who has peace, they take note. Peace in the life of another highlights their emptiness. Their darkness is exposed. And they find themselves confronted with the fact that peace is achievable.

So how's your peace these days? How's your peace holding up under the pressures associated with your various visions? The presence of peace in your life is important. From God's point of view, your vision may simply be an opportunity to showcase your peace.

2. HEALTHY RELATIONSHIPS

A second thing that causes this world to sit up and take notice is a successful relationship. We live in a relationally challenged world. I am constantly amazed at how irrational people are when it comes to relationships. Consequently, dysfunction abounds.

People are disillusioned relationally. Their relational dreams aren't coming true. Life is not as it was intended to be. People go about their lives squeezing as much love and acceptance as they can from the people around them, always coming up short.

Then they see a healthy marriage, a happy family, kids who enjoy going home for the holidays. And they are forced to wonder.

"Why them and not me?"

"What's the difference?"

"How did they get there?"

"What's their secret?"

"They're so lucky."

This is why it is so important to have a vision for your marriage, whether you are married or not. You need a vision for your family. You need a clear picture of what could be and should be relationally.

Don't sacrifice your relationships for the sake of a business or a ministry or, for that matter, for any other vision. Businesses and ministries are a dime a dozen. Even successful businesses and ministries are not on anybody's endangered species list. But strong marriages are rare indeed. Healthy families are the exception, not the rule.

There are plenty of successful entrepreneurs whose families are in shambles. Nobody concludes from those situations that without God the business plan would have never come together. There is nothing unique or divine about a business or ministry that is built at the expense of a marriage or family.

On the other hand, find me a man or woman who has built a great organization and whose family is thriving, and I'll show you an opportunity for God to draw big-time attention to himself. That's when outsiders stop and wonder. That's when people are almost forced to conclude that God was involved.

How are the key relationships in your life? What about your marriage? What about your relationship with your children? If you are single, how are you doing in the area of moral purity? Dad, Mom, do you see your family as an opportunity for God to demonstrate his power and grace to those who are watching?

"What's this got to do with vision?" you ask. Everything. We are not much of a light on a hill if we sacrifice people and purity for the sake of achieving our vision. When we do so, we remove any incentive God may have had to bless our labor. We become unblessable because we have made ourselves unusable. At that point there is nothing of significance for God to draw attention to.

Richard and Curt

I have a friend named Richard who develops condominiums. He has a partner named Curt. Through the years they have made a lot of money for themselves. Richard is fifty-two and has been a Christian for about twenty years. He is one of the most generous men I have ever met. It is evident to everyone who knows Richard and his wife that they see their business success as God's way of positioning them to invest in kingdom enterprises. His success has given him some notoriety. Over and over he has had opportunities to publicly give God the credit for all his good fortune.

The other outstanding quality Richard possesses is an unwavering commitment to do what is right. I have heard several stories of how he walked away from lucrative deals that would have required a compromise of integrity. In fact, that was the reason Curt enjoyed doing business with Richard. He knew Richard could be trusted.

In spite of Richard's faith, character, and strong family relationships, Curt (his business partner) was not interested in spiritual matters. Richard knew better than to force the issue. Instead he just continued to live the life.

For eleven years Richard prayed for Curt. Finally, on a business trip out west, Curt turned to Richard and blurted out, "I became a Christian." It was such an emotional moment that neither man could even look at the other. They just stared straight ahead without speaking a word. It wasn't until a few days later that Richard got the whole story.

Curt's family had been slowly spiraling toward disaster. He knew there were problems but didn't know how to fix them. He could buy, sell, and develop condominiums in his sleep. But when it came to rebuilding his family, he wasn't sure what to do.

When he was forced to hospitalize his son for an addiction, he finally came to the end of himself. The pressures brought on by the collapse of his family broke him. But throughout the breaking process he had watched Richard and his family. It was the picture Curt had always wanted but had been unable to achieve on his own. When the bottom dropped out, he knew his best option was to ask God for help.

Today Curt and his family are making huge strides toward putting things back together. Curt never misses church and reads everything Richard puts into his hands. His son is out of the hospital. He and his wife are rebuilding their marriage.

Don't sacrifice key relationships while pursuing your vision. It is tempting to economize relationally when consumed with the details of a vision. After all, relationships aren't urgent, while many elements of our visions are.

Remember, though, your relationships may be *the* thing that give your otherwise secular visions divine potential.

3. CHARACTER

A third thing that positions us as a light on a hill is character. For the Christian, character involves doing what's right, as God defines right, regardless of the cost.

Character is such a rarity that people eye it suspiciously. They assume a hidden agenda. Right for right's sake is unheard of. I have seen demonstrations of character that actually made people uncomfortable. It goes completely against the amoral, nonabsolutism of our society. This, of course, is precisely why it draws so much attention and has so much kingdom potential.

Like our core relationships, character is an easy thing to let slide in the pursuit of our dreams. As we discussed earlier, there are shortcuts associated with every vision. A shortcut usually demands a compromise of integrity. The ironic thing about these seemingly insignificant compromises is that they both accelerate our progress and undermine our success. The shortcut allows us to cut down on the time it takes to reach our destination. But the compromise of integrity carves the heart out of our celebration once we get there.

When you sacrifice your character for the sake of a vision, God checks out of the process. He cannot honor that which is built upon deceit. To do so would be to honor deceit. Compromise makes us unblessable. Once we compromise our character, we severely diminish the kingdom potential of our vision.

Nick and Allison

Nick is the CFO of a midsized information service business in Atlanta. When Nick got married, he made a decision not to eat with or ride in a car alone with any woman other than his wife. Nick had seen one too many "business" relationships evolve into something else. He had a vision for his marriage and family. This decision was his way of protecting his dream.

As noble as his intents may be, he is finding his decision to be very inconvenient. As CFO of the company he is expected to develop relationships with vendors and clients. That means a lot of lunches. Finding a way around lunch meetings with female account representatives is often awkward. As you might imagine, in our world of political correctness, his standard is almost impossible to explain without offending someone. Nevertheless, he continues to hold true to what he believes is the wise thing to do.

One of Nick's responsibilities is to nurture and protect his company's relationship with their bank. The account representative assigned to his company was a young, single woman named Allison. Because of the success of Nick's company, Allison was highly motivated to maintain a good relationship with her client. Consequently, she was always inviting Nick to lunch. At first Nick cordially declined with no explanation. But Allison was persistent.

Before long it became obvious to Allison that Nick was putting her off. This caused some tension in the relationship. Nick decided it would be best to explain to Allison what was up. So he told her about his decision. He assured her it had nothing to do with her and that he maintained this stance with all female clients.

Instead of being offended, Allison was intrigued. She began asking questions. The conversation quickly transitioned from business to more personal issues. She told Nick that she had never met a man who was that serious about maintaining fidelity in his marriage. In her world, the opposite was generally the case.

At one point in the conversation Nick felt the freedom to share with Allison about his faith in Christ. Again, she was intrigued. Nick went on to share the gospel with Allison. She was visibly moved. Nick ask her if she would like to receive Christ as her Savior. To his amazement, she said she would. They bowed their heads together and Allison trusted Christ as her Savior.

Only in the Movies

Perhaps you find yourself thinking, "That kind of thing never happens to me!" You may even be thinking, "I don't believe that happened to Nick!" And somebody out there is saying, "I don't even believe there is a Nick!"

Why doesn't this kind of thing ever happen to you? Well, don't take this wrong, but maybe your character isn't turning many heads. It could be that nothing about your conduct is attracting any attention—the right kind of attention, anyway. Uncompromising character in the marketplace will eventually elicit a "Why?" or a "What's up with that?" from somebody. It is just too unusual to go unnoticed.

Nick's vision for his family was the catalyst God used to accomplish his primary agenda. Namely, drawing attention to himself. When Nick made his decision to limit who he ate with, he was thinking in terms of the vision he had for his family. But that decision, along with Nick's refusal to compromise, positioned Nick as a light on a hill.

That's God's way.

A CITY ON A HILL

Have you ever prayed anything along these lines: "Father, let my light shine before men in such a way that they may see my good works, and glorify my Father who is in heaven" (Matthew 5:16)?

I don't hear prayers like that very often. Our prayers hover close to our personal visions and dreams. All too often we focus our prayer energies on trying to get God to bless something, change somebody, or grant us success with a project. He is far more interested in the consistency of your light in environments where light is not appreciated. All our projects, dreams, and visions are merely potential opportunities for the Father to draw attention and people to himself.

When you pray for your family, don't limit your request to "protection" and "blessing." Pray that God would establish your family as a light in your community. Ask him to use the family relationships you are working so hard to nurture and maintain to attract attention. Ask him to allow others to detect a divine element in your family's life and lifestyle.

When you pray for financial and business success, ask God to grant it in such a way that those outside the faith sit up and take notice. To borrow from Nehemiah, pray that the people around you would realize that your success was accomplished with the help of your God.

One of the reasons we don't take this kind of thing seriously is because we don't believe anybody is watching. Rest assured, they are. They are watching you just like you are watching them. We love to watch each other and talk about each other. It is human nature.

When you leave your neighbor's house, they talk about you just like you talk about them on the way home.

"I think they are living together."

"Did you hear how he talked to his kids?"

"Did you notice the way she looked at him when he brought up…"

"They sure seem happy."

"Do you think those carpets have ever been cleaned?"

In the office you watch the way your peers conduct business. If you are an employer, you are constantly watching the way your employees represent your company. If you are a parent, you watch the way other parents deal with their children. If you are married, you watch the way other couples treat each other. If you are single, you watch everybody.

We are all watching each other. We notice the good and the bad. We compare ourselves physically, financially, and socially. We covet. We lust. We gossip. We criticize. And we envy. Why? Because we are all people watchers. So face it: People are watching, talking about, criticizing, and at times envying you.

The question is, what do they see? Who do they see? Can they attribute all your success to hard work and good luck? Or is there something about your life that causes them to stop and wonder?

People are watching. They are looking for something authentic. They are looking for something that works. And when they see it, they will eventually ask about it.

I have a good friend named Pete. Pete has been a Christian for two years. He is from the former Soviet Union. He had never heard the name Jesus until he was ten years old. His family moved to the United States when he was twelve. His parents were agnostic and therefore had never encouraged Pete to explore anything that had to do with religion.

When I met Pete he was not a Christian, but he was full of questions about Christianity. I told him I would be happy to answer as many questions as I could. We began having lunch together every other week or so. That went on for ten months.

During our first meeting together I asked Pete why he was so interested in the gospel. This is what he said.

"I am in business with several families who have the kind of marriage I want to have some day. All of them are Christians. I know their families are the way they are because of their Christianity."

After ten months of Bible study and debate, Pete prayed to receive Christ. Why? Because several couples conducted their marriages and business in a manner that was different from the norm. And upon close examination Pete caught a glimpse of something divine. Their lives birthed a vision in Pete of what could be true of his own marriage some-day. They lived lives worth watching, and unbeknownst to them, Pete was watching.

The responsibility that once belonged to the nation of Israel has been placed upon your shoulders. You are here to be a light to your world. You are a city on a hill.

You are a beacon in this dark night.

The success God grants you is not for your sake alone. It is a means to a much greater end. A divine, eternal end. There is divine potential in all that you do. When the surrounding nations looked at the completed wall, they concluded the work had been done with the help of God. May the people in your world look at your life and draw the same conclusion.

VISIONEERING
PROJECT #15

1. What is the divine potential of your current vision(s)? What about your vision(s) has eternal consequence?

2. What can you do to enhance the kingdom potential of what you are doing? How can you be more intentional about being a light on a hill?

3. Have you lost your peace in the pursuit of your vision?

   Remember:
   - Peace generally follows perspective, so step back and regain some perspective.
   - Peace is a fruit of the Spirit, so submit to the Holy Spirit.

4. Are you sacrificing your character for the sake of accomplishing your vision?
   - Stop it. You are ruining your own celebration.
   - There is a direct correlation between your integrity and the kingdom potential of your vision.

5. Are you economizing relationally for the sake of your vision?
   - Apologize to those you have neglected.
   - Give someone permission to periodically ask you about your key relationships.

6. Begin praying: "Father, let my light shine before men in such a way that they may see my good works, and glorify my Father who is in heaven."

....

CHAPTER SIXTEEN

THE END
OF THE LINE

God always reveals himself in the midst of visions he has authored. When he does, attention generally shifts from *what* has been accomplished to *who* fueled the accomplishment. Herein is the best-kept secret regarding divinely sanctioned visions.

BUILDING BLOCK #17

THE END OF A GOD-ORDAINED VISION IS GOD.

If you are pursuing a vision God has birthed in your heart, there will be moments along the way when you will find yourself standing in awe of what he has done on your behalf. In those moments your attention will be drawn away from the work of your hands to the faithfulness of your heavenly Father.

Your visions are not only avenues God will use to do something through you. They are also avenues God will use to do something *in* you. For the natural response to his intervention is worship, surrender, and obedience.

When God shows up, everybody in the vicinity is affected. Believers, unbelievers, committed, uncommitted, it doesn't matter. The power of his presence in even small doses will leave its mark. This is why Paul could write with confidence that a day will come when "every knee will bow" and "every tongue will confess to God" (Romans 14:11). On the day of judgment his glory will be irresistible. No one will be able to stand.

In the meantime, God continues to make his presence and glory known in small, abbreviated ways. Every once in a while he shows up in our little, otherwise insignificant worlds and gives us a glimpse of his glory. And when he does, we are changed.

Remember the time Jesus asked Peter to take him fishing? Peter had been at it all night with nothing to show for it but tangled nets. The thought of rowing back out into the middle of the lake was just about more than he could bear. Besides, this time he had an audience. Jesus had drawn quite a crowd. And everybody knew you didn't fish with nets in the middle of the day. The water was too warm. The fish would be in the deeper, cooler parts of the lake. But Peter gave in to Jesus' request, and before he knew it, his net was so full of fish he had to call for assistance.

My favorite part of the story is Peter's response. One might expect something along the lines of, "Hey, look at all the fish! I won't have to work for a week." But Peter had just experienced the power of God firsthand. Luke describes his response this way: "When Simon Peter saw this, he fell at Jesus' knees and said, 'Go away from me, Lord; I am a sinful man!'" (Luke 5:8, NIV).

When God shows up, the focus shifts. Bulging nets are inconsequential when the God of heaven and earth makes his presence known. For that matter, so is the reconstruction of a wall that has lain in ruins for generations.

THE AWAKENING

Sanballat and his colleagues were not the only ones who recognized that God had intervened on behalf of Israel. The people of Israel recognized it as well. But it appears they were a little slow to catch on.

Once the wall was completed the workers returned to their homes in the surrounding towns and villages. They were ready for things to return to normal. The past couple of months had been a complete disruption of life as they had known it. Besides, there was next year's harvest to think about.

But as they attempted to return to business as usual, the significance of what had happened began to sink in. As it dawned on them that God had protected and blessed them during these fifty-two days of intense labor, they were overwhelmed with guilt and gratitude. Guilt because for years they had ignored God's Law. Gratitude because they knew that in spite of their disobedience, God had chosen to bless them. They were keenly aware that apart from God's intervention there would be no wall. Consequently, the people began to experience a deep sense of remorse for their years of spiritual apathy.

The wall was completed six days before the beginning of the new year. According to the law, this was the time appointed for the Jews to celebrate the Feast of Trumpets. But for most of the Jews in Israel at that time, the Feasts of Trumpets was simply an excuse to miss work. There was no religious significance attached to this holiday.

But on this particular New Year's Day, the conscience of the nation needed some attention. Spontaneously, with no goading from Nehemiah, the people left their homes in the surrounding towns and villages and began to gather on the square in Jerusalem. Apparently, no civic or religious celebration had been planned. This was an impromptu meeting of the people. God had touched down in their midst. And now it was time to give him the attention and devotion he deserved.

Eventually, it occurred to someone in the crowd that they needed to hear from God so they called for Ezra, the scribe, to bring out the Law and read it to them.

> And all the people gathered as one man at the square which was in front of the Water Gate, and they asked Ezra the scribe to bring the book of the law of Moses which the LORD had given to Israel. Then Ezra the priest brought the law before the assembly of men, women and all who could listen with understanding, on the first day of the seventh month. He read from it before the square which was in front of the Water Gate from early morning until midday, in the presence of men and women, those who could understand; and all the people were attentive to the book of the law. (Nehemiah 8:1–3)

For five or six hours they stood and listened as Ezra read from the law. Notice their response when he began reading.

> Ezra opened the book in the sight of all the people for he was standing above all the people; and when he opened it, all the

people stood up. Then Ezra blessed the Lord the great God. And all the people answered, "Amen, Amen!" while lifting up their hands; then they bowed low and worshiped the Lord with their faces to the ground. (vv. 5–6)

It was as if the nation woke up all at once to the reality of their spiritual condition. Like Adam and Eve, they realized they were naked. And with their realization came a pervasive sense of shame. Nehemiah says they wept as the Scriptures were being read (v. 9).

The most notable aspect of this scene is the absence of any mention of the wall. The reconstruction was clearly the catalyst for the people's renewed interest in God and his Law. But it is almost as if the wall had been forgotten. There's no mention of a celebration. Nobody suggests a party. You would assume there would at least be some sort of ceremony to commemorate the success of the project. But nobody seems the least bit interested in that sort of thing. Their attention had shifted from the vision of a rebuilt wall to the author of their vision.

This is Peter and his overflowing nets all over again. God touched down. When he intervenes, fish and brick are the last things anyone wants to talk about. They are of no consequence. On both occasions God captured the undivided attention of all those involved. This is God's way.

A FORGOTTEN FESTIVAL

After six hours of standing around and listening to someone read, you might imagine these folks would have had their fill. But on the following day, most of the men came back for another round.

As Ezra read through portions of Leviticus, they were astonished to discover that God had commanded the nation to celebrate another feast during this first month of the year. This unusual feast is referred to in Leviticus as the Feast of Tabernacles or Booths (Leviticus 23:34, 39).

This celebration was designed to remind the people of their deliverance from Egypt and of God's provision for the nation in the desert. God knew the people would eventually build permanent homes in Canaan. Once they were settled in, he knew they would forget how he cared and provided for them during their years as nomads.

The feast was to last seven days. During that time the people were to live in booths or huts made of tree boughs. These were dwellings similar to those their forefathers had used as they trekked through the desert.

Israel had not celebrated this feast in proper fashion since the days of Joshua, hundreds of years earlier. Apparently, it didn't seem important. Besides, it was terribly inconvenient to camp in your own front yard.

God had established this feast as a visual aid—a physical reminder—of his willingness to provide, protect, and intervene on behalf of those who followed him. By neglecting the reminder, they forgot his promise. Eventually, they forgot him as well.

But these were days of spiritual renewal. They got busy building booths. Why? Because God said to. That was enough. Like the nation of old, they had experienced his power firsthand. A simple command was all the reason they needed.

> So the people went out and brought them and made booths for themselves, each on his roof, and in their courts and in the courts of the house of God, and in the square at the Water Gate and in the square at the Gate of Ephraim. The entire assembly of those who had returned from the captivity made booths and lived in them. The sons of Israel had indeed not done so from the days of Joshua the son of Nun to that day. And there was great rejoicing. (Nehemiah 8:16–17)

When God intervenes, the attention shifts to him. Divine intervention, when it is recognized, results in authentic worship and unquestioned obedience. This is God's ultimate agenda for the visions he has given you. He is at the end of visions he has authored. Your visions are for his glory. He is the end of the line.

God wants to take you to the place he took the nation of Israel. A place where worship is sincere and spontaneous. A place where obedience is an overflow of a grateful heart. Vision is one of his primary tools for ushering us into that kind of experience.

All parents who have watched their sons and daughters bow and receive Jesus as Savior know what I am talking about. That is a moment all Christian parents envision for their children. Yet we live with the awareness that there is only so much we can do to bring our children to a point of decision. God must intervene in the heart of a child for that vision to become a reality.

As I listened to my oldest son Andrew ask Jesus to come into his heart, my thoughts were not centered on the things Sandra and I had done to guide him to this moment. On the contrary, I was filled with gratitude to the Father for intervening on Andrew's behalf. I worshiped as he prayed.

What I knew could be and should be was becoming a reality. But my role in the process was overshadowed by the work of grace God had so evidently done in the heart of my six-year-old son. My worship and submission in that moment was simply a response to his intervention in the life of my son. In that moment of encounter, I was brought to a place where I was worshiping God for God's sake.

It is to this "God for God's sake" place that the Father wants to take us. In those moments we worship not because we have been instructed to worship. We do so because it is the only thing that seems appropriate. In that place, faith knows no boundaries. In that place, we trust not because of *what* is promised, but because of the character of the One we are called upon to trust.

More important than the fulfillment of your vision is the fulfillment of God's vision for you. As his child, he envisions you as having matured in your thinking, faith, and conduct to the point where you could be considered conformed to the image of Christ. Someone whose character, perspective, and behavior reflects that of the Savior.

In his letter to the Christians in Ephesus, Paul casts a vision on God's behalf for all believers. He informs his audience that God's purpose in granting spiritual gifts to the church was for

> ...the building up of the body of Christ; until we all attain to the unity of the faith, and of the knowledge of the Son of God, to a mature man, to the measure of the stature which belongs to the fullness of Christ. (Ephesians 4:12b–13)

God's vision for you and me is maturity. Spiritual maturity is measured by how readily we respond to the person of God rather than the promises of God. It involves coming to the place where *who* is asking is more important than what we are being asked to do. Your vision is an avenue God will more than likely use to bring you to that place. And once there, if God says build a hut in your front yard and live in it for a week, you will start collecting branches, no questions asked.

CHICK-FIL-A

Truett Cathy, founder of the Chick-fil-A restaurant chain, is a man whose attitudes and lifestyle reflect gratitude for all God did during his pioneering years in the restaurant business.

In 1945 Truett and his brother Ben had a vision for building and operating a restaurant together. After pooling their savings, selling Truett's car, and finding favor with First National Bank of Atlanta, they were able to pull together $10,600.

In his book, *It's Easier to Succeed Than to Fail,* Truett describes the obstacles they faced in those post–World War II years when building materials were scarce. The larger contractors were first in line for whatever was available. Consequently, Truett and his brother were forced to buy used building materials. Nails were so hard to find they had to straighten old ones and reuse them.

As their building neared completion, they faced a second obstacle. They couldn't buy enough food for their grill. Again, the post–World War II economy made meat hard to come by. Larger, more established restaurants had found ways around the restrictions and government controls. But a couple of guys starting from scratch had no leverage in the tightly controlled food business.

In spite of these setbacks, Truett and Ben opened the Dwarf Grill on schedule in May of 1946. As Truett walked around the outside of the building on opening day, he was overwhelmed with God's providential care and intervention. He recognized that apart from God's help, the Dwarf Grill (which two years later was renamed the Dwarf House) would never have been more than a good idea.

> I walked around the outside alone, my heart filled with a happiness that I couldn't express. I thanked God for helping us and for giving us the courage to start and to keep going.[1]

ars that followed, Truett's vision grew. As he says, "Ideas
od—but they won't keep. They have to be acted on."[2] In
ted on his new idea. He built and dedicated his first Chick-
he years that followed, Truett and his team went on to
...op Chick-fil-A into an international restaurant chain with annual
revenues approaching one billion dollars.

Those close to Truett will attest to the fact that he has never forgotten
God's faithfulness to him in the early days. He continues to maintain a
sense of wonder at God's intervention on his behalf. This sense of gratitude is reflected in their corporate purpose statement:

> To glorify God by being a faithful steward of all that is entrusted
> to us. To have a positive influence on all who come in contact
> with Chick-fil-A.[3]

Interestingly, this statement was crafted when the company faced its
first annual decrease in sales. Almost overnight Chick-fil-A faced the kind
of economic uncertainty that drives the average corporation to abandon
its core values for the sake of what's practical and profitable. Humanly
speaking, Truett had every reason to do just that.

> I couldn't ignore the dismal sales figures—Our actual sales had
> fallen off, even though we had more restaurants. I looked at the
> problem facing us. Five malls had been scheduled to open but
> were delayed by the developers for months. We had geared our
> whole program toward the malls' target dates. That meant we had
> to pay Operators who had no restaurants....
>
> On top of that, the American economy went crazy with incredi-
> ble inflation. Interest rates shot up as high as 23 percent, which is
> what we had to pay for a period of time. I felt squeezed. I was afraid
> of debt, yet I had signed a lease on some properties and couldn't walk
> away from them. No matter what I looked at or where I turned, the
> situation got worse. I couldn't understand what was happening.[4]

In the midst of these troubled times, Truett and his staff made the decision to embrace and publicize their first corporate purpose statement. They

knew that coming out so boldly about their faith when the future of the company was in jeopardy could have been met with resistance and even ridicule from people inside the organization. But Truett and his family had experienced God's intervention on too many occasions to abandon their vision. So they developed a campaign to ensure that every Chick-fil-A Operator and staff person had a copy of their purpose statement.

Six months later the company's sales had increased 40 percent over the previous year. God honored Truett's faithfulness. Like the early days at the Dwarf House, Truett was overwhelmed with God's intervention on his behalf.

> Often we see God working only much later when we reflect on the event. And if we're not careful, we accept it all as something we have done. We forget about God's gracious involvement. I might have done so too, except for the timing of events. We made our public commitment to our Operators at a low financial point. That statement could have brought us ridicule and bad responses from our people, but we had to take our stand. And then, everything else began to fit together.[5]

Truett never forgot "God's gracious involvement." Consequently, he and his leadership team have remained faithful to their vision and purpose when circumstances made other options more appealing. It is unusual to find a company with the revenue and market share of a Chik-fil-A that is willing to publicly give credit where credit is due. Their decision to do so stems from their recognition of God's faithfulness in the early days.

THE GLORY DILEMMA

The end of a God-inspired vision is God. It just keeps coming back to him. But this notion is not without its problems or critics.

In the past, the thought of God claiming all the credit for himself made me uncomfortable. How could something that smacks of self-centeredness be an attribute of a perfect God? How is it I am instructed to be selfless, and yet the One who is doing the instructing feels free to claim all the credit?

The thought of God's ultimate agenda being his own self-aggrandizement is almost nauseating. After all, self-aggrandizement is the least desirable of all human characteristics. I can stomach almost anything easier than unabashed conceit. Yet, throughout the Scriptures God makes no bones about the fact that everything, including pain, is ultimately for his glory.

In his brilliant little book *Hot Tub Religion*, J. I. Packer addresses the dilemma of God's claim to glory.

> That God aims always to glorify himself is an assertion we at first find hard to believe. Our immediate reaction is an uncomfortable feeling that such an idea is unworthy of God, that self-concern of any sort is incompatible with moral perfection, and in particular with God's nature as love...
>
> If it is right for man to have the glory of God as His goal, can it be wrong for God to have the same goal? For if man can have no higher purpose than God's glory, how can God? If it is wrong for man to seek a lesser end than this, it would be wrong for God, too. The reason it cannot be right for man to live for himself, as if he were God, is because he is not God. However, it cannot be wrong for God to seek His own glory simply because He is God.[6]

The notion of a credit-taking God is uncomfortable. But as Packer points out, it is the only logical option. And it is the only safe option. When we lose sight of God's ultimate purpose, his glory, we inevitably begin trying to claim what is rightfully his for ourselves. Once we cross that line there is a sense in which it becomes risky for God to intervene on our behalf. To do so is to set us up for further offense.

Our innate desire for approval, credit, attention, and glory is the thing that causes many well-meaning visionaries to hijack God's vision for their own selfish ends. We have all seen it. From nationally known leaders to men and women in our communities.

The pattern is pretty much the same. God gives a man or woman a glimpse of what could be and should be. They cast a compelling vision. People rally to the cause. Things begin falling into place. Soon they are enjoying the notoriety and rewards that come with success. And then something snaps.

The leader develops spiritual amnesia. He begins to take the blessing of God for granted. Little by little he begins to edge toward the spotlight. In time he comes to believe he is indispensable to the vision.

This is generally followed by an erosion of character. Quite often men and women who lose sight of God's involvement in their journey toward the completion of a vision begin to play god themselves.

But it doesn't have to be that way.

FINISHING WELL

Our generation has the privilege of watching one of God's choice servants finish well. For over fifty years, Dr. Billy Graham has remained faithful to the vision God gave him. His faithfulness has resulted in opportunities to personally preach to over two hundred million people. Millions more have been impacted by his ministry through radio and television. Dr. Graham's perspective on his achievements is refreshing.

> I have often said that the first thing I am going to do when I get to Heaven is to ask, "Why me, Lord? Why did You choose a farmboy from North Carolina to reach so many people, to have such a wonderful team of associates, and to have a part in what You were doing in the latter half of the twentieth century?"
>
> As I look back over the years, however, I know that my deepest feeling is one of overwhelming gratitude. I cannot take credit for whatever God has chosen to accomplish through us and our ministry; only God deserves the glory, and we can never thank Him enough for the great things He has done.[7]

The end of a God-ordained vision is God. When he intervenes, you, too, will find yourself asking, "Why me?"

VISIONEERING
PROJECT #16

The sense of awe that follows an encounter with God is only as far-reaching as our memory. Personal experience attests to the fact that it is easy to forget God's past faithfulness. When his faithfulness and our faith intersect, we walk away confident we will never be the same, and we will never doubt him again. But time and circumstances have a way of blurring the past. New challenges birth fresh doubts.

For this reason you need a written record, a detailed account of the times when God came through on your behalf. You need to journal.

Chuck Swindoll describes a journal as "an intimate record of the journey that the Lord and I are travelling together."[8] A journal is the story of your life with God. It is a way of documenting the lessons God has taught you as well as the experiences he has brought you through.

> Furthermore, our journal entries give us rallying points...historical, dated markers that specify God's dealings deep within our souls as well as His workings on our behalf. We need to preserve a written record of such divine interventions.[9]

The reason we don't record these experiences is because we can't imagine we could ever forget them. But we do, especially the details.

Worse than forgetting, we have a tendency to reinterpret events in our past. When God seems distant, it is easy to think back on events to which we had attached special spiritual significance and question whether or not it was really God we experienced. But a detailed written account is compelling. It is much easier to argue with our memory than words on a page.

Divine intervention, when it is *recognized*, results in authentic worship and unquestioned obedience. Divine intervention, when it is *remembered*, can have the same results. Journal and remember.

CHAPTER SEVENTEEN

MAINTAINING
YOUR COURSE

*The final test of a leader is that he leaves behind in others
the conviction and will to carry on.*
WALTER LIPPMAN

When I was a kid, our family owned an eighteen-foot travel trailer. Every summer the four of us loaded up and headed to the beach. Our favorite place to camp was on the stretch of beach outside Naples, Florida. Back in the mid-sixties there was nothing there but sand. No houses. No condominiums. And no sanctioned campsite. We would simply drive out on the beach along the tree line until we found a spot that suited us. Often we would go for days without seeing another living soul.

The water along that portion of the Florida coast is beautiful, but the undertow can be fierce. If you aren't paying attention, you will find yourself hundreds of feet down the beach from where you put in. It is more frightening than dangerous. As a kid, I can still remember looking back at the shore and wondering why Mom and Dad had moved the campsite.

As a precautionary measure Dad would pile up a dozen or so coconuts about forty yards down the beach from the trailer. He instructed us to stay between the trailer and the coconuts. If the tide took us past coconuts, we were to get out of the water and walk back up the beach until we were even with the trailer before getting back in.

Every once in a while we would glance back toward the shore to make sure we were still in bounds. If so, we went right ahead with whatever we were doing. If not, we waded back to shore and walked back up the beach.

In your pursuit of the various visions God has placed before you, you will be prone to drift. In one sense we are all like children playing in an undertow. We live, work, and play in an undertow. There is a current that is constantly pulling us toward compromise, self-sufficiency, and expediency. Without a clear point of reference it is easy to rationalize and justify just about anything. This is especially true when compromise appears to be a necessary means toward the completion of your vision.

In order to compensate for the constant tug toward moral and spiritual compromise, you must develop a clear standard of beliefs and behaviors to refer to along the way. Your core beliefs and behaviors function like that stack of coconuts. They serve as moral and ethical guardrails as you pursue your visions to completion.

RAISING A STANDARD

Last time we looked in on our Jewish friends they were camping in their yards. As the Feast of Booths was coming to a close, it occurred to several community leaders that it was time to make some practical changes in the way the community was being run. They recognized that the momentum of their spiritual breakthrough was not enough to keep them from slipping right back into the spiritual lethargy they had just come out of. They needed some coconuts on the beach.

These leaders understood that their problems stemmed from their ancestors' decision to abandon God's Law. They were wise enough to acknowledge that disobedience, not military weakness, was the ultimate reason their borders had been overrun. The leaders of the community knew that if God allowed the wall to be torn down once, he was not beyond allowing it to be torn down a second time.

So they developed a written covenant between themselves and God. In the covenant they pledged their devotion to the Lord God and his Law (9:38). The leaders signed it and everybody took an oath swearing to uphold their end of the deal (10:28–39). This was their stack of coconuts.

The document would serve as a clear, objective standard against which their behavior and beliefs could be measured.

The covenant dealt with three specific areas that had been at the root of Israel's moral and spiritual decay in the past: their relationship with foreigners, their respect for the Sabbath, and their care of the temple.

To follow through with their pledge, the people were forced to take some radical steps relationally and financially. Relationally, they were not allowed to marry or in some cases even associate with foreigners. This was particularly awkward for those who already had foreign wives.

Financially, they made several costly concessions. To begin with, they agreed to close down their businesses on the Sabbath. Their biggest financial concession had to do with their agricultural practices. The people decided to honor God's command in Exodus regarding a Sabbath rest for the land (Exodus 23:10–11). This law forbade farmers from planting crops every seven years. The idea behind this law was to force the people to trust God to sustain them by his hand rather than through their labor. As you might imagine, this was not a law anybody was eager to abide by.

If you take the time to read through the entire account, it is apparent the people living in Jerusalem had a renewed vision for their nation. They were beginning to see Israel as it could be and should be. Consequently, they were determined to maintain the momentum developed during the reconstruction process.

They were beginning to identify with the Israel of old, the nation they had grown up hearing about. The Israel whose devotion to God served as an open invitation for divine intervention; the nation known for its dependence upon and allegiance to the Lord God.

Nehemiah and his governing council were wise enough to recognize that time has a way of eroding the initial passion associated with a spiritual breakthrough. Developing the covenant was their way of safeguarding the vision. It was their way of keeping the dream alive. If they would steer clear of foreign influence, trust God to provide economically as well as agriculturally, and reestablish the temple as the centerpiece of the community, they would be a blessable people. With these things in place they might live to see the day when Israel would once again fulfill the role God had established for her.

Israel's social and religious reorganization points to an axiom that is absolutely critical to the success of any vision. Namely, visionaries must establish and adhere to a set of core behaviors and beliefs.

BUILDING BLOCK #18

MAINTAINING A VISION REQUIRES ADHERENCE TO A SET OF CORE BELIEFS AND BEHAVIORS.

To keep a vision moving in the right direction, those involved must embrace a mutually agreed-upon code of conduct. In the world of business these tenets are usually referred to as values. Regardless of the terminology one chooses, it has been established through observation and experience that behavioral boundaries must be maintained to protect the integrity of a vision.

In his best-selling book, *Built To Last,* Jim Collins presents the results of a six-year quest to identify and research the development of what he terms "visionary companies." Marriott, 3M, Boeing, Merck, Sony, and Walt Disney are just a few of the companies that show up on his list.

> Visionary companies are premier institutions—crown jewels—in their industries, widely admired by their peers and having a track record of making a significant impact on the world around them.[1]

The question Jim's research sought to answer was, what makes a visionary company a visionary company? What is it about these companies that enabled them to remain at the top of their industry for so many years?

He found several characteristics, common denominators, shared by each of the visionary companies. One of those characteristics is an uncompromising commitment to a set of core values. He defines these values as the "organization's essential and enduring tenets—a small set of general guiding principles."[2] In visionary companies it is understood that these principles are never to be compromised, even for the sake of financial gain.

Collins includes a quote from Tom Watson Jr., a former IBM chief executive, that underscores the importance of a guiding set of principles to an organization's vision.

I believe that any organization, in order to survive and achieve success, must have a sound set of beliefs on which it premises all its policies and actions. Next, I believe that the most important single factor in the corporate success is faithful adherence to those beliefs....Beliefs must always come before policies, practices, and goals. The latter must always be altered if they are seen to violate fundamental beliefs.[3]

That sounds like something I would say to my congregation. "Beliefs must always come before policies, practices, and goals." In order to maintain your vision you must adopt a set of what Tom Watson terms "beliefs." These beliefs establish the guidelines within which you and your team will operate while pursuing your vision.

Jim Collins and Tom Watson have stumbled upon a principle that has been in place since God put Adam and Eve in the Garden of Eden. It is core beliefs and the behaviors that follow that have held the church together for two thousand years. This cause and effect dynamic that Collins and Watson have observed functioning in the marketplace is a part of every enduring relationship and organization.

Jesus stated it this way: "Any kingdom divided against itself is laid waste; and any city or house divided against itself will not stand" (Matthew 12:25).

The terms *organization, family,* or *ministry* could be substituted for *kingdom.* None of those institutions can survive division. In chapter 12 we discussed the issue of alignment. There we made the point that visions thrive in an environment of unity. They die in an environment racked with division. A vision cannot stand up under the pressure of prolonged periods of disunity among team members.

Unity can only be maintained where there is agreement about and adherence to a set of core beliefs and behaviors. These beliefs and behaviors establish expectations among team members. When they are violated or abandoned, the foundations of the organization or family are shaken. No one knows what to expect anymore. Trust has been violated. The vision suffers.

THE BLESSABILITY FACTOR

But unity is not the only thing at stake. As Nehemiah and the nation of Israel discovered, there is another important dynamic that leaders cannot afford to overlook. Adhering to a predetermined set of beliefs and behaviors makes your visions blessable. There are certain things God chooses to bless. Obedience, for example. And there are things he refuses to bless. Disobedience, for one.

Israel's problem was that their disobedience put them outside the sphere of blessability. Loved, yes. Blessable, no. Furthermore, their disobedience caused them to lose sight of the vision God had established for them.

As a visionary, it is imperative that you remain blessable. Translated, you must adhere to and lead your team to adhere to a set of beliefs and behaviors that reflect the tenets of Scripture. Your business or ministry may want to develop specific applications of these tenets that set you apart from competitors or similar organizations. But at a bare minimum, you must embrace the standards set forth in the Scripture. Reflect on the implications of the following verse as it relates to your various visions.

For the eyes of the LORD move to and fro throughout the earth that He may strongly support those whose heart is completely His. (2 Chronicles 16:9a)

How important is it to you that the Lord strongly support what you are doing? If it is important, then your heart must be completely his. When we embrace what is important to him, we bring our heart into alignment with his. When your heart is completely his, you are blessable.

Your core beliefs and behaviors can be divided into two categories: general and specific. *General* beliefs and behaviors are those every believer should adhere to. Things like honesty, purity, and integrity should be embraced regardless of the nature of our vision. These and similar qualities are critical to the success of any God-ordained vision. After all, God doesn't bless dishonesty and impurity.

Failure to adhere to general standards of honesty and purity have caused countless visions to come apart at the seams. We have all seen visions damaged by mishandled finances and unresolved relational conflicts. These two things, along with moral failure, account for just about every failed vision I know of.

In each case, someone (or someones) wandered outside the boundaries of blessable conduct. They forgot what really mattered. In Tom Watson's words, they allowed practices to come before beliefs. When you are consumed by a vision, it is easy to sacrifice ethics for the sake of progress. But when you do, you step outside the realm of what God will bless.

Specific beliefs and behaviors are specific to your particular vision. Truett Cathy believes all Chik-fil-A stores should remain closed on Sunday. That is a belief specific to Chik-fil-A.

Years ago Billy Graham elected not to receive personal speaking honorariums. All honorarium checks are to be written to the Billy Graham Association. He asked his associates to do the same. This is a standard they believe is important for maintaining the financial integrity and thus the vision of the ministry.

Some time ago I asked our church staff not to meet alone off campus with members of the opposite sex. We set this standard to protect the moral integrity of our vision. We believe it is appropriate for our particular setting. It may not be applicable to yours.

MAKING YOUR LIST

At the end of this chapter you will be given an opportunity to develop a list of beliefs and behaviors for each of your visions. One way to determine these is to ask the following two questions of each arena where you believe strongly that something could be and should be. They can be asked as a team (we, our) or as an individual (I, my).

1. What could we do that, if done consistently, would provide the greatest potential for our success?
2. What could we do that would guarantee we never see our vision materialize?

Thinking through these two questions will help you narrow the scope of what's absolutely critical to the success of your vision.

Sandra and I have a specific vision for our family. We envision a day when we will have a mutually enjoyable adult relationship with our children. Practically speaking, we want our children to enjoy spending time with us once they are grown and gone. That's our vision as parents.

As we discussed how to get there, we determined that if we could teach our children to show respect for those they liked and disliked, it would prepare them for the kind of relationship we envision in the future. So we adopted respect as one of our core family behaviors. In fact, "Treat Momma with respect" is the number one rule around our house.

Visions, by nature, are exciting in their initial stages. But it takes more than excitement and determination to successfully complete what God has birthed in your heart to do. What could be and should be will not be apart from clear moral and behavioral guidelines. Maintaining your vision requires uncompromising commitment to a set of core beliefs and behaviors. Assembling these is no easy task. It is not an afternoon's work. Consequently, few people take the time to work through the process.

By investing the hours required to think through and record your core beliefs and behaviors, you sensitize yourself to the boundaries that safeguard your vision. Equally as important, you sensitize team members. What is "assumed conduct" by you is in all likelihood not "assumed conduct" by everyone on your team. And on those occasions when you need to call the team to account, there must be a predetermined standard.

In most cases, developing your lists will be a matter of unearthing what you already expect of yourself and those laboring with you. Scripting your beliefs and behaviors brings clarity. Sharing them with members of your team or family helps avoid the otherwise inevitable collision of conflicting expectations.

It is easy to get buried in the details of any vision. You need an unchanging standard by which to check yourself along the way. From time to time you need to glance toward the shore. Only then will you know that you are still operating in blessable territory.

VISIONEERING
PROJECT #17
Answer the following questions for each vision you are pursuing.

1. What could I do that, if done consistently, would provide the greatest potential for the vision's success?

2. What could I do that would guarantee I never see my vision materialize?

List the beliefs and behaviors that you believe are critical to the success of your vision. Think in terms of general versus specific. Specific values or beliefs are those that pertain to your particular vision.

1. Family

       General:

       Specific:

2. Ministry

       General:

       Specific:

3. Career

       General:

       Specific:

....

CHAPTER EIGHTEEN

THE LEADER'S MANDATE

STAY FULLY ENGAGED AND ACT BOLDLY

*Leaders must challenge the process because systems will unconsciously
conspire to maintain the status quo and prevent change.*
THE LEADERSHIP CHALLENGE

Leading people is difficult. Whether you are a single mom leading your teenage son or a CEO leading a corporation, leadership is difficult. People don't act right. They keep coming up with impractical ideas. And they have a hard time seeing past their own most pressing need.

There is no autopilot in the enterprise of visioneering. Sustaining a vision's forward motion requires the visionary's constant attention. Preserving the integrity of a vision demands that the navigator be fully engaged.

Due to no fault of his own, this was the one principle Nehemiah violated.

AN UNTIMELY RECALL

When Artaxerxes gave Nehemiah permission to leave his service to rebuild the wall, he set a time limit (Nehemiah 2:6). Apparently, Nehemiah was considered a valuable asset by the king. Artaxerxes had no intention of permanently releasing Nehemiah from his royal duties.

We don't know how long the king intended for Nehemiah to be gone.

We do know he stayed in Jerusalem twelve years before finally returning to Susa. When he said farewell to the inhabitants of Jerusalem, all was well. The Law was being read aloud in the square on a regular basis. There was an eagerness among the people to sustain a spirit of submission and dependence upon the Lord God. The temple was reemerging as a centerpiece of the society. Everything was in order. Nehemiah must have felt good about leaving.

The Bible doesn't tell us how long he was with Artaxerxes in Susa. But eventually he asked the king for permission to return to Jerusalem (13:6). Once again the king was gracious and allowed Nehemiah to leave his service.

We can only imagine what Nehemiah must have felt as he made his way back toward Jerusalem. No doubt he reflected on his first journey. On his initial pilgrimage he had no idea what to expect when he arrived. This time he expected to find things much the way he left them.

But he was in for a surprise. It seems he underestimated the significance of his presence in the city. He was a catalyst for sustained change. With him out of the picture, the spiritual and social climate deteriorated. By the time he got back, conditions were disconcertingly similar to what they'd been the first time he'd ridden into the city.

BUILDING BLOCK #19

VISIONS REQUIRE CONSTANT ATTENTION.

To begin with, the men who were to maintain the temple had not been given their allotment of food (13:10). They had no choice but to go home and provide for themselves. With the temple in disarray, respect for the Sabbath began to lapse as well. When Nehemiah arrived, the Sabbath had become just another workday (v. 16).

To top it all off, the men of Judah were marrying foreign women again (v. 23). Their children were being taught the traditions and customs of their immigrant mothers. In some cases, these kids didn't even know how to speak Hebrew (v. 24).

There was one thing different about the city this second time around. The debris was missing. The debris that for over one hundred years had served as a reminder of what happens when God's people abandon him. But now the reminder was gone. In its place stood the wall. The wall that was once nothing more than an idea, a vision. The wall that never would have been built apart from God's intervention. It served as a visual reminder of God's remarkable grace and power. Yet there in its shadow the people forgot.

When Nehemiah saw what was going on, he was ticked. And rightly so. He had risked his life by asking the king for permission to come to Jerusalem in the first place. He'd poured everything he had into the construction project. His life had been threatened repeatedly while the work was being done. And once the operation was complete, he had gone to great lengths to right the social and spiritual wrongs that had led to the destruction of the city in the first place. In short, Nehemiah had invested heavily in the city and people of Jerusalem. He could not stand by while the whole thing spiraled back into chaos.

So Nehemiah did what every competent visionary does when a vision veers off course. He exercised bold leadership. When he found out the Levites had been forced to abandon their posts at the temple because they had not been taken care of properly, he "rebuked" the officials of the city (v. 11). Then he called the Levites back in from their fields and reassigned them.

He was equally proactive when it came to dealing with the abuse of the Sabbath. This was not a time for mercy. Too much was at stake. What could be and should be was never going to be unless extreme measures were taken.

> Then I reprimanded the nobles of Judah and said to them, "What is this evil thing you are doing, by profaning the sabbath day? Did not your fathers do the same, so that our God brought on us and on this city all this trouble? Yet you are adding to the wrath on Israel by profaning the sabbath." (vv. 17–18)

When merchants from surrounding areas camped outside the gates in an effort to skirt the recently instituted Sabbath prohibitions, Nehemiah threatened them with bodily harm. His threat was so menacing they never came on the Sabbath again (v. 21).

But none of this compares to the action Nehemiah took against those who had married foreign women. Nehemiah knew this sin posed the greatest threat to the nation. Israel's history bore witness to the fact that when foreigners were introduced into the social fabric of the nation, it was only a matter of time before their religion filtered in as well. Nehemiah's response?

> So I contended with them and cursed them and struck some of them and pulled out their hair, and made them swear by God, "You shall not give your daughters to their sons, nor take of their daughters for your sons or for yourselves. Did not Solomon king of Israel sin regarding these things? Yet among the many nations there was no king like him, and he was loved by his God, and God made him king over all Israel; nevertheless the foreign women caused even him to sin. Do we then hear about you that you have committed all this great evil by acting unfaithfully against our God by marrying foreign women?" (vv. 25–27)

That's bold.

Nehemiah drew a line in the sand. When someone takes a moral stand in an atmosphere of declining standards, it will appear extreme to the one whose behavior is being called to account. For a parent who sees his teenager's chat time interfering with study time, reducing phone privileges is a no-brainer. But the average thirteen-year-old girl will view such action as extreme.

A similar dynamic occurs anytime a man or woman with a vision acts boldly in an effort to salvage the dream. A call for extensive change will always seem extreme to those who are comfortable with the status quo. What is considered conventional wisdom to the visionary is often viewed as radical to the people in the trenches. That's to be expected. Visionaries see things differently.

When the time comes for you to start calling down curses and pulling out hair, here are two things to keep in mind.

1. BOLD LEADERSHIP MUST BE VISION BASED.

Major changes must be anchored to a vision. The severity of the change must be matched by a clarity of connection to the vision. If it is not, the decision will easily be interpreted as a quest for power or control. Leaders who fail to follow this principle are often accused of making decisions for personal gain.

Nehemiah was quick to tie his harsh reaction directly to the vision they had been pursuing all along. Notice his response to the people's violation of the Sabbath rest.

> Then I reprimanded the nobles of Judah and said to them, "What is this evil thing you are doing, by profaning the sabbath day? Did not your fathers do the same, *so that our God brought on us and on this city all this trouble?* Yet you are adding to the wrath on Israel by profaning the sabbath." (vv. 17–18, emphasis mine)

The trouble he refers to is the destruction of the wall. Allow me to paraphrase. "Wake up, folks! Neglecting the Sabbath was a big part of the reason the wall was torn down in the first place. If you keep this up, God is liable to send another wave of destruction, and all we have done will have been for naught. So knock it off!"

This wasn't action for action's sake. It wasn't change for change's sake. Nehemiah's decision was not born from personal ambition or preference. Violating the Sabbath threatened the vision. Something had to be done. To deliver on your vision, you must be willing to make bold—and often unpopular—decisions for the sake of what could and should be.

In the course of teaching my boys American history I ran across the following event from the life of Abraham Lincoln.

On December 20, 1860, South Carolina declared its independence from the Union. The state called on custodians of all federally-owned property to surrender their holdings to the newly elected state convention.[1] Major Robert Anderson, commander of the Federal forces at Fort Sumpter sent word to Washington asking for instructions. In the meantime, Confederate troops under the command of General F. W. Pickens trained their guns on the fort.

With only three months remaining in his term, President Buchanan declined to take decisive action. During those weeks of indecision, the situation in South Carolina continued to deteriorate.

When Abraham Lincoln finally took office in March of 1861, the stage was set for the first battle of the Civil War. He had two choices. He could pull Federal troops out of South Carolina, thereby recognizing the state's sovereignty. Or he could refuse to surrender the fort, knowing good and well that such a decision would force the hand of the rebel state. The result would no doubt be war.

His cabinet, fully aware of the consequences of either decision, suggested a third alternative. In true-to-form political fashion, they advised him to do nothing.

Immediately following his inauguration, President Lincoln began receiving pressure to liberate the slaves, to use his presidential power to decree the emancipation of slaves in both northern and southern states. As much as he hated slavery, ending this barbarous practice was not his ultimate agenda. His vision was not a slave-free nation. His vision was a unified nation. In a letter to one of his critics he wrote:

> My paramount object is to save the Union and it is not either to save or to destroy slavery. If I could save the Union without freeing any slaves, I would do it; and if I could save it by freeing all the slaves I would do it; and if I could save it by freeing some slaves and leaving others alone I would do that.[2]

Lincoln was gripped by a lucid image of what could and should be. A united, United States. Secession, in his mind, was worse than slavery. He was determined to do all in his power to keep the Union intact. So President Lincoln did what all good leaders do when gripped by a vision, he acted boldly.

Lincoln sent a letter to General Pickens. He informed Pickens that a ship full of provisions had been dispatched to Fort Sumpter for the purpose of resupplying the dwindling food stores. The message was clear. Lincoln would uphold the Union at any cost. Pickens responded by firing on the fort. So began the Civil War.

Could the battle have been avoided? Sure. But it would have required Lincoln to abandon his vision of a unified nation. Instead, he acted boldly. But it was not boldness for boldness' sake. His decision was grounded in his commitment to what could and should be true for his beloved nation.

As a leader, it is essential that your decisions be anchored to your vision. But there is a second thing to keep in mind when circumstances merit a bold response.

2. BOLD ACTION MUST BE CARRIED OUT AGAINST A BACKDROP OF CLEARLY DEFINED BELIEFS AND BEHAVIORS.

Your core beliefs and behaviors serve as the standard against which the actions and decisions of those partnering with you are to be measured. When the time comes for bold action, you will more than likely be calling people back to what you understand to be the core beliefs and behaviors associated with your vision. If these aren't clear to begin with, there will be no identifiable context for your actions.

Your predefined beliefs and behaviors determine the expectations for those you are working alongside. This is true for your family, business, ministry, or any other type of organization you are involved with. If these are not clear, you will not have the leverage needed to bring about reform.

When Nehemiah called for reform in Jerusalem, he wasn't introducing anything new. These weren't recent ideas Nehemiah was espousing. He was calling them back to a previously agreed-upon list of beliefs and behaviors.

Nehemiah had the advantage of a historical precedence. He knew from Israel's experience what the consequences were for abandoning the temple, the Sabbath, and God's restrictions on marriage. He was quick to incorporate all of this into his call for reform.

> Did not Solomon king of Israel sin regarding these things? Yet among the many nations there was no king like him, and he was loved by his God, and God made him king over all Israel; nevertheless the foreign women caused even him to sin. Do we then hear about you that you have committed all this great evil by acting unfaithfully against our God by marrying foreign women? (vv. 26–27)

A call for change without the benefit of clearly defined core beliefs and behaviors is like conducting a job performance evaluation on an employee who has never received a job description. The employee walks away with a semiclear understanding of what failing at his or her job looks like. But no real understanding of what it means to succeed.

It is not enough to communicate, "Things need to change around here." That's akin to kicking over an ant bed. To get things back on course, the course must be exceedingly clear.

MAINTAINING A VISION REQUIRES BOLD LEADERSHIP.

One might get the idea that this principle flies in the face of grace, sensitivity, love, and other New Testament values. After all, we teach our children not to curse, hit, or pull people's hair, yet here's this man of God doing all three.

But this principle is not outside the boundaries of Christian conduct and character. In fact, Jesus Himself modeled this type of leadership in one of His more famous encounters.

> And Jesus entered the temple and drove out all those who were buying and selling in the temple, and overturned the tables of the money changers and the seats of those who were selling doves. (Matthew 21:12)

I think that falls in the category of bold, don't you? And notice what Jesus said to justify this peculiar behavior.

> And He said to them, "It is written, 'MY HOUSE SHALL BE CALLED A HOUSE OF PRAYER'; but you are making it a ROBBERS' DEN." (v. 13)

He anchors his actions to the Father's vision for the temple and a belief as old as the prophet Isaiah (cf. Isaiah 56:7).

Jesus knew what every visionary eventually discovers: Being nice doesn't always get the job done. And waiting around for people to catch on by themselves can be devastating to a vision.

Eventually there are trends that must be reversed, wrongs that must be righted, issues that must be resolved, and conduct that can't be tolerated. When problems surface, the leader must rise to the occasion and take decisive action.

YOUR CALL

You will have opportunities to step up to the plate and call for change. If you are the leader in your home, don't shirk your responsibility to call for reform when things begin to slip. You know best what could and should be in the family God has blessed you with. Don't settle for anything less than that. Yes, it will be awkward. No, not everybody will understand. So what? Think about what's at stake. Lead boldly.

If God has given you a vision for a ministry or a business enterprise of some kind, don't be content to let things drift in a direction other than the one God birthed in your heart in those early days. Don't be afraid to hold people accountable to previously agreed-upon standards. If you have never formalized your beliefs and behaviors, begin immediately. They provide the leverage to bring about change when things are sliding in the wrong direction.

Don't tolerate those things that have the potential to derail your vision. Deal with them. If you don't, your tendency will be to begin distancing yourself from the problem people and the unaligned environments. Things will only get worse. After all, what is unmanaged generally becomes unmanageable.

Visions demand constant attention. Stay fully engaged.

Visioneering calls for bold leadership. Develop a healthy intolerance for those things that have the potential to impede your progress toward what could be and should be—those things God has put in your heart to do.

VISIONEERING
PROJECT #18

1. What is going on now in your family, business, ministry or other organization that if left alone has the potential to derail your vision?

  • Family

  • Career

  • Ministry

  • Other

2. What action needs to be taken to correct this?

3. Is it time for action?

4. What do you have to lose by acting?

5. What do you have to lose by doing nothing?

6. If you aren't sure what to do, sit down with someone who is further down the road and get his or her input.

CONCLUSION

E verybody ends up somewhere in life. Nehemiah ended up somewhere on purpose. What he believed could be and should be became a reality. The wall was rebuilt. The people responded to his call for social and spiritual reform. The temple was operative. And the Sabbath was revered as God intended.

When his vision had been completed, Nehemiah ended his message this way: "Remember me with favor, O my God" (13:31b, NIV). We are reminded once again of Nehemiah's sense of destiny. He never lost sight of the divine nature and significance of his work.

MORE THAN IMAGINATION

Like Nehemiah, you have a destiny to fulfill. God has placed before you opportunities and responsibilities that are brimming with divine significance. He has given you gifts, talents, and relationships that are waiting to be exploited on behalf of his kingdom. You have a multifaceted mental picture of a preferred future. You have vision.

But as Nehemiah's story illustrates, it takes more than imagination and passion to make what could and should be a reality. A vision requires more than a singular encounter with God. For even those experiences where he clearly births an idea in your heart will not provide you with the tools nor the momentum necessary to see it through to completion. Hopefully, the previous eighteen chapters of this book have made that abundantly clear.

Visioneering requires patience, investigation, and planning. Visioneering requires faith in God's ability to work behind the scenes. Confidence that he will orchestrate what he has originated.

Visioneering will call for risk-taking and sacrifice. More than likely you will need to cast your vision to others. In those moments of public disclosure you will discover how committed you are to what you believe could and should be.

Things won't always work out the way you expect them to. Be careful not to confuse your plans with God's vision. Remember, plans are often revised. Don't be afraid to alter your strategy as circumstances around you change.

Like Nehemiah, you will have detractors. Some will find your visions threatening. Change can be unsettling. Respond to criticism with prayer. Prayer will help you stay focused on the source of your vision.

From time to time you will be tempted to compromise your character for the sake of expediency. Resist. Maintain your moral authority. Your moral authority is what makes you a leader worth following. Abandon the vision before you abandon your moral authority. Protect your moral authority and the moral authority of your team by developing a set of core beliefs and behaviors. Live and work within those boundaries even when doing so impedes your progress. In this way you remain blessable.

There will be seasons when you feel like you are making little if any progress. In those times it will be easy to get distracted. This is when you must join with Nehemiah in declaring, "I am doing a great work and I cannot come down." Whether your visions are family, ministry, or business oriented, they require constant attention. Stay focused.

Most importantly, remember that there is divine potential in all that God has put in your heart to do. The end of a God-ordained vision is God. His glory is his ultimate agenda. Allow your heavenly Father to exploit the visions you are pursuing for his glory.

STARTING AND FINISHING

Every Fourth of July over fifty thousand runners assemble in front of Lenox Square Mall to take part in the Peachtree Road Race. The course of this celebrated 10K takes runners through the heart of one of Atlanta's major business districts. Every March the *Atlanta Journal Constitution* publishes an application for the race. The first fifty-five thousand applicants to get their completed forms to the Atlanta Track Club are allowed to participate. The race is generally full the day after the application is published.

One year I decided to run in the Peachtree. I mailed my application and check—only to have it returned a few weeks later. That's when I discovered that you need to get the form in the mail before the ink on the newspaper has had time to dry. I never bothered to apply again. But I have participated in the race for the past six years.

I learned an important lesson that first year. There are a whole bunch of wanna-be runners who never get past the application process. My guess is they expend so much energy getting their applications in on time they are too tired to train. Consequently, when race time rolls around, there are plenty of available race numbers for those of us who don't have an inside connection to the Atlanta Track Club or who don't live next door to the post office. One year I had two numbers I couldn't even give away.

Anybody with a pen and a stamp can decide to run the Peachtree Road Race. But not everybody with a pen and a stamp can run six miles. Only those who pay the price to prepare for the race.

Everybody has a mental picture of what could and should be for his life. But not everybody will pay the price to turn that mental image into reality.

If you are consumed with the tension between what is and what could be, if you find yourself emotionally involved...frustrated...broken-hearted...maybe even angry...about the way things are, and if you believe God is behind your anguish, then chances are you are on the brink of something divine. Something too important to walk away from.

Pay the price.

Embrace the vision.

After all, everybody ends up somewhere in life.

You have the opportunity to end up somewhere on purpose.

Chapter One

1. Orville and Wilbur Wright, "The Wright Brothers Aëroplane," *Century Magazine,* September 1908.

Chapter Three

1. Jim Bakker, *I Was Wrong* (Nashville, Tenn.: Nelson Books, 1996), 22.

Chapter Eight

1. James M. Kouzes and Barry Z. Posner, *The Leadership Challenge* (San Francisco: Jossey-Bass Publishers, 1987), 107.

2. *Defining Moments Series.* Taped interview with Bill Hybles and Lee Strobal.

Chapter Nine

1. Larry Crabb, *Connecting* (Nashville: Word, 1997), 65.

2. Ibid., 52.

Chapter Ten

1. Taken from *What is Vision,* a tape by John Maxwell.

2. Taken from *A Committed Heart,* a tape by Karen Bennett.

3. Ibid.

4. Ibid.

5. Ibid.

Chapter Eleven

1. *Built to Last,* 147, quoting Sam Walton with John Huey, *Made in America* (New York: Doubleday, 1992), 70.

Chapter Thirteen

1. Ascension Research Center, www.ascensionresearch.org/teresa.html.

2. Subir Bhaumik and Meenakshi Ganguly/Calcutta and Tim McGirk/New Delhi, "Seeker of Souls," *Time,* 15 September 1997, 81–82.

3. Peggy Noonan, "Still, Small Voice," *Crisis,* February 1998, Vol. 16, No. 2, 12–17.

Chapter Sixteen

1. S. Truett Cathy, *It's Easier to Succeed Than to Fail* (Oliver Nelson Books, A division of Thomas Nelson Pub. 1989), 50.

2. Ibid., 119.

3. Ibid., 155.

4. Ibid., 154–5.

5. Ibid., 160.

6. J. I. Packer, *Hot Tub Religion* (Wheaton: Living Books, Tyndale House 1993), 27–8.

7. Billy Graham, *Just As I Am* (San Francisco: Harper Collins/Zondervan, 1997) 723.

8. Charles R. Swindoll, *Intimacy with the Almighty* (Dallas: Word, 1996), 65.

9. Ibid.

Chapter Seventeen

1. James C. Collins and Jerry I. Porras, *Built to Last* (Harper Business, 1994), 1.

2. Ibid., 73.

3. Ibid., 74. Quoting from Thomas J. Watson, Jr., *A Business and Its Beliefs* (New York: Columbia University Press, 1963), 5–6, 72–3.

Chapter Eighteen

1. Paul Johnson, *A History of the American People* (New York: Harper Collins, 1997), 460.

2. Ibid., 461.